From Hitler Youth
to
American Soldier

A Prisoner of Hope

*The Story of a Young Boy's Journey from
Tyranny to Freedom During and After WWII*

Herb Flemming

written by

Timothy King

From Hitler Youth
to
American Soldier

by
Herb Flemming

God bless you

Herb Flemming

Golden Morning Publishing
Winchester, Virginia

Unless otherwise indicated, all Scripture references are from the King James Version Bible

From Hitler Youth to American Soldier: *The Story of a Young Boy's Journey from Tyranny to Freedom During and After WWII*

© 2009 Herb Flemming

Published by *Golden Morning Publishing*
P.O. Box 2697, Winchester, VA 22604

Produced by Richard Choy

Library of Congress Cataloging-in-Publication Data

Flemming, Herb
        From Hitler Youth to American Soldier: The Story of a Young Boy's Journey from Tyranny to Freedom During and After WWII

Library of Congress Control Number 2009902307

ISBN 978-1-889283-18-0
        1. Non-fiction—Autography—History—Christianity

Printed in the United States by Morris Publishing
3212 East Highway 30
Kearney, NE 68847
1-800-650-7888

Contents

Acknowledgements

I would like to thank Timothy King, who actually wrote my story, and his wife Tammy, who transcribed most of our interview tapes, for all their labor in putting this work together. Without them, this book never would have been written. I would also like to thank my wife Frieda for her incredible patience during the five years it took to write my story, and I would like to thank Rudy Schaack and several other people who provided important details about their parts of the story.

Dedication

I dedicate this book to my children and grandchildren. By reading it, I hope that they will better understand not only our family history, but also how God can work in their lives.

Author's Note

Incidents that are marked with an asterisk probably did happen as I described; however, I don't remember exactly in these particular situations. There were many people that certainly did have what I described happen to them. I ask that you pardon my memory for any discrepancies that you may have noticed if you were there too and remember things differently from how I have written them. Thank you, and God bless you.

Foreword

The wonderful life stories of Herb Flemming and his family remind us there are authentic people who give us hope through their examples. His passion for God and his family affirm values which offer strength and protection for those who live in a threatening world culture.

This family provides a legacy of faith from one generation to the next, inspiring one to believe our future is brighter than our past. His stories cross cultures and continents while reminding us our choices determine our providence. This incredible journey will warm your soul!

Pastor Larry Hickey
Potomac District Superintendent - Assemblies of God

Introduction
"Prisoners of Hope"

I am struck by the remarkable narrative of this author and the accompanying story of his family. Herbert Flemming, his parents and siblings, have been held by the redemptive bonds of a divinely given hope evident throughout their lifetime. This book is more than a gripping saga of struggle, survival, and ultimate victory. It conveys a quintessential message for its readers which is timeless.

The story is that of a young boy growing up in a tightly knit community situated on the Baltic Sea in East Prussia, before and during World War II, and then of the challenges to life and limb while his family were refugees after the war. The trail of Herb's young life is traced through all the adventures which young and curious boys experience.

Herb had his older brother Karl, a cadre of friends and secret hiding places, Tom Sawyer-like haunts, and a host of personal discoveries to hold his inquisitive mind captive. He notes the bumps and bruises and lessons learned in his journey of growing up. Throughout all this there was also the strong, positive, parental influence of his father Otto and mother Maria. They were there with and for him in all his roller coaster trip. It makes for exciting reading and has something to say to families of our current generation.

For Herb, the usual progression from innocent childhood to adolescence to young adulthood was brutally interrupted when the Great War came to them.

For years most of its affect had been distant, but towards the end of the war the Russians drove ruthlessly and relentlessly westward, and Herb's hometown was in the direct path of their bloody fury. The slow pace of life in his quiet village suddenly turned tumultuous as refugees and soldiers and then the fighting itself descended upon them. Herb's family left home in a harrowing but divinely protected exodus to the relative safety of northern Germany. As one reads the story, the evidence of divine Providence is inescapable.

Herb's life and story is also heartwarming. His separation from his family at age twelve so that he could work on a farm and relieve the burden on his mother tears at your heart. His search as a young man for truth and reality finds fulfillment when he makes Jesus Christ Lord of his life. His hunger for a walk with God and his earnest seeking of God's will for his life speak volumes for his integrity. And how at the end, God provides a life partner for him in the person of Fraulein Frieda Gatzke is touching and romantic.

Herb's autobiography includes his experience of emigration to the United States of America, his return to Germany as a US soldier, and much more. But through all this, the power of his hope, a God-given gift, was overwhelming. It was as if Herb and his family were held captive by their hope through all their years of trial. Herb was indeed, a "Prisoner of Hope."

Not only that, but the entire narrative brings us face to face with gnawing questions which are universal and as old as the human family. What is the human race looking for? Where is it conducting its search?

When they think they've found it, do they recognize whether the answer is true? How do they take satisfaction and hope from that discovery?

These questions are not peculiar to a single culture. The Bible is filled with stories of people on such a quest. Among them was Solomon, fabled King of Israel. He prided himself on his works, wealth, wine, women, and wisdom. Having gained more than any of us could ever hope, he concluded "Vanity, vanity, all is vanity and vexation of spirit." These universally sought goals turned out to be lighter than air.

There are some commodities in short supply in our world. The most needful and satisfying of these cannot be found in the big stores, the avant-garde shops, or on the internet. When we talk about love, joy, peace, forgiveness, patience, and personal understanding, this world has only one major vendor. In order to find these commodities in abundance, we must turn to God Himself, our Creator, our Eternal Father, and the worthy Architect of our future. This was the all encompassing discovery made by Herb and his family. It is embodied in these simple yet profound words, "God gives hope." The Bible reads in Hebrews 6:19, "We have this hope as an anchor of the soul, firm and secure."

It was my privilege to serve as pastor to much of the Flemming family from 1957 to 1962, at the First Assembly of God church in Albany, NY. By this time, the four eldest children were married. Otto served much of that time on our church Board, and we grew very close to them.

We had many long conversations, the Flemmings and I. Otto went through a Job-like experience, having lost everything. He was a lay minister, a blacksmith, a forward observer in the military, and a commanding figure as a father and husband. He lost his church and his vital place of leadership in his small town. And worst of all, he lost his family after they fled by sea to Germany, and he was captured by the Russians. As a Russian POW, he was subjected to his captors' political indoctrination classes, or brainwashing sessions. One of his most memorable quotes to me arose from those classes as they tried to foist their atheistic anti-God philosophy on him. Otto said with profound faith, "God's Word rose up in my soul, and my mind could not surrender." They had his body, but not his mind, not his spirit, not his faith, and not his heart. He too was a "Prisoner of Hope."

Maria Flemming was also a Prisoner of Hope. With unwavering faith, she shepherded her eight children, Hildegarde, Karl, Horst (Herb), Ruth, Marianne, Waltraut, Ursula, and Gerhardt, through their flight as refugees. She was carrying her ninth child, Ulrich, as well, as she boarded the refugee ship and left her beloved Otto on the docks of Pillau. Ulrich, however, was born very ill and had but a short life in their ultimate place of refuge. All through that, Maria never sacrificed her hope for Otto's safe return, even though it took nearly five years before she saw that hope fulfilled. She committed that sturdy faith to Herb, as well as to her other children.

I stood by Maria in the Albany Medical Center as she bade us farewell and slipped into Heaven in 1959. Years later, I saluted Otto when God called him to his eternal home as well. Both were prisoners of hope. Could their voice be heard today, they would join their children and say to you who are still on your quest, "Look to the Primary Source! It is God Who gives us Hope!"

And that is the heritage of Herb Flemming. What follows now is Herb's life story, told in his own words. It is a remarkable story, from a remarkable man. He makes himself open and vulnerable to you, as even now he is a prisoner of the hope that his testimony will help guide you to the Answer that you are seeking in your own quest.

Thank you.
Rev. Almon M. Bartholomew
Superintendent Emeritus
New York District
Assemblies of God

1

Escape From Pillau

The roads in Pillau were jammed. Wagon after
wagon lined the streets, with an occasional sled,
automobile, or Army truck mixed in between them. The
wagons were piled high with people's belongings. It
wasn't just clothes and furniture in the wagons, either.
It was valuable stuff, like expensive paintings and boxes
of jewels. But it was all abandoned by the side of the
road. The people who owned this treasure had fled
towards the harbor. More people constantly passed by
too, but they just ignored what was in the wagons,
completely focused, as they were, upon making it to the
docks.

We had to leave our own wagon by the side of the
road as well. It was completely impassable. Up ahead,
someone's wagon had overturned in the middle of the
road, and the father and older son of that family were
trying to get their horse under control. It kept on
rearing up, terrified at being confined and not
understanding what was going on. Finally, they just cut

1

the traces and let the horse go free. Dozens of other horses roamed around as well, their owners already having freed them. My father and his friend, Oskar Audehm did this with their horses now too.

We joined the throng of people streaming down to the harbor. It wasn't a panic, at least not yet. But no one was wasting any time either. The sky was bright with sunshine on this early February day, in 1945, but no one was laughing or standing out enjoying the sunshine. No one was selling fish or bread or anything else. No one was talking in pleasant tones, and what was said was hushed and urgent. In the distance, you could hear the whistling scream and reverberating thuds of the Russian artillery shells, driving us on.

My father, Otto Flemming, and his friend Oskar, were members of the local Marine Artillerie unit, a part-time coastal artillery battery on the coast of the Baltic Sea, in East Prussia. Papa, as we called him, and Oskar were assigned to the squad that manned the observation post just south of Rothenen, where we lived. Their unit had fallen back into Pillau, along with most of the rest of the army, but they had persuaded their commander to let them return to Rothenen to get their families. Now, after rescuing us and bringing us back to their headquarters on the outskirts of Pillau, their commander had given them a couple of young soldiers to help us. One of them, Kurt, knew the Pillau area. He was our guide and was helping us get down to the harbor to find the ship that hopefully would carry us and the other refugees to safety in north central Germany. The other one, Markus, was carrying Gerhardt, my youngest brother. Rumor had it the German Navy was trying to evacuate the entire Samland Pocket, so people were flocking to the coast trying to escape from the advancing Russian Army.

The street we were on was so packed with wagons, horses, and people, that it was very difficult to make progress, and Papa was growing frustrated. We constantly had to pick our way back and forth between the wagons. Even keeping our footing was difficult, since the cobblestones were covered with ice, and the street was bowed in the middle, so water would run off into the gutters on the side of the road. Several wagons had crashed into each other, creating roadblocks in places, and sometimes you'd even see horses falling down, because their hooves slid out from under them on the ice. Finally, Papa asked Kurt if he knew a better way to get to the harbor. Kurt said he did and motioned for us to follow him.

We cut off to the left, taking a narrow side street, all twenty of us. Besides Markus and Kurt, there were my father, my mother Maria, my older siblings, Hildegaard and Karl, ages thirteen and twelve, myself, Herb, at age eleven, my younger siblings, Ruth, the twins Marianne and Waltraut, Ursula, and little Gerhardt. That made eight kids in the Flemming family, though there would soon be nine, since Mom was eight months pregnant and about ready to burst. Then there was Oskar Audehm, his wife and daughter, and the Schaack family. They had Rudy, age fourteen, his father, who was also in the military but out of uniform, Rudy's mother, and his two younger sisters. They had been fleeing on foot, when we caught up with them on the outskirts of Pillau and invited them to join us.

We trudged on and on, for nearly an hour, taking first one street and then another, going left and right in alleyways and around dark corners. When we finally came out onto a main street, Kurt admitted he just didn't know where we were, but after a while Papa looked around and saw we were on the same street we had started on, just downhill from where we left it by about two hundred meters. Papa was really getting angry with Kurt now, but he was in too much of a hurry to do anything about it right then, so we plunged back into the crowd heading down hill towards the harbor.

It took us another hour of slipping and sliding down the crowded street to reach the dockyards. There before us lay mountains of suitcases and bags and boxes that people had thrown away because there wasn't room for them on the ships. Long lines of people snaked between the piles of discarded luggage, the abandoned wagons, the wandering horses, a bombed out freight car on a rail siding, and several warehouses and fish factories, most of which had considerable bomb damage. There were also heaps of rubbish, rotting food, and feces, whose smells overpowered the faintly pleasant aromas of fish and seawater. Oddly, there were even some shade trees lining the water's edge and some of the streets, but they seemed out of place in this mayhem.

The lines of people went down to the water where the largest ship that I'd ever seen was docked at a stone quay. It looked like a big passenger liner, and it had a gangplank going steeply up the side of it onto the deck, where people were fanning out, trying to find a place to spend their imminent sea journey. I just could make out the name, General von Steuben, under the bow. Already, the entire deck seemed covered with people, and not just the main deck, but also the decks on the superstructure, all the way up to the top. The ship seemed to be very full and rode so low in the water you couldn't see the waterline painted on the hull.

"Over here. This is the way," said Kurt, as he headed off towards one of the lines of people. As we obediently followed him, we noticed that people in the

4

other lines seemed to queue up tighter as we passed, as if to keep us from cutting in front of them. Many of them still carried heavy suitcases and other belongings in some vain hope that they'd be allowed to keep them once they boarded the ship. We saw many other ships in the harbor too. Some of them were military. Some were freighters or fishing boats. But all of them seemed to have a line of people leading up to them and piles of discarded belongings at various places along that line.

Once we were in the proper line, Papa said to Kurt, "You stay with us until we board the ship. I want you to help Maria up the gangplank." We spent another hour in line, talking with the Schaacks, swapping our stories of how we each made it out of Rothenen and past the police cordon around Pillau. It was comforting having them with us, even though we weren't really friends. We were encouraged just having someone else from our hometown along with us. Papa and Oskar would not be able to come with us, of course, since they were in the military, and we thought Rudy's Papa was helping his family the same way, so we needed encouraging.

We began to get excited as we got closer to the ship. It would be such a relief to be on board finally, and to get underway and escape from the Russians. But just as we neared the gangplank, with only another ten or twenty people left before us, someone yelled down from the ship, "No more! No more! The ship is full! The ship is full! Nobody can get in here anymore!" And then they pulled the gangplank up and began throwing off the big mooring ropes, so they could move out into the channel.

We all just stood there at first, too shocked to do anything. This was our last chance to escape from the Russians, and a sense of despair and dismay began

5

spreading through the crowd. We could hear the artillery shells crashing in the distance, and we all wondered whatever would happen to us, trapped in Pillau, with the 39th Guards Army bearing down on us.

2

Around Rothenen

We moved to Rothenen, in the county of
Samland, when I was just one and a half years old,
towards the end of 1934. Papa had been working as a
blacksmith on a large plantation in Dorhtenenhoff with
his father, who was also a blacksmith, but Papa had a
dream of having his own blacksmith shop, and
Rothenen was a place where he could do that. At first
Papa had to work for a local farmer, while we rented a
house from the shoemaker. Papa would do all the
smithing for the farm, and then he was free to do work
for his own customers. That way he was able to build
up a business. Eventually he bought some land at the
north end of town and built a house, and later on, he
built his own blacksmith shop and began working for
himself full time.

Rothenen was a small town - actually just a
village - but it was a wonderful place for a boy to grow
up. There were wide fields on all sides of it, with only
dirt roads leading into town, and just a short walk west

of town was the Baltic Sea, where one could go swimming or watch the fishermen tend their nets.

What few streets there were in town were cobblestone. The main street formed the junction between two wyes in the road, making a sort of dog bone or bow tie shape, with the town running north to south in the straight part between the forks. The road to the northwest went to Nodems, which served and was mostly owned by an aristocratic plantation with large land holdings in the area. The road to the northeast led inland to Grebieten and Germau, where the local creamery was. On the south end of town, the road that angled to the east went to Osterau, while the road that ran southwesterly along the coast went to Saltnicken and passed the coastal observation post where Papa had his military duty. Our house stood just below the junction on the north end of town.

Across the street from our house was the Daniels' Store. They also had a theatre, dance hall, and inn. On our side of the street, just south of us, lay several rental houses for farm workers, including one that we called the Villa, owned by farmer Dagott, which had a pond out in back of it. On the other side of the street a network of small roads funneled into a track leading to the sea. Among these roads, but still along the main street, were the Wittkau farm and house, where my best friend Alfred lived, then the Romey house, the Hübner's bakery, the Hinz' house, and the Burgermeister's house, who was also the wagonmaker and carpenter, Mr. Eggert. Just beyond this lay the town's fire department and jail, sharing the same building, and the town plaza, which we used as a playground and sports field. Across the street from the plaza, on the inland side of town, stood the town's two-room schoolhouse. This was on the south end of town, just above the Saltnicken - Osterau junction.

Most of the children of the families in the area settled in the same town, so you had several families that each had several houses in town. This was true of the Dagotts, the Wittkaus, the Niemanns, the Hübners, the Audehms, the Schaacks, the Schocks, the Baumeisters, the Growes, and the Strausses. Most of their homes were scattered through the network of roads feeding into the road that went to the sea, but the Niemanns' house and farm was next to the school. They owned a lot of land and had quite a number of workers on their farm. The Growes owned the only other general store in town, which was right where the roads came together on the way to the sea, but the Schaacks had a vegetable stand right next to them too. Most of the families that lived closer to the sea were fishermen and owned boats that they kept down on the beach, sometimes with several families sharing one boat.

The farmers in town had fields extending mostly from in back of their houses. They grew potatoes, peas, turnips, beets, wheat, and various other vegetables. In the late summer and early fall, we would help them harvest their crops, with their large, expandable, horse-drawn wagons. This was hard work, but it was also fun, especially when we got to race each other with the horses, back to the barns, or when we got to take the horses into the ponds to bath and drink. It was beautiful there, with the sun shimmering off the fields and the smell of hay, earth, and growing things mixing with the smell of the sea blowing in from the coast.

Rothenen was about 20km north of Pillau, which was the big city on the coast, and which was also at the end of the channel that led to Königsberg, the capital of East Prussia. Every now and then, we could see ships coming or going from there, from our vantage point on the bluffs overlooking the beach near Rothenen. These bluffs were a good 10-20 meters over the beach, so we could see quite a ways from there. The farmers' fields extended right up to the bluffs, but the beach below was of beautiful, soft, white sand, even though boulders and debris often fell onto the beach from the bluffs during storms.

The road from town to the beach split into three steep cuts of sand and dirt as it went down through the bluff to the water. The fishermen would bring their longboats up onto the beach with special rollers, which were mounted on boards to keep them from getting in the sand, and then they would keep the boats in place and upright with triangular chock blocks. Usually they just left them on the beach, but when a storm came up, they would use the rollers and a hand winch, which they had installed in a ravine, to pull the boats further inland, off the beach. They also had railings alongside where they kept their boats, and they would spread their nets across these railings for them to dry and also to allow them to mend the nets. All this took up quite a bit of the beach, but there was still plenty left for us to play on and swim from.

Our house was one of the newest houses in Rothenen, where, as in most of Germany, even in the 1930's, the average age of most houses was over 100 years old. Our property was in the northeast corner of town, with one side of our house facing Main Street and the north side facing a side street that went off towards the village of Korjeiten, due east from Rothenen. This street joined Main Street at right angles, right where the roads from Nodems and Grebieten made a fork in the road. Papa built the blacksmith shop between our house and this street, so that the shop had road frontage on two sides of it.

In front of the house, Mom had a rose tree, which was her pride and joy. It bloomed in July, just in time for the birth of my twin sisters, Marianne and Waltraut. On the south side of the house, she had also trained a pear tree to grow up, as if it were on a trellis. In the southeast corner of our property, up against the low chicken wire fence that separated us from farmer Dagott's worker houses and the Villa, we had a garden, and then along our back fence, we had gooseberry and sour cherry trees alternating with red current bushes, with a few apple trees sprinkled throughout the back yard. That made for a very nice affect, as well as providing us with a number of fresh fruits through the year. There was also a picket fence running between the shop and the house, with a gate in it right next to the house, and there was a woodshed out in back of the blacksmith shop.

Papa's blacksmith shop served more purposes than just to provide him with a place to work. He had his shop on the side that faced Main Street, but on the backside of it, there was a pig pen in the south corner, with a chicken coop on top of that, with a wooden ramp with cross pieces on it, for traction, running up to the coop in back of the shop. Then, in the north corner, there was a wash kitchen for Mom to wash the kitchen utensils in. Also in this kitchen was the big oven in which she would bake bread. This oven was on the inside corner wall and was backed up against Papa's smith forge on the other side of the wall, so they could share the same chimney. The door to the blacksmith shop itself, was on the side of the building facing Main Street. Just to the right of there, as you came in, was the work bench, with several vises on it. Over in the corner on the left was the Oxygen tank and a carbide generator for welding things, since Papa's work as a

11

smith was much broader than just shoeing horses -
back in those days, a blacksmith was more like a
general machinist and metal worker. On the wall
beyond them was Papa's 16-speed drill press, and then
on the back wall was his forge. The anvil for that was
just to the left of the forge, and then there was a big
metal scrap pile in the corner on the left, since
whenever he needed a piece of metal for something, it
was better for him to look for it among the pile of used
pieces than for him to try to make something new.
There was another pile of larger pieces of scrap just
outside the shop, on the side by the Korjeiten road.
Also, in the corner beyond the work bench, there was a
side door that led over to the house. Around back of the
shop, on the corner by the Korjeiten road, was the
outhouse.

    Our house was built of brick for the walls and of
red Spanish tile, which you see on so many houses in
Germany even today, for the roof. There was only one
entrance, which was through the kitchen, facing out
into the back yard, but later on, Papa extended that by
putting a glassed-in porch, which we used as a dining
room, around the kitchen door, with the exit now facing
the blacksmith shop. We had two stories and a
basement, which was mostly only used for storing
vegetables and so on; the stairs were in the kitchen by
the door. From the kitchen, you could go either into the
living room or into the master bedroom, which was
facing the front of the house. In the living room, on the
far wall, was a chaise longue; there was a large table in
the middle of the room; and there was a ceramic tiled
stove and heater in the inside corner, which shared a
chimney with the kitchen stove too, much the same as
the setup in the shop.

    Upstairs were the bedrooms for us children.

There was a large foyer area where the stairs came up, on the side facing the blacksmith shop, over the kitchen, and there were two bedrooms off of that, exactly paralleling the rooms downstairs. The bedroom facing Main Street was for my sisters, and the other bedroom was occupied by the various apprentice boys that Papa employed by virtue of his being a Schmiedemeister, or Master Smith. When Gerhardt came along, he slept with Mom and Papa.

Karl and I shared a bed out in the foyer. There wasn't any dropped ceiling out there, so we could see right through to the rafters. There wasn't even any plywood roof under the Spanish tiles, so we could see right through to them too, and we could even see through to the sky outside, through little chinks in between the tiles. That made it extremely cold during the winter, so that the top blanket would freeze over from our breath. When it snowed, we would wake up, and our bed would be covered with a light dusting of snow. Our bed was just a straw mat, covered with a burlap bag and two down blankets, which we slept between.

As is true for most people, our lives were shaped by our parents and a few close friends as we grew up. Mom had received Jesus Christ as her Lord and Savior as a young girl in Schmiedenen, and she and her family, the Helmdorfs, belonged to an evangclistic Pentecostal group known as the Blau Kreutz (Blue Cross), who preached a lot against drinking and swearing. She was of average height, though she may have been a little on the heavy side too. She was a quiet person and a hard worker. She would do all the cooking and household chores, plus keeping Papa's books for his shop and making clothes for us kids. She brought order and serenity to our family, and later when we were refugees without Papa, her faith and strength of character kept our family together and provided the example that we needed as teenagers during those desperate years after the War.

Papa was a powerfully built man, a blacksmith and the son of a blacksmith. He was from Schmiedenen too, but my grandPapa was a real drinker, and in his early 20's, Papa was following in those footsteps as well. Many of the girls in Schmiedenen wanted to go out with Papa, but he ignored them, preferring someone who was hard to catch and who was also worthy of the hunt, namely, Maria Helmdorf, but since Papa wasn't a Christian, she told him that she couldn't go out with him. Papa's sister, Elfriede, however, was a Christian, and she and Papa were close friends. He frequently waited for her at her church, just to be with her, even though he didn't like being there, and eventually, someone invited him in for a service, and he received Jesus as his Savior too. After that, he went back to his favorite bar and announced to all his friends, including the farmer's boy who always had drinking contests with him, that he could no longer drink with them because he'd become a Christian. Then he started holding street meetings too, because of how powerfully God had touched his life, so everyone thought that he'd gone crazy - everyone, that is, except Maria Helmdorf, who now became interested in him and soon became his wife.

The touch of God's hand on Papa's life was strongly evident throughout the time that I knew him. Papa had an incredible temper, which would often send us kids scurrying to get out of his way, but when things would quiet down, we always found him praying and talking quietly with Mom, asking her forgiveness and setting things right. Papa was always amazed at the fact that God loved him and had sent His Son to die for him, and he spared no effort telling people about this wondrous love that God had for him. In fact, Papa even became a lay preacher and preached in several churches during the time we were living in Rothenen. It was so beautiful, getting up on Sunday mornings and hearing Papa singing Gospel hymns while we were getting ready for church.

From Hitler Youth to American Soldier

3

The War Starts

The summer of 1939, after I had turned six years old, was a wonderful, magical time. Papa was able to take some time off from his work now and then, and he took us to the beach, where we would build sandcastles and roughhouse with him. Us kids would climb all over him on the beach, trying to tackle him, and then he would throw us in the water or bury us with sand up to our necks. At other times, Karl and I and perhaps some of the others would run through the fields and the streets of Rothenen, chasing each other. In the mornings, or sometimes when Papa was working, we could hear him singing Gospel hymns, and we knew that he was happy, and that made us happy. He would take us to Sunday School, and then we would listen to him preach afterwards, and there was always our morning devotions.

I was so happy on one particular Sunday morning, after devotions, because I suddenly realized that Jesus had indeed lived and walked on this earth. As we walked to church that morning, I was gleefully skipping along, because I thought that perhaps Jesus had even walked that very same path that I was on right then. It didn't occur to me that He had lived in Palestine and that I was in East Prussia. That wasn't important to me back then. I was just happy to know that Jesus had actually been alive and on the same earth as I was.

The summer went by without my even knowing it. There were so many things to do and experience and get into. We chased bicycle rims, pushing them with a stick, up and down the streets on some days. Other days we played rabbits, burrowing under one of the farmer's haystacks and chasing each other through there - that is, until one of the other boys brought a lighter with him and lit the haystack on fire because he was angry that the Easter Bunny wouldn't come out of his hole. And still other days, we would amuse ourselves by making mud balls from one of the local ponds, putting them on the end of a stick, and then whipping the stick so that the mud balls would fly up and hit the metal roof of the farmer's barn, and make a big banging noise as it hit.

Then one day in early September, the magic changed. It was mid morning, and I was playing in the front yard, out by Papa's blacksmith shop. Papa had been working inside with a customer, and as he got done, he and his customer came back out, as the customer was getting ready to leave. I wasn't paying any attention to them at all, so I didn't really notice as two of his other customers from town walked up to him in the yard and joined the conversation. But I felt the change.

The air got cold all of a sudden, or it seemed to. Things seemed to stop and hang in mid air. I couldn't hear what Papa and his customer were talking about with the two newcomers, but their mannerisms changed. They became tense, and their talk was hushed and nervous. They were scared. So I became scared. I knew right then that something great and dreadful had happened and that it was happening to us as well.

That evening, Papa did something he hardly ever had done before. After dinner, he announced that he had to listen to the radio. He strode quickly into his bedroom, reached up onto the mantle where it was, and turned it on. The reception was scratchy, and it was hard to understand. Karl and I followed him in though, so we heard it. The man's voice was high pitched and strained. He was excited and angry. His voice rose and fell, like the waves of the sea, and he seemed to mesmerize us. I couldn't understand the meaning of the words that he was saying, but it was obviously very important, by how my Papa focused on listening to him and hushed us up whenever any of us said anything. I'll never forget the sound of that man's voice on the radio, the voice of der Fürher.

The days that followed that day just had more of the same. Papa became more and more tense, and he seemed distracted or pre-occupied with other things whenever we tried to talk to him. Mom was worrying as well, though she just kept it inside. Papa always listened to the radio after dinner from then on, and he always told us to be quiet whenever we made the slightest noise while it was on. He was so intense when he was listening to it.

We heard reports of some Samland-based Army units being sent to Poland, which was only 150km south of where we lived, to fight against the Poles. Things began to change around town, and Papa suddenly became a great socialite. He volunteered to become the town's Fire Chief, and then he also volunteered to be the Civil Defense Coordinator. People started holding meetings in town. Then, some people came by and asked whether Papa was going to join the Nazi Party, but he used the excuse that he was too busy doing all these other things to be able to do that too. There were recruitment drives to join the Army too, but Papa managed to get out of that as well, because he was a blacksmith. That exempted him from service, because he was already in a vital national security occupation, supporting the farmers. Nonetheless, it wasn't long after that before Papa joined the local reserve unit, a Marine Artillerie unit that had observation posts up and down the coast, from Pillau to far beyond Rothenen. He knew that if he was a part of this coastal defense unit, he would never get called away to fight in the conflagration that was just beginning.

4

The Early Days

That did not keep Papa from being sent away to a base near Denmark for eight months of training though. He had to leave in November, 1939, and he could not return until June, 1940. However, unbcknownst to us, he made some acquaintances during that time that would later give us a great deal of help, economically, after the war was over. Of course, his business languished for a while, but since he was on active duty, he got paid enough that we could scrape by without the blacksmithing income for a while, though we did keep Papa's apprentices on, and they were able to do some of the more routine work. Later, when he returned, because everyone was very patriotic, as well as just wanting to support us, he was quickly able to regain his customers and even a few new ones.

I had other things to think about though. School had started just before the war, and I was still trying to adjust to that. We had a 2-room schoolhouse at the other end of town, so I had to walk through town every morning after eating breakfast. Then, when it was lunchtime, I would go home for lunch, only to return to school for a couple more hours before the class day ended.

Our classes were divided up with grades 1-4 in one room, with one teacher, and then grades 5-8 in the other room, with the other teacher. Our studies were the usual reading, writing, arithmetic, and so on, that you would expect for a first grade class, and our teacher was stricter than what teachers are today. But we still managed to have fun and carry on, as kids will do.

During recess and after school, we would play Schlagball or various other games in the sports field across the street from the school, next to the Fire Department building. Schlagball is like baseball or stick ball. We used a broom handle and a tennis ball to play. The batter would have the ball, since we didn't have a pitcher. He'd throw the ball up and try to hit it with the broom handle. If he hit it, he'd try to run to base, and the outfielders would try to catch the ball in the air or touch him out with it if it hit the ground before they caught it. We only had one base, which was a pair of birch trees at the far end of the field. So if someone got on base, the next batter could drive him home, but it was further away than what the bases are for baseball. We enjoyed playing it though. We also played dodgeball, which we called Fölkerball, and soccer, and various other games, but Schlagball was our favorite game. Of course, back when I was just beginning school, I was lucky just to be allowed to play.

One time, while we were playing Schlagball, and I was waiting for my turn at bat, I got hit in the eye as the batter cocked the broom handle back, because I was standing too close behind him. Actually, it hit me just above my eye, but everyone thought that it had hit me in the eye, because I fell down on the ground, screaming and covering my face. One of the other kids ran back into the school and told the teacher that I'd been hit in the eye with the broom stick, and that my eye was running out of my face, but by the time the teacher came out to investigate, I'd gotten back up and had run home. The teacher got on his bike and followed after me, only to discover that I was okay except for the scratch and bruise over my eye. Oh, boy, did that hurt, but I was very thankful that it didn't hit my eye.

After school, we would run back home, often stopping to play with friends or what not. Mom would make supper for us, and then we'd have to do our homework. Supper was not our main meal back then. Lunch was. So we would have something light for supper, like fish chowder or leftovers from lunch.

Mom was a good cook, and most of the time, I liked what she served. For instance, she would use some of the leftover rye dough or sourdough from baking bread, and she would roll it out thin on a cookie sheet and then put layers of sour cream and sugar on it and bake it. Oh, my, that was so good, just thinking about it made my mouth water. Another thing that she did very well and that we had fairly often was Königsberger Klopse, which was boiled meatballs, cooked in a gravy sauce, with peppers in it, served over steamed potatoes. Many times we would also have pork chops, milk soup, and of course, potatoes. We almost always had potatoes. All kinds of potatoes. The Italians had their pasta, but the Germans had their potatoes. And fish. Mom would buy buckets full of fish from the local fishermen, and she would find all kinds of ways to cook it. But it was good, and we ate well.

There was one thing that she would cook that I really didn't like though, and that was Sauerkraut. We would eat our meals out on the veranda, which had windows on three sides. Most of these windows were in pairs, but on the corner by the house, away from the outside door, there was a place where there was only one window, and below that window, Papa had built a door for the ducks to get under the house with, so that they would have a place to live. Now, since all of these windows could swing out, I soon learned that if I would sit next to this one window whenever we had Sauerkraut, and if I would wait to eat it until everyone else was finished eating and had left the table and Mom was starting to clean up, that I could fling the Sauerkraut out the window with my fork, bit by bit, and my Mom would think that I was eating it. But in reality, the ducks were eating it. They cleaned up the evidence, so no one ever found out that I was doing that.

Everyone had their chores to do as well. Once Papa came home from his training in Denmark, it became my job to polish his boots every day. Papa's boots were the typical German Army boots, made of leather, that came high up on the calf and didn't have any buckles. They used to call them "knobel becher," the "gambling cup," or "wirfel becher," which was "dice cup." When they were polished correctly, they were very shiny and really looked good on him, so if I missed a spot, he'd find it and make me do that part over again. That happened pretty frequently, but I didn't mind too much, because Papa looked very handsome in them, and that made me proud of him.

Another chore of mine was to build the fire for Mom to make bread with on Fridays. Our bread oven was in the wash kitchen in back of Papa's shop, so that its flue could use the same chimney as Papa's forge. I

could fit about 15 pieces of split wood into that oven,
which was quite massive for a woodstove. It was built
out of firebrick, rather than just iron, so it could get
hotter than a regular woodstove designed for heating.
Mom would keep a grapefruit-sized ball of dough from
last week's batch under a towel in her big wooden
kneading trough near the oven to seed the new batch
with. After it had set for a week and soured in the
dough, she'd add more flour and so on to it and knead it
together to make the dough for this week's batch. Then,
while she let that sit for a while to let the yeast rise, I
would stoke a good, hot fire in the oven, and once it had
burned down, I'd rake the ashes out with a hoe so that
she could put the bread in the oven. Papa had made
some large sheet metal baking pans, and Mom would
divide the dough into 12 loaves and put them in these
pans to bake. She always made sure that she made
enough dough that there was that ball of it left over, so
that there would be yeast for the next week's batch.
Otherwise, she'd have to buy some more yeast at the
store.

Mom also did the laundry on that woodstove,
though she used the smaller oven above the bread oven
for that. She'd boil the wash water in a huge kettle over
the stove, and then she would put all our clothes into it
to boil the dirt out. Today, that would be a lot of work,
but back then, we didn't have very many clothes, so it
was just one or two loads of laundry per week, even
though she had eight kids and a husband to do laundry
for. We wore our clothes longer without washing them
back then, so each of us might only use one or two sets
of clothes during a week.

Once we were done with our chores and
homework, and frequently on Saturdays too, I would lay
out in the yard or in one of the fields nearby and just

25

watch the clouds go by and listen to the surf pounding
in the distance. My favorite place to lay was on the bluff
overlooking the Baltic sea, because the sky was so
much bigger there, you could see all the way down to
the sea, and the noise of the waves was relaxing, even
mesmerizing. I was fascinated by the clouds. They
were so beautiful. And as many people do, I would
imagine that they formed pictures of one thing or
another. One time, I saw Jesus in the clouds, sitting on
a chaise longue, like we had in our living room. Then
He stood up and walked towards me, with His hands
stretched out towards me. Of course it was just a cloud
picture, but it left a very powerful impression on my
young mind.

As we grow up, there are many things that leave
such impressions on our minds, that affect us for the
rest of our lives, and one of the most consistent things
like that as I was growing up, was of my Papa singing
and praying and glorifying God as he went about his
work every day. He was a happy man, my Papa was.
He would sing and talk to God while he was working in
his blacksmith shop or while he was getting dressed in
the morning, and he would do this even more as he was
getting ready for church on Sundays, as he was also
asking the Lord for what he should preach, since he was
a lay minister. Papa would pray a lot and ask God to
use him and to help him give his testimony and to help
him minister to the people. Papa was so moved by the
thought that God loved him and had sent His only Son,
Jesus, to die for him, that he just loved talking about
Jesus with people, and he did this at practically every
opportunity.

One of Papa's favorite songs, which I remember
him singing nearly every Sunday morning, was
"Wunderbar, wunderbar! Gottes grosse Liebe ist

wunderbar! Uns allen ist sie gleich uns alle macht sie reich. Gottes grosse Liebe ist wunderbar." (Wonderful, Wonderful, God's great love is Wonderful. It's the same for everyone, and it makes everyone rich. God's great love is wonderful.) I'm very grateful to my Papa for that heritage which he gave me. Through his daily habits of righteousness and integrity, he shaped the basis of my life.

From Hitler Youth to American Soldier

5

Images

The next few years were times of contrasting impressions and competing images. I was growing up and learning lessons about how to work and how to live for the Lord. Times were generally good, and we had a lot of fun playing games and getting into trouble. Yet there were days that seemed out of place, days that seemed to stop in mid sentence, days that left you wondering.

One of those days was a Saturday morning, not long after Papa had returned from his military training. I was out in the front yard, playing, when my school teacher came riding along on his bicycle. He came up pretty fast, so I wasn't able to run off and avoid him, since as his student, he wouldn't normally be someone that I would choose to socialize with. Instead, I decided to be pleasant and respectful, so I turned and offered a cheery, "Good morning!" I was expecting him to reply with an equally cheery, "Good morning, young man," and then he would just continue riding through town. But he stopped. Quickly. And he got off his bike and very determinedly walked over to me. Then, with a stern look on his face, he wagged his finger at me and proclaimed, "It is not 'Good morning.' It is 'Heil Hitler!' Do you understand!?" In somewhat of a state of shock, I slowly nodded my head, not knowing what else to do and not at all understanding why he said that. Then he got back on his bike and rode off. I stood there, looking after him, dumbfounded, until I remembered my feet, and I ran into the house and hid for a while.

The next Monday morning, in school, it was as if that had never happened.

Most days weren't like that though, and it was easy to forget that we were at war, at least for us kids anyway. My best friend, Alfred Wittkau, and I, for instance, would take old bicycle rims, with the spokes pulled out, and we would take a bent stick and use that to push the bicycle rims along the street. Since all of our streets were either cobblestone or dirt, and since the cobblestone ones were bowed in the middle to let the rain run off of them, keeping the rims moving that way was quite a challenge. We had great fun doing that though, racing each other from one end of the town to the other. We hardly ever wore shoes back then, except for school and on Sundays, so all this running was in our bare feet. We would do that for hours, and then, when we would stub our toes on one of the paving stones, peeling the skin way back and bleeding a lot, we would run just outside of town to a dirt road where there was a lot of sand, and we would shuffle through the sand on the road to make our foot stop bleeding. If there was any cow or horse manure around, we'd step in that too, so the sand would cake up around the cut, and it would stop bleeding. Mom would yell at me when

I got home, saying that I could get an infection that way, but it served my purposes, which was just to get it to stop bleeding.

Alfred and I were great friends. He would call me "Butzer," which meant, "Someone who makes noise with a hammer;" and I would call him "Feter," which was short for Alfred. Sometimes people would also call me "Pasekel," meaning "Sledgehammer." I guess they would call me that because of my Papa being a blacksmith, and because I was a pretty big boy myself. Feter and I would do everything together though, and we would get into all kinds of trouble. Sometimes we would take sticks and make wooden guns out of them to play soldier with, which we probably would've done even if there wasn't a war going on right then, and other times we would play horse and farmer by tying strings to the arms of one of us, the horse, who would then lead off walking, while the farmer held other end of the strings and followed along behind. We also liked to make little mud balls out of the clay from the sides of farmer Dagott's cow pond. We would then stick sharp sticks through them and use those sticks to fling them at his metal-roofed barn, so that they would make a loud banging noise. Other times we'd just throw gravel rocks at each other, sometimes at other boys in town too, by dividing up into two groups. I remember getting hit in the head several times from that, but I dished it out at least as badly as I got it.

One of our favorite things to do was to sneak up into the attic, or Rumpel Kammer, in German, of this old farm house. We would sit up there, looking out the window and telling each other ghost stories, or stories about witches, goblins, ravens, and so forth. It was really creepy up there, since the attic was filled with old furniture, travel chests, pictures of old people, clothes, and other stuff, and it was all covered with a thick layer of dust and connected to each other with networks of cobwebs. It was stuffy and dark, and since we weren't supposed to be up there anyway, it was the perfect place to tell scary stories. We would make stuff up as we went along, always trying to out-do each other in scariness, until finally, both of us would get so scared that we would run out of there, fleeing for our very lives.

Another thing that we did, which I am not proud of, was to torment the local farm cats. Feter had a Saint Bernard, who would ignore a cat if you were holding it in your arms, but as soon as you would let the cat go, the Saint Bernard would chase it for all he was worth. So we used some rope and made a harness for the dog and tied him to Feter's sled. Then we would catch a cat from somewhere and hold onto it while we sat down on the sled behind the dog. Finally, we would throw the cat over the dog's head, and when it would land, the Saint Bernard would chase it, pulling us frantically along behind, until the cat managed to dash under a building or into a barn. Oh, that was a lot of fun.

We tormented our own cat too, this time by tying a pig's bladder to its tail. When either my Papa or Feter's Papa would slaughter a pig, we would make sure that we retrieved the bladder intact. We would tie off one end of it and then stick a straw into the other end and blow it up. We would also put little pebbles or dried peas into it through the straw, and we'd tie off this end too and hang it up to dry once we'd done all this. When it was dry, it looked somewhat like a balloon. Next, we would tie a string to one end of the bladder and tie the other end of the string to our cat's tail and then let him go. He would walk along a little, and the bladder would follow him, tugging at his tail and making a rattling noise. Of course, that scared him, so then he would

32

run, but the monster on the end of its tail would follow
him every step of the way. Soon the cat was in a frenzy
and was literally climbing the walls, on the curtains,
and was running all over the house, pitifully screaming
MEOW, MEOW! We just rolled with laughter at that,
but if my parents caught us, they'd holler at us, and
then they'd give me a whipping if the damage from the
cat was bad enough. Needless-to-say, today I know that
doing that sort of thing to animals is cruel and wrong,
but we were kids back then, and we didn't know any
better.

Our parents wouldn't approve of it either, but we
could get away with starting it at least because Papa
was usually in his shop or outside, and Mom spent
quite a bit of her time outside with the animals or the
garden, or in her wash kitchen behind Papa's shop.
Once it got going though, we made such a ruckus that
someone always found out. After all, our house wasn't
very big, and we had a lot of people in it. Besides my
seven brothers and sisters, all of whom were more than
eager to tell on me to my parents, we also had two or
three apprentice boys with us most times.

These apprentice boys, who were in their teens,
were an inexpensive way for Papa to have employees.
We provided them with room and board, but beyond
that, they were only paid a few pfennigs per week. They
would stay with us for three years, until they took their
Journeyman's test and moved on to work as a
blacksmith on someone's farm or whatnot. Papa had
them staggered so that we would only lose one of them
per year, and then he would hire another to replace him,
since the Blacksmith Apprentice high school vocational
course was a three-year program, where the boys would
be in school one day a week and then would work in a
blacksmith shop for the rest of the week. Not all the

boys came from our immediate area either. Sometimes Papa would have boys or their parents approach him to ask about employment, but he also sometimes went into Pillau or Königsberg, to the guild shop, to inquire if there were any boys seeking work.

That was how Papa hired a Jewish boy one time. This boy had been seeking an apprenticeship for quite a while, but because he was Jewish, no one else wanted him. Also because the boy was Jewish, Papa had to sign some special papers saying that he wanted to hire him, and this marked my Papa as a friend of the Jews. Perhaps because Papa was a Christian, he felt a special responsibility towards them and was willing to take some risks for them, but if you asked him, it was only because of the boy's work credentials. There were many occasions when Papa would compliment him or say to someone else how proud he was of the boy's handiwork. Papa liked to tell people that this was the best apprentice boy that he'd ever had, and he continued to say that even after the boy had taken his test and left us. I sensed that Papa was under pressure about this though, because he was almost too eager to say good things about him, and then once, I heard Papa telling Mom that his coal vendor had confronted him while he was buying coal and had shaken his finger at him and warned him that once "they" were finished dealing with the Jews, they would come after the Judengenossen, or friends of the Jews. Sometimes I would also hear Papa talking about how much harder it was for him to get supplies than it was for other blacksmiths, and he implied that this was because of his being a friend of the Jews.

Papa was allowed by his guild to employ apprentices because he was a Master Smith, or Schmiedemeister. About five years after he'd become a

Journeyman, he'd gone to school in Königsberg and had taken a test for this, right about the same time that he became a Christian. So now, he had people coming from not just Rothenen, but from all the surrounding towns to get their horses shoed or their wagons repaired and so on. He did sheet metal work, fixed people's tools or made new ones for them, welded things, made the suspension and steering system for wagons and the rudder and keel for fishing boats that the carpenter might be working on. People liked his work, and they liked him too. He would even fix horses' hoofs, when they were cut or got an infection in them. He would coat the wound with creosote to protect it, and then he would put a poultice of clay, cow dung, and vinegar over it. Then he would wrap it in a burlap bag and tie it to the horse's hoof. This would draw out the infection.

Papa was very versatile like that, in his work, but one thing that he did not like to do was ask people for money. If it hadn't been for Mom going to visit all his customers now and then, to collect what they owed him, he never would have made enough to live on. He always felt that he was charging people too much for his work, but Mom would reassure him that this was the going rate and that people were happy to pay it for his services. We always had a lot of people coming by the house for something, either as Papa's customers, or for some of the other things that he did, or just to stay at our house for a while, as in the case of several relatives of ours, so that they could spend some time at the beach without having to pay for a hotel. In spite of that though, Mom enjoyed her times when she went out to collect Papa's charges, since this was really the only time that she could call her own, get away from us kids, and where she could go here and there and just talk with people - other adults, that is - at her own pace.

35

I mentioned before that Papa was also the Fire
Chief and the Civil Defense Coordinator. One of the
things that he used to do in those positions was
conduct training exercises. The Fire Department had
these fold-down 4-person-carry pumps with gas engines
back then, and they'd have to carry them to the scene of
the fire. They had a small water tank on them, so if you
were going to use very much water, you'd have to run an
intake hose from there to a pond, to supply the pump
and the fire hose with water. These training exercises
usually included a service to someone in town, such as
pumping out an old well or pond, or something like that.
One time they were doing this, and the local prankster
showed up and was making fun of them, so Papa shot
him with the fire hose and knocked him over with the
water pressure. They had a good laugh about that. The
only time they had a big fire to put out though was
when the Gut ("Goot," an inherited land holding
belonging to nobility) plantation barn burned down,
killing several of their horses. Thankfully, most of the
horses escaped. I tried to go see it, since you could see
the flames from the other side of town, but the firemen
wouldn't let me get close, because I was only about eight
years old.

I was always trying to do stuff like that, that my
Papa was involved with, because he was my Papa, just
like any boy will do. I was too young to be one of his
apprentices, but I helped him out in his shop as much
as I could anyway, and so I learned how to do a lot of
things that blacksmiths do. Papa always told me
though, that I was not allowed in his shop if he wasn't
there with me. Of course that didn't really stop me from
doing that anyway. One time, Papa and Mom were away
for the weekend, when a farmer came by and wanted to
pick up his plow, which he'd left with Papa for

sharpening. Papa hadn't done it yet though, and he wasn't there either, but I knew how to do it, and I was confident of that, so I to built the fire up and used the hammer to thin out the blade, sharpen it, reheat it, and then put it in the cooling water to harden it up. Everything I did was right, but Papa was furious with me anyway, when he found out about it, so I got a good spanking out of that, because I had disobeyed him.

There was another time that I really wished that I had listened to him better. Feter and I, and often my brother Karl, sometimes would go into Papa's shop to play around. One of our favorite activities there was melting lead in his forge and then dribbling it into a bucket of water with a ladle, because it would fizz and steam and make funny shapes as it hardened. That may have been what we were doing on this particular day, because I needed the forge turned on for whatever we were doing. Papa had both a manual bellows and an electric fan to heat his forge with, and I was going to turn the fan on. The switch was on the wall to the right of the forge, housed in a Bakelight casing, but there was a large hole in the casing, so that you could see the wires. Well, it was dark in the shop, and I wasn't really looking at what I was doing anyway, so I ended up sticking my fingers into this hole. The next thing I knew, I was waking up on the scrap iron pile on the other side of the room, and I was sore all over. Thankfully, no one saw me, because I would've gotten in a lot of trouble for having done that.

Sometimes we played in there with bullets too. We'd take a rifle cartridge and take the bullet out of it. Then we'd put the cartridge in a vise grip and hold a center punch up to the primer cap with a pair of tongs, and we'd strike the center punch with a hammer. This would set the primer off with a bang, and it would burn out the powder too with a big flash, so it was pretty exciting to us. We also had a key, one of those old keys with the hollow centers, and we'd scrape match heads off and put their filings into the hollow end of this key, and then pack it down. Then we'd take a nail and cut the point off flat and whittle it down so that it would fit into the hole of the key. With the nail stuck in the key like that, we'd tie a 20-inch piece of string to them and then swing them in an arc, so that they'd hit a wall or tree or something. If you did it just right, the nail would set off the match head filings and make a small explosion. We liked things that went bang. We were just typical boys.

Papa also kept carbonite around for one of his torches, so sometimes we'd take that, and put it and some water in a can, and then put the lid on the can and hold it down until it blew the lid off. Sometimes we'd go fishing with that too, by putting the carbonite and water in an old beer bottle, sealing the buckle clamp over its mouth (similar to how a Mason jar works), and then throwing it in a pond. It would go off under water and stun a lot of fish, carp usually, and then we'd pick the fish out of the water when they came to the surface.

One time we were out by farmer Daniel's barn, on the path that went up to his hand crank well, and we were playing with pistol bullets. In this case, outside, we'd take the bullets out of the cartridge and then hit the primer with a rock until it went off. At some point, I hit it just right, and when it went off, the primer cap flew up and hit me in the leg, which was bare, because it was summer, and it buried itself under my skin just above my ankle. Feter and Karl prodded around in my leg, looking for the primer, but they never did locate it. We got scared and ran off after that, because we weren't supposed to be playing with bullets like that. As far as I know, the primer is still somewhere in my leg, but thankfully, it didn't bleed much.

Of course, the biggest bangs and the most fun came from real firearms, and since there was a war on, there wasn't any shortage of them around. Partly because of that, and partly for political reasons, all of us kids in town, both boys and girls, were required to join the Hitler Youth. This was sort of like German Boy Scouts to us. We were young, and we didn't know the political implications of all this. It was just fun, and everyone was doing it, so we joined in enthusiastically, when we turned ten years old, along with everyone else.

The meetings were held in our schoolhouse or outside. We would stand at attention and parade around town in our column of two's, learning facing movements and singing cadences. The girls wore white blouses, black skirts, and white socks, and they looked nice in their uniforms. We boys wore light brown shirts, black pants with a black belt, and black knee socks. The leaders, who were usually just the older boys, also wore a black shoulder strap that went from the left side of the belt, across your chest, and under the epaulet on your right shoulder, and from there onto the back of the belt. We also wore a square kerchief, folded from corner to corner to form a triangle and then rolled up to go around your neck like a tie. You held the ends together with a leather knot that you slid up over them, much like the Boy Scouts do. I was proud to wear that uniform, but again, that was what everyone was doing, and I didn't know any differently.

Now, each town had its own Hitler Youth unit, or troop, and ours was designated "Ost Ostland Fähnein sieben dreiundvierzig," or East Prussian Unit 7-43, which meant that our unit was the 7th troop in district

43 of East Prussia. We had this Ost Ostland 7-43 unit identifier on a shoulder patch on our shirts, and we had epaulets with 43 on them, while the shoulder straps had the seven on them. Our unit also had a small triangular flag, or guidon, with our unit name on it, that we carried with us when we marched around. It was a great honor to be allowed to carry to guidon, but I never got to do that because I was too young and too new in the troop.

We had meetings about once or twice a week, after school. At the start of the meeting, we'd always have a little ceremony, and we'd march around some, and then afterwards, we'd break up to do various activities. If it was sunny out, we'd play games outside, or we'd work on our gardens. Each of us had a garden, in a plot next to the school. The cadre would teach us how to plant and care for vegetables, and they'd explain the value of doing that, both for supporting the war effort, and also because Hitler was a vegetarian and wanted people to get back to nature, though I never quite understood all that. I had a row of kol rabi and a row of carrots. Sometimes they'd also explain about health and hygiene or various other things. On the other hand, if it was raining out, we'd stay inside and shoot air rifles. We had these metal boxes, or bullet traps, with paper targets attached to their fronts, sand inside of them, and a cloth hung in back of them, that we'd set up at the end of the classroom where the chalkboards were, and we'd sit or lay at the other end and shoot at the targets. The pellets would make a loud clang when they'd hit the boxes, so we got a kick out of that. The cadre also explained about gun handling and safety and how to clean and care for guns. That was a lot of fun, and we always looked forward to those days.

Once a year, in the summer, we used to get together for a county-wide Jamboree, in Germau, not far from us. They had games, almost like the Olympic games. We did javelin throwing, shot put, the hammer throw, high jumping, pole vaulting, running, and other types of Olympic games. There would be several hundred kids there, over a long weekend. We slept in tents and ate in a mess hall, and everybody dressed up in their uniforms. I only attended one of these Jamborees, since things started to break down the year after that.

At the end of the Jamboree, we had a massive capture the flag game, where we divided into two teams, one of which had to hide and defend the German flag, with the Swastika on it, and the other of which had to attack and try to find and capture the flag. This was a much more aggressive game than what Boy Scout troops in the US play today. We didn't play flashlight tag or touch tag, etc, where you have to fall down and play "dead" for a few seconds. You became dead by getting in a fight with another boy, and the first one to get knocked down was declared dead by the cadre. It was a free-for-all, where defenders had a half hour to hide the flag however they could, and then the attackers used whatever means they could to find and capture it. I was on the attacking team. We won, after discovering that one of the defending boys had the flag hidden underneath his shirt. There were a lot of fist fights, punching, and tackling, and some boys got hurt, though the cadre refereed and kept it from getting too rough. Yet the cadre intended for us to be rough. It was intended for us to learn to fight and be aggressive, defending or fighting for, our flag. They got us fired up before the game, by talking about how we were the German people and how we had to do whatever was

41

necessary to win and to prove how good you were.

The other place where we could play with guns, real guns, in this case, was at my Papa's Army post, which was an observation post for the Marine Artillerie, or coastal artillery. They had an ammo bunker, a small wooden barracks for the twelve to fifteen men that were stationed there, and a forty foot observation tower. The tower had an enclosed observation deck, or room, with windows and a trap door, so you could get into it from the stairway going up to it. There were four wooden pilings, or legs, with diagonal braces, and a stairway running up between them that had three landings before it got up to the deck. The whole thing was brown, and the legs and braces had creosote on them to protect them. They had a chicken wire fence around the post too. Later, when the Russians got closer, they built trenches between the buildings and put some concertina wire along the top of the fence. The trenches would go about fifteen feet and then have a ninety degree turn, so they progressed in a zigzag fashion, so that enemies couldn't fire down the entire length of the trench.

The men that were stationed there were all reservists. They would pull duty there for twenty-four hours at a time, and then they'd have twenty-four hours off, during which time, they'd go home and tend to their farms, businesses, and families. All of them at this particular post were from Rothenen or one of the other surrounding towns, so they all knew each other and were friends. They knew that they had to help the war effort, but the war was something that was distant and vague to them. Their primary concerns were the concerns of everyday life, so things like the formalities of rank and command structure were rather winked at and ignored.

It was that sort of mentality among them that allowed Feter and me to run out there to play and/or bring our Papas their lunches on a semi-regular basis. Mom would pack Papa his lunch, give it to me, and then I'd meet Feter, and we'd head on out there. Once there, and after handing over the lunches to our Papas, we'd spend most of the afternoon playing. We'd run up and down the stairway, look out the windows at the sea, play soldier in the trenches, and generally have a good time. The men there just ignored us for the most part, until the day that we got into their rifle rack and took some of their rifles. They had this rack outside their barracks, and they stored their rifles, which weren't Mausers, but rather were Belgian guns that looked like an American M1 carbine, there. One day, they'd left it unlocked, and we noticed it, so we took a couple of them and chased each other around the trenches, shooting at each other. Thank God, they weren't loaded, because we would've killed each other - after all, there was a war going on, and the Russians were making a lot of progress against our forces, so the men were quite likely to have had their ammunition close at hand. Of course, when they saw us out there, playing with their rifles, one of them came out and yelled at us and took the rifles away from us.

You can't really blame them for ignoring us like that though. After all, they had a rather boring mission, and very little ever happened there. Their mission was to call back to their company headquarters in Pillau whenever they saw a ship or plane or anything unusual. They also had regular daily reports to make, for things like the temperature, wind direction and speed, sea state, and so on. They had weather station instruments there, and on the walls of the observation deck, they had maps and sea charts and posters with pictures of airplanes and ships on them, to help them identify whatever they saw out there, since they'd likely be very far away. It was a nice, quiet, sort of duty, which went very well with the quiet village life that we led.

Yet, just as the war produced many contradictions and conflicting images, so there were days when all was not quiet in sleepy Rothenen. Rothenen, along with most other towns, had several foreign prisoners of war that had been resettled there. They weren't really even prisoners anymore, as they had been captured by the German Army during the early days, when they won all the battles they fought, and the Army was so confident of winning that, instead of keeping these prisoners in regular prisons, they were farmed out to various towns and cities all over Germany and were settled among the population. So it came to be that we had several Belgian, French, and Polish prisoners that lived in Rothenen. They mostly lived in the Insthaus, which was a large boarding house next door to us, and which they also shared with several of the local hired farm hands. One of those farm hands, Rudy Preval, was assigned to keep an eye on the prisoners and lock them in their quarters when their curfew was up. He was chosen for this because he was a member of the Nazi Party, but he was rather strange too, as he would dress up in his uniform and march up and down our main street, like he was someone important, even though he was all alone.

One of the prisoners, a Pole, happened to be our milkman during the war. He didn't deliver milk to us though. Usually, he picked milk up from us, raw milk, because we had a cow, and even with all the people that lived in our house, we still had milk left over to send to the creamery in Germau. He would stop by our house with his buckboard wagon and his horse, on his way out of town, and then he would stop by again, in the evening, on his way back into town, and drop off some buttermilk, cheese, or whatever Mom had asked for during his first visit that day.

On this particular day in November, after the sun had gone down and it had become quite cold, he came rushing up to the house and banged heavily on the door. Mom let him in because Papa was still on duty at the observation post. He was breathing hard, and so was his horse. He was a big man and had a big, long, scraggy beard, which was all covered with ice from his breath and the cold air. He dashed into the house and collapsed on our veranda dining table, not just exhausted, but frantic and nearly hysterical. In between gasps for air, he stammered in broken German, "I don't know what happened! I don't know what happened. I see here and there some dead people on the road, and they all had the yellow star on them, painted on them, and they were all shot through the head!"

Mother tried to console him, while all of us kids gathered around and silently stared at him, wondering what he'd really seen and whether it meant anything to us, but knowing in our hearts that it must have been dreadful, to make such a big man as this break down and cry, sobbing and babbling as he was.

We brought him a blanket and some hot coffee, and after a while, he quieted down and began to tell us what he'd seen. He'd been on his way back from Germau, passing near Nodems, which was a Gut town, just a kilometer away, owned by the Von Distelburg family estate, when he saw first one body and then another and another, until he had passed eight bodies, along the side of the road. They had all fallen haphazardly, their bodies contorted like rag dolls. They were gaunt and bedraggled and looked like wraiths, mere shadows of humanity. They were dressed in tatters and didn't have nearly enough clothing to keep warm, but that didn't matter anymore, because they'd all been shot through the back of the head. And every one of them had a yellow star painted on his or her shirt.

He also said that even though it was very cold out, their bodies were still warm, and he could see steam rising off of them, so this hadn't happened but a few minutes earlier. That was what got him scared, more than anything, because he knew who it might be that would be killing Jews, and if they found out that he knew about it, perhaps they might come after him too, after all, he was a Polish prisoner of war. The older ones of the rest of us were thinking that they might come after us too, if they knew that he was telling us, because Papa had received threats from the Nazis about this, because of his acceptance of the Jews and his hiring of the Jewish apprentice boy. So all of us were very uneasy about this.

Mom and I were thinking about an even more disturbing possibility as well, since she'd told me earlier that year about her trip to the county clerk's office when Papa was getting promoted to Master Sergeant. In order to become eligible for promotion, he had to submit documentation proving that he had no Jewish blood in his ancestry back to at least nine generations, so she had to go to the clerk's office and request a trace of his ancestry. While she was there, she had a rather unsettling experience. The clerk read through the required nine generations without encountering anything Jewish-sounding, but then she stopped and asked in a very terse, but suggestive, tone of voice, "Mrs Flemming, how far do you want to check?" Taking that as a hint that there might be something after that that she wouldn't want to hear, Mom asked her to stop reading, and the clerk prepared the certification based only on what she'd read. Whether that was a hint or not though, we do have some Jewish blood in us, because on my Papa's mother's side there was a person by the name of Cohen, but they never asked about the mothers' names, only about the Papas.

About an hour went by, as the Polish milkman talked with us and rested. When he finally left, Mom sent us to bed early, as she wanted some time to think by herself, and she didn't want to have to answer all our questions about this either.

The hours dragged by, and neither Karl nor I, in the same bed upstairs, were able to sleep. We heard every little movement that Mom made downstairs. She wasn't going to bed. She was nervous and kept the light on, finding little piddly things to do here and there, probably waiting for Papa to come home from his duty, as he was let off at midnight.

Finally, just as we were starting to drift off to sleep, Papa came home, but the sound of his voice held horror in it, and we were instantly awake and listening. Papa was crying and stammering, just like the milkman. It was difficult to understand what he was saying, but Mom made him repeat it until we'd both heard it as well.

That evening, just as it was getting dark, Papa and two other soldiers were up in the observation tower, when the gate buzzer rang, indicating that someone was at the gate, wanting to get in. They'd earlier heard some shooting down on the beach and were alert to find out what it might have been, so they could make their report back to Pillau. When they looked, it appeared to be a woman, but since it was dusk, they couldn't see her very well. One of the other soldiers was a lieutenant and told Papa to go down and see what she wanted, so he grabbed his helmet and rifle and walked down the stairs and out to the gate.

As he got closer, the first thing he noticed about her was the big yellow star painted over her right breast. Then he saw how poorly and thinly she was dressed and how gaunt she was. And finally, he saw her arm, or what was left of it, hanging by a thin thread of skin and muscle, the entire upper part of it, including the bone, having been shot away. There was blood dripping all over it, and her bone stuck out weirdly from the stub of her shoulder, underneath a poorly done tourniquet, moving as if she was trying to gesture with it. He clamped his hand over his mouth and bowed over, as if someone had struck him in his gut, struggling to keep from wretching. This was the first time he'd ever seen anything like this.

Upon reaching the gate, he managed to compose himself somewhat and straightened up enough to look at her and ask what she wanted, as if that was necessary. She said, "Sir, please, cut the arm off. It hurts so much."

Now tears leapt from his eyes, as the irony and desperation of both of their situations hit him with full force. She was a Jew, having been shot by the Gestapo just a few meters away, on the beach, and she was risking what was left of her life to beg for such a little thing as to have the remnants of her arm cut off. He was a Christian and wanted very much to help her, yet back in the tower, there was an officer, a representative of the German state, and if he showed even one ounce of mercy to this pitiful, dying, member of God's chosen people, he could be implicated with her and could be sent to prison, depriving his own family of his help and sustenance. He held the power of life and death over her, and yet she held it as well over him.

He started to mouth some words, but then in shame and fear, just shook his head and numbly turned and walked back to the tower. Once back among his comrades, he simply said that the shooting had been the Gestapo. The other two looked at each other knowingly. They would not be reporting that particular incident that night.

All this, Papa related to Mom through tears and sobs, finally ending by saying, "I couldn't help her, because she was Jewish. I couldn't help her. I would've been shot, or I would've been in trouble." And with that, he moped off to bed, though we could hear him groaning, as if he was sick, for a long time afterwards.

Karl and I looked at each other in the dark, shivering, knowing without saying anything, what the other was thinking. When you are young, and you see your parents afraid and convulsed by guilt like that, it makes a profound impact on you. You get this helpless feeling, a very vulnerable feeling of fear that becomes a knot in your stomach and goes with you everywhere for a very long time. We learned to live with that fear.

The next day, Papa slept late, claiming that he was sick. The story of what happened had gotten around town though, and Karl and I soon found out more of the details. A squad of Gestapo had been marching some Jewish prisoners from somewhere near Germau and then through Nodems to the beach, and from there they were heading towards Pillau, past Rothenen. When they arrived opposite our village, they encountered the town's fishermen and tried to get them to take their prisoners out to sea, to throw them overboard to drown, because "the Jews weren't worth a bullet." The fishermen refused, so the Gestapo forced the Jewish prisoners to continue marching towards Pillau, every now and again shooting one or two of them that fell from exhaustion. The woman that Papa encountered somehow managed to escape after being shot at close range. I don't know what ever happened to her, but the fishermen and some of the townspeople buried as many of the bodies as they could in the sand of the beach, hoping to erase their memory and keep anyone else from finding out.

There were other times that bodies were found on the beach as well. Sometimes a submarine or some other ship would be sunk in the Baltic Sea, and some of the victims would float in to shore where we were. Feter and I found several ourselves one morning, as we were out playing around and looking for bernstein, or amber, which commonly washed up on the beach, and which many people would comb the beaches for in the mornings. Four German sailors washed up on the beach together, all intermingled, their skin bleached white and their bodies bloated from the water, causing their rings and watches to eat into the flesh of their hands. It was a terrible sight, and we rushed into town to tell someone. Another time, although he didn't wash up on our shore, Hans Hübner, one of the fishermen from our town, who was serving on board a submarine, was killed at sea when his sub sank. He was never found, so when they erected a grave stone for him in the Germau cemetery, the epitaph read, "Von Feindfort nicht zuruek gekommen," "From Patrol against the Enemy, not returned."

Karl and Feter and I were good friends with those fishermen, the Hübners, especially. There were several of them in town, and they owned a couple of fishing boats, but the ones that befriended us the most were the two principal brothers, who shared one of the boats.

50

They would frequently take us out fishing with them during the summers. Altogether there were about six fishing boats in town, with four of them out on any given day, plus the fishermen also had a rowboat, which Feter and I used to steal sometimes when no one else was around. We'd row out about 200 feet off shore, and then we'd drop anchor and go diving off the boat. It was beautiful down there. It was so clear that you could see nearly as far as you could see on land. There was a wide, sandy bottom that seemed to go on forever, and as we got down near it, we could see flounders hiding in the sand, and when they saw us, they would take off, scooting along just above the bottom, leaving rooster tails of sand behind them, as if they were hydroplaning racing boats. In other places, there were piles of rocks with seaweed clinging to them, waving in the current like trees in a high wind. It was beautiful, even magical down there.

When we would come back to the surface to rest, we would just lay in the boat and watch the sea and the clouds until we figured that it was time to take the boat back so that we didn't get caught. Other times, we would sit on the bluff overlooking the beach, eating peas that we'd just picked from one of the farmers' fields, and which we'd carried in a fold of our T-shirts, and again, we would just sit there and watch the day go by, the waves pounding on the beach below, the clouds scudding along, changing shapes as they went, and the sun moving through the sky, warming our bodies in the grass. Sometimes we would kick sand up with our feet and watch it fly off in the wind. It was an idyllic time that seemed to go on forever.

The boats that the fishermen took us out in were about twenty-five to thirty feet long. They were just a ribbed shell of a boat, shaped like a bullet, and made of oak, but they had a small platform in their bottom, so that you could walk the length of the boat without having to worry about tripping over the ribs. There wasn't any cabin or any other shelter on them, except for the engine housing in the center of the boat. The engine was diesel, and it turned a single propeller shaft, which was exposed, and which traveled along the bottom to the stern, where it went out through the hull and ended in a small propeller. The fishermen let us sit in the back, near the tiller, which was fun, because sometimes they'd even let us steer the boat for a while, though other times, if they didn't want to be as bothered with us, they made us sit in the front. We felt very special that they would let us come with them, since we never saw them letting any of the other boys in town go with them.

The fishermen would catch several different kinds of fish, and they had a couple different sizes of net and trot line to do it with. Sometimes they would use a small net for catching minnows, which they would then put on hooks on their trot line for catching eels or larger fish. But when they took us out, they used their larger nets, which they had for catching Strömlinge with, which was like herring, only a bit smaller and blue, instead of green. They would take us out with them in the mornings, and they would set their nets out and then return home or go fishing for eel or flounder or something else during the day. Their nets floated with glass buoys, which were marked with colored flags, so the fishermen could tell their own apart from someone else's, the net bottoms being weighted down with lead weights. In the afternoons, the fishermen went back out to collect their nets, and they would catch thousands and thousands of these Strömlinge. The fishermen went through the same routine when they fished for eels, except that they anchored their trot line with a couple of rocks, or an old iron wagon wheel. They didn't let us come with them to collect their nets and pickup the fish in the afternoons in either case though, because we would be in the way, with all the Strömlinge or eels in the boat too.

It always amazed me how the fishermen could find their way on the sea. They had names for their fishing areas, and they would talk about going to this or that bank or flat, and they would run along the coast until they were opposite a particular tree or house. Then they would line that tree up with another object, such as our house or the blacksmith shop, further inland, and they would turn out to sea, keeping those two objects lined up perfectly, while timing themselves. They never used a compass though. Sometimes we would go for half an hour or an hour beyond where you could see land, so that the water rose up in a curve, like a hill, to where at first it seemed like you were looking down on the distant shore, and then the water would cover it up. Then they would stop and announce that we were at that fishing bank, and they would start throwing their nets overboard. I could never figure out how they could be so sure of where they were, but they spent all their time on the sea, so I suppose that they just knew it that well.

At the end of the day, when the fishermen would bring their catches back to shore, their wives and older children would meet them at the beach and help them lift their nets out of the boats and onto the sand. Then they would use winches, which were anchored in a ravine up in the bluff above the beach, to pull the boats up on rollers in the sand, until they were near the top of the beach, where they would prop them up and store them. Their whole families would gather around then and help sort the fish into various buckets, and then a fish vendor would take the buckets to the market in a truck. After that, the fishermen would stretch their nets out on some high racks or railings near the boats, to dry, and they would spend that evening or perhaps the whole next day, sitting around and repairing their nets.

One day, they caught so many fish between all of them that the fish vendor didn't have room for all the fish in his truck. So he asked one of the fishermen if he could take some of the fish by boat to the market in Pillau Of course Feter and I were there watching, so we immediately asked if we could come along for the ride. The fisherman said that would be fine, but we'd have to run and get our parents' permission first, so off we went. We ran with all our might through the town to where our houses were, so by the time we got there, we were all out of breath and panting. Then everyone wanted to know what was up, and when Karl and Feter's older brother, Alfred, heard what was going on, they begged to come with us too. Both our parents said it would be okay, as long as it was okay with the fishermen, so the four of us then ran back down to the beach. Upon hearing that our brothers wanted to come with us, the fishermen cautioned that the boat might be too low in the water, but as long as the extra weight didn't sink them, it was okay with them. They'd pretty well finished loading the boat by that time, and they already had it out in the water, so we waded across to it and sat down where the fishermen told us to sit. The fisherman was right about the boat riding low in the water. It came up almost to the gunwales, but after motoring around in a circle a couple of times without swamping the boat, they were convinced that it would be okay, so we took off, heading south along the coast.

We'd been gone for several hours when a most extraordinary thing happened. We passed a submarine going in the opposite direction, U-109. It had a fresh coat of light gray paint on it, and the periscope masts were a mottled black, white, and gray. There were several crew members in the sail and on the deck, and they waved to us as we waved back and shouted our greetings. We were so thrilled by this, and we were talking about it so excitedly that no one noticed, several minutes later, when the submarine's wake hit us and dumped several gallons of water into the boat. That cooled us off real quick, and we had to grab some buckets and start bailing out the water. We took on enough water from the wake that the boat was lowered in the water sufficiently that several other waves were able to come over the side too, and then we started getting scared that we might sink. We shoveled water with those buckets with all our might after that. Thankfully, it worked, and we stopped taking on water and were able to finish the trip without any further incidents.

Only about an hour after that, the Pillau lighthouse came into view, and soon after that, we were going up the channel and then into the harbor of Pillau. The channel crossed at right angles to the harbor and continued on towards Königsberg, so to enter the harbor, we had to turn 90 degrees to port and cut across the oncoming lane in the channel, trying not to get swamped by any more wakes from passing ships. The lighthouse was built on top of a stone sea wall, just over half the distance down the channel to the harbor, and at the mouth of the harbor, the sea wall also made a 90 degree turn to the north.

Just as we crossed into the harbor, the first thing we noticed was a huge white ship, a passenger liner,

moored next to the quay. We had to pass it anyway, so
the fisherman at the tiller, having seen our mouths drop
in awe at this mammoth ship, took us as close to it as
he could, passing merely ten or twenty feet from it. We
looked up in utter amazement at how high the port
holes and the deck were above us, with the sea gulls
gliding majestically to and fro among the life boats and
superstructure or sitting on the hand rails and watching
anxiously to see if there were any fish near the surface
of the bay. We were overwhelmed and speechless, able
only to utter gasps of wonder as each part of the ship
passed by us. The fishermen with us, on the other
hand, pointed out to each other things like the large red
cross painted on the side, noting that it was a hospital
ship, or the large amounts of guana, rust, and lichens
that had accumulated on the ship, and the fact that
sand bars had grown around its ends, indicating that it
had been there for a long time, and they wondered why.
As we passed the bow, we all noticed that its name was
the General von Steuben.

As we turned away from the General von
Steuben, across the harbor, we saw the silouhette of a
great battleship, and again we were awestruck. It was
almost completely covered by gray camouflage netting,
strung from the shore, across its superstructure, and
ending in several buoys. The netting looked like a giant
spider's web, and it made it difficult to see much detail,
though we made out the towers, the funnel, and the two
big gun turrets. One of the fishermen said that he
thought it must be the Scharnhorst, but he couldn't tell
for sure.

We felt so small in the presence of such great
ships, in our little fishing boat, like a tiny ant among
giants. We were quiet for the rest of the trip, which
wasn't far, as the fishing dock was only a few hundred

meters further into the harbor.

There were several other fishing boats moored at or around the fishing dock, though most of them were larger than ours. We pulled up and hailed someone to help tie us up to one of the pilings. It took an hour or so for us to get all the fish unloaded and turned over to a local fish vendor, but once that was done, we refueled and got ready to go back the way we'd come. Much to our chagrin though, the fishermen noticed that a storm was starting to come up, and since they'd already had such a close shave with the submarine's wake, they decided that we boys would have to go home by train. So they walked us over to the train station and booked us on a train bound for Germau, paying for the tickets out of their own pockets. At first, we were excited about this too, since it was our first train ride without our parents, but it was already early evening, and we were exhausted from our long voyage, so we all slept nearly the entire way home. Only the fact that the fishermen had instructed the conductor to stop at Godnicken to let us off saved us from going to Germau or Palmnicken. We still had to walk several miles in the dark after getting off the train though.

Those were wonderful times, when we could go out to sea with the fishermen. It was so peaceful there, and the sky was so large, and there was always some sort of adventure to be had or to imagine out there.

It was even an adventure watching the fishermen and the carpenter build their boats, which they did with some help from Papa for the propeller, shaft, and metal fittings. There was this low grassy spot next to the road, across the street and just beyond the school house where they used to do this. This was the same spot where the carpenter would assemble house frames with 6x6 timbers and tongue and groove mortises, just like in the old times, before transporting them to where he was building a house. They would lay out all the necessary wood, and he'd set up a big frame for assembling the boat, with a huge kettle on a fire next to all that. Another frame and a covering would go over the kettle, but it would have a hole at either end to allow the boards to pass through it. They would keep a board in this frame over the kettle, heating it up and allowing the steam from the kettle to loosen it up so that it could be bent into the correct shape to fit in the hull frame. Once they got a board done, they'd bend it and put it into the frame and fasten it down. When they got the hull done, they'd caulk the seams with occum and paint the underside with tar to keep the water out. They'd put in usually three benches, and then they'd paint the whole thing white. Papa would secure the engine and its housing in the center and put the propeller and its fittings on too, along with the tiller. The whole thing took several days to complete.

We kids made a boat of our own once too. Feter and I were the ringleaders for this, as usual. We used a flat bottom, with a wood frame, straight sides, and a triangular, rather than curved, bow. It was only about six by three feet, and it was very heavy, but it floated, even with two people in it, though it rode very low in the water. We made an engine for it with a gear box that Papa gave us from a milk separator. It used hand power from a crank that came out of its top, and it had a propeller shaft from there out the back end. We used a bunch of marmalade buckets with their bottoms punched out and their sides flattened to make sheet metal sides, which we nailed to the wood frame, along with several other pieces of sheet metal that we found laying around, from old signs and so on. We tarred the outside of this to make it water proof. It only took us a couple weeks of intermittent work to build it. We called it Bertha, because it was so heavy. It floated though, and we sailed around in it a little. Not long after we started using it though, Karl and another kid were out in it, about fifty feet from the beach, with three-foot waves, and they took a wave in the boat. They were already running low in the water, so more water started coming in. The rest of us on the beach yelled encouragement to them, but they got scared and jumped out of the boat, and it sank after that. We weren't too sad though, because it was really too heavy, and it was too much work to use to really have fun with.

There was another boat around that we got a lot more usage out of than that one. This boat was a beached wreck that we found up the coast a bit from Rothenen. It wasn't much bigger than the fishermen's boats, but it had an old cast iron potbellied stove in it, with two burners on top. We got to playing around with this stove and found that we could take it out of the boat. After a bit of thought, we ran back to Papa's blacksmith shop and convinced him to give us a couple wheels from some old plows, plus a plow axle, a long handle, and some hardware and tools. We took these out to the top of the beach where we'd left the stove, and we proceeded to build an Army field kitchen, with wheels and a tow handle, out of it. When we then wheeled it back into town, it immediately attracted the attention of all the other boys in the area, and soon we had a gang of about ten boys that wanted to play Army with us. Our next stop was at my Mom's, where we convinced her to outfit us with Army uniforms. Well, they weren't quite uniforms. She had some old shop coveralls and jackets laying around, and she tore these up to make belt satchels out of them, similar to what the German soldiers used for carrying food or ammunition. These satchels were really just big pockets, with a button-down flap and slots in the back where you could slip your belt through to carry them with. The ones from the shop coveralls were deep blue, and the ones from the jackets were whatever color the jackets were, which made us look rather odd, but in our minds, we were all dressed in Army field gray. Lastly, we also made some gas mask containers, the fluted black canisters that the German soldiers carried, out of empty cardboard oatmeal cylinders, with ropes strung through them and over our shoulders, and we carried our water bottles that Mom also gave us in them. Thus properly fitted out, we grabbed our field kitchen, some supplies, and some sticks for guns, and we set out to conquer the world.

Just south of town, near the beach, about halfway to Papa's military outpost, was a Schlucht, or ravine, called the Kraig, after the stream that ran through it. This ravine grew wide as it neared the beach, and its walls were a good 15m high, so it formed a small valley for about 300-400m inland from the beach. At one place, where the stream bent around to the south, there was a rise in the ravine floor, forming a large mound, where legend has it that the old Germanic tribes used to meet to celebrate the Winter Solstice, or Sonnenwendefest, and to have their pagan feasts and so on. Anyway, this was where we headed with our little troop of soldiers, and over the next few days and weeks, we built a bridge over the stream and a bunker and an observation tower for our base of operations.

There was a trail that led down into the ravine from town, since during years of drought, the spring that fed the Kraig was the only source of fresh water in the area, so people from town would go down there to fill up buckets and bottles of water. This particular year though, there had been sufficient rain, so people weren't going down there for that. We, however, took our field kitchen down the trail to the mound, where we set up a temporary camp, and then we started cutting down small trees, limbing them, and laying them across the stream as the foundation for our bridge. We tied these logs together and staked them down, laying the branches across the top of them and then covering all that with sod and grass, to form a passable road bridge across the stream. Next, we hauled the field kitchen across the bridge and started blazing a trail up the steep wooded slope of the south side of the ravine. We worked our way about two-thirds the way up the slope, cutting a couple of switchbacks into the trail to keep our path from being too steep for the field kitchen. Then we cleared a small area, dug a shallow pit there, big enough for all of us to fit into, felled more trees, and piled their logs around the sides and on top of our pit to form a military bunker of sorts. We finished it off by covering the top with small branches, sod, and grass, similar to how we'd done with the bridge. We put the field kitchen inside our bunker, along with our supplies, and then we went to work on an observation tower nearby. This we located in a tall tree, or trio of trees, which joined at their base to form a triangle-V, and whose crowns were high enough that you could see over the top of the ravine from them. We built a ladder up the side of one of these trees by driving spikes into its trunk, and we constructed a platform near their top, between them, from which we could see all the fields around us, to the south and west of the ravine. Our last act of genius was to string a wire between the observation platform and the bunker, where it was connected to a clapper in a tin can, which would rattle when the troops manning the observation platform pulled on the wire, forming a sort of warning and communication system between our two outposts.

For the next several weeks, we whiled away the summer of '44, spending almost all our time playing in and around our bunker. It was the perfect place for boys to play in. In between fighting off hordes of Russians, British, and Americans, or Vikings, or Romans, we would lay around watching the clouds go by or joke with each other, plotting against the girls in town, and daring each other to do things we shouldn't, but never really intending to do any of them. We even cooked and ate meals there, bringing supplies in from our homes and preparing them on our field kitchen. We were quite impressed with our little bunker and with our engineering abilities, and everything was absolutely wonderful, until one day...

Feter and I were up in the observation tower, watching out for the other boys down in the bunker, on a beautiful, warm, sunny day, when Feter all of a sudden, punched me in the arm. "Horst!" he whispered, "Who's that?" he said, pointing far away, down in the potato field, towards Saltnicken. I'd been looking out towards the sea, wondering for the umpteenth time what it must've been like to sail with the Vikings, so it took me a while to locate who or what he was pointing at. There was a man walking through the field towards us, and he was carrying something long and black and shiny in the crook of his arm. He was still a long ways away, but he was walking fast, with determination and purpose.

"He's got a gun," said Feter, with his voice beginning to rise in pitch. "Oh, he's probably just a hunter," I replied, not quite following where Feter was going with this.

The man was nearly half way through the field by

now, so we were beginning to be able to see what he was wearing. It was just the typical coveralls, white shirt, and suspenders that any farmer or fisherman would wear while at work around there. Feter gripped my arm, "He's not a hunter, he's a farmer, and he's coming to get us!"

I turned towards Feter, and our eyes met. "Oh no!" I said. "He must be the farmer that owns this land. He must've seen us yesterday when we were up in his field, stealing potatoes!"

Feter could hardly contain himself. "He's gonna kill us! Let's get out of here!"

We turned and yanked frantically on the alarm wire, causing the clapper down in the bunker to knock violently in its can. We'd played with that many times before, sending out alarms of the invading barbarians of some imaginary army, but this time there was a special sense of panic in the way we pulled on it. The other boys in the bunker quickly spilled out and looked up at us. "What's going on?" asked Karl, as Feter was already scrambling down the ladder.

I hoarsely whispered, "The farmer that owns this land is coming, and he's got a gun! We've gotta get out of here!" In all of our playing and fort building, we'd never really caused any ruckuses or bothered anybody, but we had cut down several dozen trees, and we were on some farmer's property, and we hadn't asked him or anyone else for permission, and we all knew that. So when we saw what we thought was the owner of the land coming, we knew that it was time to leave, and quickly.

Karl turned and began barking orders to the other boys, telling them to grab their supplies and food and so on, while he and another boy picked up the tow handle of the field kitchen, which we had outside the bunker that particular day, and turned it around towards the path down the hill. I got to the bottom of the tree just as he was getting the stove into motion, while most of the other boys had already run down the hill. It was going to take a lot of work to get the stove to the other side of the stream, and it would be dangerous too, but it was our most prized possession, so we felt it was worth it.

Once they got the stove moving, it quickly picked up speed, and then the job became braking it enough to go around the first switchback. The stove went up on one wheel as it careened around that turn, but they just managed to keep it barely under control. I was hot on their heels and feeling very uncomfortable at being the last one down the hillside. "Hurry!" I implored.

Now in the longer stretch of path, Karl and the other boy moved faster, allowing the stove to pick up more and more speed. The second switchback was fairly close to the stream below, and there was a very steep drop off between the path there and the stream. When they reached the turn and swung the front end of the stove around to the right, the stove again went up on one wheel, but this time, its body just kept going straight, tipping it over and right off the embankment. They turned and tried to hold onto the handle, but the weight of the stove, and its twisting motion, ripped the handle from their grasp, and the stove fell, end over end, down the bank and into the stream, landing with a huge splash and quickly sinking out of sight.

Dismayed at the sight of losing our precious stove, the three of us momentarily just stood there, watching the place where the stove had fallen into the water, the ripples spreading out from there across to the other side of the stream, and the water spray landing all around us. All the other boys, on the bridge and on the other side of the stream below, turned and looked back at the sound of the splash. One of them looked up at the top of the hill and pointed, shouting, "RUN!!"

Karl, the other boy, and I looked back up the hill, just in time to see someone's silhouette disappear down from the crest, in our direction. All thoughts of trying to rescue the stove vanished, and we broke into a dead run, clearing our four-meter long bridge in about three steps, dashing across the open space around the mound, and charging up the trail on the other side of the ravine. We didn't stop running until we'd gotten home, and then, because we didn't want our parents to see us this way, we stayed outside, pretending to play, but heaving and panting, utterly exhausted from the run, but victorious, because we were alive.

As I think about all that, we were so afraid of that farmer with his gun that we never did stop to think that it could've been anybody. Most of the men back in those days dressed the way he was dressed, and we didn't know who owned that land anyway. But it was exciting, and we loved adventure and getting into things, so this was a wonderful adventure for us, and we talked about it for days afterwards.

We did a lot of work with the farmers there, especially that last summer and fall that we were in Rothenen, even though my family weren't farmers. You know, there weren't many people in Rothenen, and everybody knew each other, and what was important to one person was important to everyone, so when it came time for the harvest, and the farmers needed help, everyone just pitched in to help them. That was the way it was. My brother Karl and I helped the Dagotts more than the other farmers. They lived just beyond where Feter lived, and he only lived across and down the street from us.

During hay season, or during the wheat harvest, or also rye or whichever other grain was in season, we would help the farmers by driving their wagons that collected the sheaves of wheat. In one sense, it was similar to today's practice, where you've got a tractor pulling a big hay wagon, picking up hay bales, and the combine or harvester tractor is going ahead of it, forming and dropping the hay bales. Very few farmers back in those days, at least in our area, had tractors though, so they still did it the same way that they'd been doing it for hundreds of years. The farmers and their families would go along on foot, with their scythes, and they would cut the hay and tie it into sheaves. There would be a couple of them or more working together on a row, and they would lay the sheaves against each other in a row, so that they would stand up. This helped the sheaves to dry out and ripen faster, and it also made it easier for them to be picked up and put into the wagons. Those farmers that did have tractors just used them to mow their fields with a sickle bar, but then people still had to follow along behind on foot to gather the hay into sheaves and stack them against each other into rows that could be picked up.

After a few days had passed to let the hay dry out, the farmers would come and get us, and we'd all go out with their horse-drawn wagons to pick up the hay. This involved a process we called "weiter fahren," or "moving forward." They would have a team of four horses pulling each wagon, but the wagons weren't the kind that you could just ride in. They were special, expandable wagons that had a huge center beam that could be pushed out or telescoped to separate the front and rear axles further. They also had slats, instead of planks, for the floor, and they had large, interconnected ribs that could be stood upright or laid down at an angle, depending on what kind of a load they were carrying. That way, when the farmers were harvesting beets, potatoes, or turnips, which are all relatively dense and heavy, they would compress the telescoping center beam and bring the ribs upright, so that the wagon could carry a smaller, but heavier load. Later on, during hay or wheat season, since those are relatively light and voluminous, they would expand the telescoping beam and lay the ribs out at an angle, so that a far larger, but lighter, load could be carried.

As we moved along the rows of sheaves in the field, we would have a couple of guys walking alongside the wagon, picking up the sheaves and throwing them up to a couple more guys standing in the wagon or on the ribs, who would then stack the sheaves in the wagon. My job, since I was younger, was to sit on the lead horse, which was usually the front left one, and tell the horses when to stop and when to go. We would stop the wagon to allow the men in back to pick up some sheaves, and when they were done, I would tell the horses to go, and we would move forward a wagon length or two and then stop again for the next section of sheaves to be picked up. When we got to the end of the row, we would turn around and go down the next row, and so on, until we'd done the entire field. I didn't actually turn the horses. I just sat on them, while one of the men grabbed the bridle and led them around. By the time we got done, the wagon was stacked as high as a house, so we had to be very careful driving it forward, though they did tie it down when we were moving back to the barn.

Us kids didn't get paid or anything for doing this. We were there, a part of the community, and it was fun, so we did it. It was beautiful, being out there in those hay fields, in the warmth of a late summer day. As we moved forward, we would scare up bunches of bugs and so forth, and then birds would come along and try to catch them. When we stopped, I could watch the clouds and daydream. We would do this all day long.

Just sitting on the horses was fun too. It made me feel like a grown-up, because I had a great responsibility. And when we were done for the day, and we had put the wagons away in the barns after unloading the last load of hay, we got to take the horses over to this pond out behind Dagott's barns, so that they could drink and cool down. We usually had two or three wagons out in the fields at the same time, so we would have eight or twelve horses to lead down to the pond. Karl and I would ride on the lead horses, and the other ones would just follow along. Sometimes they would walk down into the pond, so that their bellies were getting wet, and we would have to bring our feet up to keep from getting wet too. Once in a while, the horse would lay down in the water and roll around, and then I'd have to jump off, but the pond wasn't that deep, so I just got wet, and it wasn't any big deal.

While we were driving the wagons around in the fields, picking up hay, the farmers had saddles on the horses that Karl and I were riding, but after they'd put the wagons away, and we were about to take the horses down to the pond, they took the saddles off, so while we were in the pond, and again while we were leading the horses out to pasture, we were riding bareback, and we loved doing that. This was the most fun part of the day, because we got to ride the horses bareback, where and how we wanted to. Well, Karl got to anyway. He was a couple years older than I was, so he was allowed to gallop and run with them, but I had to stay at a walk or trot. I was jealous of him for that, but it was a lot of fun to watch him galloping off down the dirt road towards the pasture, with a cloud of dust rising up behind him.

One time, my sister, Ruth, who was two years younger than me, was out there with us while we were getting ready to take the horses out to pasture, so someone put her on a horse so that she could come out with us. Of course, she was riding bareback just like the rest of us, but she wasn't as experienced or as strong as the rest of us were, so she had trouble holding onto the mane. Well, we started off through town towards the pasture, and pretty soon, we got up to a trot. Ruth was doing ok up to then, but when a horse trots, its back end bounces a lot, so Ruth got bounced around, and since she didn't really know what to do, she started sliding backwards down the horse's back. All of a sudden, she slid off the horse's butt and was dragging along, holding onto the horse's tail, screaming and crying and carrying on. When the rest of us saw her doing that, we laughed and laughed, and to this day, we still tease her about how she slid off the horse's butt.

After we got done harvesting the hay, Karl had another job, which he used a smaller horse for, a beautiful tan horse, with a brown stripe running down its back. He would hitch a hay rake, one of the large, wheeled variety, with curved tines that could be raised or lowered with a lever, and that had a metal seat on it, to the horse, and he would go out and rake all the extra hay up that had fallen and been scattered around, and he would make rows of it at the ends of the field, so it could be collected too. Once he was done with that and he'd put the hay rake and bridle away, he'd take off on that horse and just ride around. The horse was very spunky and high-spirited, and we loved watching them prance around, dashing here and there, through the fields and around town.

During the evenings, after a day of harvesting wheat, the Dagotts would thresh some of the wheat with their big threshing machine, which they kept in their barn. They threshed most of the wheat during the winter, when they didn't have anything else to do, but there was usually too much wheat and hay to be stored in the barns, so they would thresh what they couldn't store. Their barns were large and open, and they would pile the hay all the way up to the rafters. Most of the area in the barns didn't have a second floor, though all of it was tall enough to have one, so that they could pile more hay in there. But where they did have a second floor, they used the rooms underneath that to store their potatoes, turnips, and beets in.

Now just across the street from Dagott's barn, and down a little, was Wittkau's barn, and it was in Wittkau's barn that Feter and I sometimes sneaked in some cigarettes and secretly smoked them there. Wittkau's barn was large and L-shaped, being on a street corner, and in one leg they kept their hay and straw, and in the other leg, they had their cow and horse stables. At the far end of the horse stables was a room where they kept turnips to feed to the animals, and they had a chipper machine in there to chop up the turnips to make them easier for the animals to chew. The chipper had a hopper in it, which led down into the cutting chamber, which was powered by a motor on top of it. This all stood up against the foundation wall, which was made of bricks. Since the barn belonged to Feter's family, we were in there a lot, and one day, we found a brick that would come out of the foundation wall, next to the chipper. So when we started stealing cigarettes from my Papa - who didn't really smoke, but he did get cigarettes as part of his military rations, and he would keep them in his bedroom drawer until one of his customers wanted to buy some from him - we started hiding the cigarettes and matches in the cavity behind this brick, since that seemed to be the natural place to hide them.

We didn't smoke the cigarettes there though; we only hid them there. We smoked them on the other side of the barn, the side where they stored the hay, even though that wasn't very smart on our part. In that leg of the barn, they had a large bay, with huge double doors at either end of it, so you could drive the big hay wagons in one side and out the other. They would offload the hay into the bins and balconies on either side of the bay, and then they would drive the wagon out to make room for the next one. When it wasn't hay season, they used this bay to park the wagons in, and they also stored a large sled and a riding wagon, or coach, there. This riding wagon was like a stage coach, but without the walls and roof. It was very formal and nice, with a front seat and a back seat, and soft leather cushions to sit on. It also had covers, like blankets, but made of sheepskin leather, with fur on it, that attached to the frame or back of the seat in front of you and then stretched out over your lap and hooked to either side of the exterior of the wagon with straps and hooks, into a pair of grommets. When they weren't using this wagon, they left the lap covers attached to the grommets, so they covered the seats. It was under these lap covers, on the floor of the front seat of that riding wagon, that Feter and I hid while we were smoking. I'm sure our parents would have beat us to within an inch of our lives if they knew we were smoking in that barn, since we could've burned down that whole barn in an instant, with all that dry hay in there. Thank God, He spared us from our own stupidity.

One of the other barns in town, down the street from us, but not Wittkau's or Dagott's, was a refuge for a different sort of activity. A couple of Jews from somewhere were hiding in there for a while. People used to bring them food and water, and they just let them live there. No one thought much about it, and I never really heard anyone talking bad about them in town. But there was this one girl in Rothenen, who had a bad, rather lewd, reputation, and when she found out about these Jews, she went and told some strangers about them, perhaps so that she could gain some kind of favor from them. The next day though, while us kids were playing Schlagball over by the school, we noticed a couple of freshly dug pits, about six feet long, two feet wide, and a foot and a half deep, down at the end of our field, next to the birch trees. We'd already heard that the Jews had been found and rousted out of their barn, so we speculated that these pits might be graves. Later on that day, after school was over, I was walking around, just outside of town, when a couple of gunshots rang out, and I thought, "Uh oh, somebody got shot. They killed those two people." Sure enough, by the time I got back to the schoolyard, those graves were filled in with dirt. That made me feel kind of strange and cold inside, knowing that they had been shot, and their bodies were now in those graves at the end of our sports field.

It was a dilemma for us, as Christians, when we thought about what to do concerning the Jews. Perhaps if Hitler had treated both the Jews and the Christians alike, persecuting them equally, then maybe the Christians would have responded differently. But since Hitler was not persecuting the Christians for the most part, even though the Nazis did talk about dealing with the Christians after they were done dealing with the Jews, individual Christians had to make their own decisions about what to do, about how much support to give the Jews, and about what it would cost them.

This is not to say that Hitler simply ignored the Christians. On the contrary, he did several things to control the church, though perhaps the most insidious thing was that he did not persecute them like he did the Jews, thus effectively dividing the Jews and the Christians and limiting the possibility of public backlash against his policies. Even before Hitler, the German government basically owned at least the facilities of the Catholic and Lutheran churches, and they still do to this day, supporting them with payroll taxes. So the Catholic and Lutheran churches were the accepted, or official churches, and if you didn't want to have taxes to support them withdrawn from your paycheck, you had to sign a Declaration of a Different Faith. One of the things that Hitler did do to the Christian community was require that if you weren't a Catholic or Lutheran, you had to become a member of the "Evangelische Freie Gemeinde," or Evangelistic Free Church, but the "Free" part meant that they were "free" from government support, as well as regulation. Most Baptists, Methodists, and even some Pentecostals allowed themselves to be grouped into this denomination, which also meant that the individual churches had to be registered with the government. The more independent Pentecostal churches, and some others, refused to do this, so they had to go underground. But even though Hitler used that method to try to establish some control over the non-official churches, they still allowed churches within that group to worship pretty much as they wanted to, or at least I never heard of anyone running into trouble with the government over anything like that. They even allowed

Catholic and Lutheran priests to teach religious classes in the public schools, even during the war.

My family was Pentecostal, and most of the time, we attended the Pentecostal Church in Powayen, which was a home cell church associated with the Elim Pentecostal Church in Königsberg, and which was also part of the Evangelische Freie Gemeinde. There were about 30 people in that church, including kids, and my Papa was the lay pastor for that cell group.

My Papa loved the Lord more than anything or anyone else, and he loved talking and preaching about Him too. There was no other subject - not even blacksmithing - that he loved to talk about so much. The thought that God had sent His only Son to become a Man and to die for us, for our sins, for him, Otto Flemming, so overpowered him that he would choke up with emotion and often even cry when he talked about that. Papa knew the things that he had done earlier in his life, when he would have drinking contests with one of the farm kids in town, and so on, so he was acutely aware of how badly he was in need of a Savior, and he was just in awe of the love of God and of His mercy on us. Papa was like this all the time. He had his times when he became angry with us or with Mom - as he did have quite a temper - but God was nearly always on his mind, and the Name of Jesus was nearly always on his lips. He would sing too, or hum, getting ready in the mornings, or even while he was alone in his blacksmith shop. His favorite song was "Wunderbar, wunderbar, Gotte grosse liebe ist wunderbar, uns allen ist tich gleich und alle mache die reich. Gotte grosse liebe ist wunderbar." "Wonderful, wonderful, God's great love is so wonderful, for everyone it's the same, and everyone it makes rich. God's love is so wonderful." We grew up with that. Papa was always singing or talking about the

74

Lord like that, and it was wonderful. I personally didn't receive Jesus as my Savior until after the war, but Papa taught us so much about the Lord and how to live for the Lord that it set me on the right track for my entire life.

So we went to church and Sunday School at this house church in Powayen every week, and most of the time, it would be Papa that was preaching. He loved to preach, and he was very passionate about it too. It was exciting to hear him preach, because it was as if he had just gotten done talking with the Lord, which he probably had, and now he was telling us about what he and his best Friend had talked about. There were also some Sundays that, instead of going to Powayen, we went to a Baptist Church in Palmnicken, about 6km up the coast, particularly if Papa had been invited to speak there. I remember one time he was speaking there, and he was in his German Army uniform, because he had to report for duty right after the service. He preached about why God would choose someone like him to be saved. He said that he couldn't understand it, but God loved him so much anyway, that He chose to save him. Here he was, in his pressed and starched German Army uniform, up in front of a Baptist Church, preaching the love of Jesus, with tears streaming down his face. That impressed me, and I have always respected him for that. It took a brave man, who didn't care what other people thought of him, to do that.

I suppose that my Papa had his times, when he did wrong things, just like everybody else does, but I remember him being a very righteous man. Whenever he got angry at Mom, he would always ask her to forgive him later on, and I never really saw him drinking or anything, except once, when he made some wine from the fruit of a cherry tree that he grew in our backyard.

He had cared for and tended this tree for such a long time, and then he was so excited and proud when he was able to make cherry wine out of the cherries. My cousin, Werner Neumann, who was a Luftwaffe pilot, had come over to visit us while he was on leave, so he and Mr. Daniels, who owned the store across the street from us, helped Papa drink his cherry wine. They gave us kids a little sip of it as well, and gave us some crackers to go with it so that it wouldn't affect us. I remember how good that wine tasted, but I think Papa and the others had a little too much of it to drink, as he was bragging about it and carrying on a lot, and afterwards he even went to a bar. But despite times like that, Papa was faithful and just and righteous, and I remember that all during my childhood and even after I got married, I wanted to be like him. He was a good man, and I loved him.

Other people liked him as well. It seemed like we always had people coming over to our house, from all over Germany. Most of the ones from further away were relatives who wanted a free stay at the beach, since we lived so close to the Baltic Sea, but there were others who would come from all around East Prussia to visit with Papa. One of these people was a man named Uncle Besler, though I don't think we were really related to him. Papa had met him one night on his way back from Königsberg. It had been snowing so hard that Papa's train was forced to stop until they could clear the tracks, so Papa had to find a place to stay overnight. Well, there was a church near that station that had a guest room, where people would stay overnight if they'd come a long ways to go to church, or during the week for other things as well, so Papa went to stay there. As he opened the door to the room though, a cloud of smoke poured out, as if something was burning there.

Papa rushed in to see what was happening, and he found this guy, who turned out to be Uncle Besler, asleep on the bed, with smoke backing up out of the coal stove. Apparently, the snow had blocked the flue. Papa quickly woke him up and got him outside where he could clear his lungs. If Papa had arrived a few minutes later, he would've suffocated, so he was very grateful to my Papa. And every so often after that, Uncle Besler would come by our house to cook for us or to babysit while my parents went somewhere together or just to spend time with them.

My Papa must have truly endeared himself to Uncle Besler and the others who came by, because it was not always an easy thing to stay at our house. We were a family of eight children, and our house was rather small for that, so it was very crowded. Also, besides the fact that my parents always had a lot of work to do, Papa's work was out in the blacksmith shop, so they couldn't really keep an eye on all eight of us at once, and my parents frequently would use visiting relatives or close friends as babysitters, so that they could escape from the din and confusion that we created. Perhaps because we sensed something playful in his personality, we were especially rambunctious with Uncle Besler, and we teased him incessantly. His attempts to quiet us down just egged us on to further exploits, until we practically drove him mad. One time, he even came after us with an iron frying pan. It was a miracle that he ever came back.

Karl and I were always fighting with each other as well. He was two years older than I was, so he should've been able to best me easily, but somehow I managed to grow faster than he did, so I was actually bigger than he was. So I was always challenging him, and we would go round and round, sometimes just teasing each other, and sometimes in an actual knock-down fight. We slept together too, so we could continue fooling around even after going to bed. We couldn't make too much noise though, because if Papa heard us and came up after us, we knew we were goners.

We collaborated on a lot of stuff too, of course, like the times that we would sneak through a hole that we'd cut in the wire fence that separated the road from farmer Dagott's yard out beyond Wittkau's to steal apples off his apple trees. One time he met us there with a shotgun, so that ended that. Other times we stayed outside playing, until just before supper, and then we would feign tiredness after supper and go right up to bed, without doing our homework, so that we could play or talk with each other in bed. That worked on Mom, but when Papa came home after military duty, he would always check on us, calling upstairs to us to see if we'd done our homework yet, and if we hadn't, not only did we have to come down and do it, but we also got a whipping to go with it.

It wasn't just Karl and me that would fight and fool around, either. All of us got involved, and sometimes several of us would gang up on just one or two of us. This type of thing usually only happened when Mom and Papa were off to Königsberg and had left us with a babysitter, and we usually managed to keep it a secret from them once they did get home. But if I was the one that everyone else was ganging up on, I had a thing about me where I would break off the fight and run and hide somewhere, feeling that they were all against me. Sometimes I actually avoided getting into these big fights by sneaking off to my room just as it was getting started. One particular time though, the fight got so bad and was going so badly for me that I jumped up and declared that I was going to kill myself, because they were all against me. To prove it to them, I ran off to find something to do it with too. When they saw that I might be serious, their attitude towards me changed, and they began to beg and plead with me not to hurt myself. Well, when I saw what affect my act had on them, I really hammed it up, threatening to cut my throat with a knife that I'd picked up. They started crying and begging me to put the knife down and not hurt myself, but I kept it up until they'd done what I wanted them to do. Even though that act worked for me, I never did it again, because I saw that my brothers and sisters really did love me, and I was impressed by that.

Another time, when Mom and Papa were away and had left the oldest of us kids, Hildegaard, who was fifteen, in charge of us, Karl and I were fighting over a length of string. It was a long piece of string, and we each wanted it for some project or other, so we'd wrapped it around our fists, and we were pulling on it against each other and sometimes hitting at each other too. Well, we were doing this in the kitchen, where Hildegaard was making sandwiches for lunch for all of us, and she was using a sharp knife to cut the sandwiches with. She told us several times to stop pulling on the string, but since she was just our older sister, we paid her no attention. So finally, when she'd had enough, she came over with the knife to cut the string in half, thinking that this would solve the problem. But I was one of the middle children, so I was always conniving to get more than my fair share, and I was never satisfied unless I got it too. When I saw what she was about to do, I reached out with my free hand to grab the string closer towards Karl, thinking that I would get the bigger half when she cut it. She didn't see me do this in time to change her direction though, so when she cut down with the knife, she cut my thumb instead. Oh, I hollered, and blood was streaming out all over the place. Usually when something like that happened, no matter who did what, we would all sense the danger from our parents, and we would come together and all promise each other not to tell our parents anything about what happened. This time though, since Hildegaard had to put a bandage on my thumb, there was no way to hide it from them once they got home, so Karl and I got a scolding. It was really something though, how no matter what happened, even if we were tearing the house apart, we would always manage to unite and quiet down and keep everything a secret once Mom and Papa got home.

Now, if it was just me that was doing something, or even if it was someone else, but they - usually one of my sisters - thought that they could blame it on me, then they would be sure to tell our parents about it. I seemed to have a knack for getting in trouble like that, even if I hadn't done anything at all. Since I was always getting into something or starting something anyway, I guess I was the natural person to blame everything on. I just seemed to attract spankings that way.

There were so many things that we did like that. We were just normal kids, playing around, having fun. We hardly even noticed that there was a war going on around us, except for those few times when it touched someone in Rothenen. But as I turned ten and then eleven, the fortunes of the German war machine reversed. There was a particular annual event or gathering in Rothenen that seemed to symbolize what was happening and how we felt about it. The whole town came out for this and made a day out of it. It was the largest event of the entire year, and it happened in the winter, just before Christmas.

This was the town hunting holiday, or
Jagdfreiertag, and everyone looked forward to it for
weeks. Back in those days, even in Europe, there was
more undeveloped land than there was developed land,
so the local wild animals tended to get out of hand,
population wise, and they would eat the farmers' crops
and cause problems. So the Jägermeister, or town
hunting warden, would organize an annual animal drive
and hunt to keep their populations down, and also to
provide meat for the winter for the townsfolk.

On the appointed day, the whole town would
gather out by Papa's blacksmith shop very early in the
morning. The Jägermeister and the Burgermeister, or
mayor, would organize everyone into teams, so that
everyone had a job to do. The women and younger
children would go over to the Daniels' general store and
meeting hall across the street from us, and the men and
older children would split into two teams. One of these
teams would go back through town to the south, while
the other headed out of town to the north. Each team,
once it got out of town, would spread out into a long
line, moving east and west, and then the ends of the
lines would begin to circle back around towards each
other, forming two giant circles. The men, of course,
were armed with shotguns and rifles, and some of them
had a particular three-barreled gun, with two shotgun
barrels on top and a rifle barrel beneath and between
the shotgun barrels. Each of the men would have three
to four children assigned to him as beaters, and they
would all spread out, roughly equidistant from each
other, moving out in opposite directions in a curve, until
the ends met. One of the men at the head of the line
had a bugle, and once he saw that the lines were in
position and everyone was far enough apart from each
other, he would blow the bugle as the signal for

everyone to stop.

The circles that they formed like that were about a kilometer or more in diameter and encompassed most of the land surrounding the town. Once everyone was in position and had stopped expanding the lines, they would turn towards the inside of the circle, and the hunt would begin. Most of the children had metal pots and pans, sticks, and buckets, and it was their job to make noise and beat the bushes, which would scare the animals out of their hiding places as we moved along, and then the men would shoot them. Some of the older children would have heavy sticks, and when a rabbit or other animal would get shot but hadn't died yet, it was their job to take the animal by the hind legs and hit them over the head with the stick, to put keep them from suffering any longer than necessary. This was great fun for us, doing the things we loved most, making noise and chasing things, but the men kept things orderly and made sure that no one got ahead of the circle, as that would be too dangerous.

Meanwhile, the women, back at Daniels' store, were cooking pea soup. This wasn't like you buy in a can today. This was a rich, heavy, pea soup, with ham and onions and so on it in. Mmm. It was delicious. They made huge kettles of it and then prepared long tables with plates or bowls for everyone to eat from. I'm not sure why they always prepared pea soup. It was a tradition that dated back hundreds of years probably.

Anyway, as the circle slowly closed in upon itself, we eventually began to see the opposite side coming towards us, and about that time, the leader would blow his bugle again, and everyone would stop again. This time, the men turned and faced outside the circle, and the children continued on towards the center of the circle. The men were turned to the outside to prevent anyone from getting shot, since we were so close to the opposite side by that time. Since the threat of being shot was gone now, the children were free to race into the middle of the circle, whooping and hollering and beating their pots and pans with all their might. Whatever animals were left in the circle became terrified, and they would run for their lives. Some of us kids would try chasing them for a ways, but as soon as the animals got outside the circle of men, the men would turn and shoot them.

As all of this was happening, the men would keep a record of which and how many animals they had shot. After it was all over with, we would go around and throw the animals together in piles, and then someone with a wagon or a sled would go around and collect them all to be taken into town. Each type of animal was worth a certain amount of points. For instance, rabbits may have been worth two points, ground hogs worth three, foxes worth five, and rae deer worth seven. This was because the men had a contest going, to see who was the best shot.

Once we were done collecting the animals, we would all assemble back at Daniels' store to find the results of the contest and also to celebrate. The mayor would address everyone and congratulate them on another successful hunt and express his thanks to everyone for all the hard work they'd done. Then the Jägermeister would announce the totals of animals killed and who had won the prize for best hunter. This was a great honor, as he would become the Jägermeister for the next year's hunt. When all the formalities were out of the way, the Jägermeister turned us over to the woman in charge of lunch, and she would tell everybody where to get their soup and where to sit and so on. It was a wonderful time for people to socialize and catch up on the news and for the kids to play with each other. This would go on for the rest of the afternoon, until it was time to clean up and go home.

For the animals though, for the rabbits, ground hogs, foxes, rae deer, and so forth (There were also elk and moose, but we didn't shoot any of them; we didn't even find any that I knew of), it was a terrifying event that inevitably ended in their deaths. The circle would get closer and closer, and they would hunker down further in their holes and hiding places. Some of them would run and get shot, and the others would learn that to run meant to die. So they may have crawled further into the circle to avoid detection, or they may have tried to hide and let the line pass them, but always, the children would find them and scare them out, and they would be killed. The hunt was relentless and unstoppable, and it closed in, further and further, like a noose, tightening around their necks.

And so was the Russian Army to our German forces. All that we could do was not enough to stop them. Time and time again, we outmaneuvered them and killed thousands upon thousands of them, and hundreds and hundreds of their tanks, but there were always more where those came from. They were relentless and unstoppable. They came closer and closer, until by mid-1944, we were beginning to see refugees and retreating military units coming through Rothenen on their way to Pillau.

6

Retreat!

A few days after we had to abandon our fort in the Kraig, Feter and I were walking dejectedly down the road through town towards the beach, looking for something to do, when Karl ran up behind us, shouting for us to stop. When he caught up to us, with his chest heaving, he whispered, "Guys, you gotta come see this. There's some soldiers coming into town from Nodems, and they look really weird. They're all beat up and everything."

Curious, we all ran back, but just as we were passing Feter's house, we stopped all of a sudden, allowing the dust we had been kicking up to pass us. There were half a dozen German soldiers gathered in front of Daniel's store, and another half dozen meandering past our house, and maybe twenty more, plodding slowly down the hill beyond our house, strung out in a long line.

These were not the kind of German soldiers that I was used to seeing, the Marine Artillerie soldiers in my Papa's unit, some with pressed uniforms and some that were wrinkled, but all of which were always clean, and all of which were always worn with pride. No. These soldiers' uniforms were torn and thread bare, caked with mud, sweat, and blood, with an aura of dust around them. The men who wore them were gaunt and had hollow expressions in their eyes, like they were looking through you towards something very far away. Several were wearing helmets, and several others wore their garrison caps, but nearly half had no hats at all. Their hair came down unkempt nearly to their necks, and their faces were scraggily with beards that hadn't been shaved for days. About three of them carried rifles, but none of the rest were armed at all. Some carried packs of one sort or another, and nearly every single one of them had some type of cast or bandage on, or they were limping or using crutches.

Feter and I just stood there in the street, staring at them with our mouths open. Other children, and adults too, were beginning to notice them and gathered to watch them. Karl walked slowly towards them, but on the other side of the street, and walked past them towards our house, as if he was going to fetch Mom and the girls.

The door to the store opened about this time, and Papa and Mr. Daniels came out with another of the soldiers, an officer. Mr. Daniels told them, "Yes, come in. You can stay in our dance hall. Just spread out on the floor there. I'll bring you some food and some water or something in a few minutes. Yes, go ahead on in. It's to the left there." The officer, who looked just as bad as the rest of them, began waving them into the store.

Papa turned to me and said, "Horst, have your Mother get some food ready to help the Daniels feed these men. Get your sisters to help, and you help too. I've got to go talk with the Burgermeister. I'll be back in a while." With that, he turned and strode off at a fast pace towards the other end of town.

Several of the people that were standing around watching now came forward to help also, while others went up the street to help some of the soldiers who were struggling more than the others with their wounds, while still others turned and went home to gather supplies or to tell more people about what was going on. Soon the whole town had become abuzz with the news, and people were showing up all the time at Daniels' store, carrying loaves of bread, meat, potatoes, fully cooked meals, bottles of water, and various medical supplies.

But the soldiers kept coming too, and by evening, there were over 100 of them crammed into Daniels' store and dance hall. Some were talking with each other or with the locals. Most of them just lay sprawled out on the hardwood floor, sleeping with their head on their pack, not having prepared any bedding or anything, as if this was just as comfortable as their bed back home.

Papa was in Mr. Daniels' back office, talking with him, the Burgermeister, the officer and another soldier, and a couple other men from town. It was well past our bedtime, but Feter, Karl, and I were still up, talking, whispering, and fooling around just inside Daniels' door. We could hear Papa and the others talking, but we couldn't make out much of what they were saying. Mostly it sounded like they were trying to figure out how many more soldiers might come through town and how they could feed and care for all of them. I'm sure Papa was asking about any news from the battle area too.

Feter, Karl, and I didn't really understand why the soldiers were in town, but from the attitudes of the adults, we knew it wasn't good. We were excited that we were being allowed to stay up so late, but we were also nervous about why, and we were uncomfortable with all these strange men there, who we didn't think were acting like soldiers at all, but rather like old men from a sanitarium or something like that. We were making fun of them, of this one because his face and arm twitched, and he mumbled while he was sleeping, or of that one, because his uniform pants had a big gash torn out of their bottoms, and although they were held together by some string, they exposed his posterior in an absurd fashion. Everyone was calling them Kurland Kampfers, or Resort Fighters, because they came from the north coast of the Samland peninsula, near the Russian boarder, which was known to be a resort area for the wealthy.

The next day, Papa called Karl and me into his blacksmith shop after breakfast, saying that he needed to talk with us. He said that the soldiers had been wounded while fighting the Russians, and that they were going to Pillau, where they would rest and recover. After they were well again, they would be joined into another unit and would go and fight again. He also said that there would be more of them and that we may have to make some sacrifices to help them. Mr. Daniels had already sent in an order for additional supplies from his vendors, along with a request for reimbursement from the government. Papa said that there may be groups of civilians come through as well, warning us to be careful of them, because we didn't know who they were or what they might do. Up until this point, we were a mixture of curiosity, apprehension, and excitement, but what he said next confused us and caused us to feel the first tinge of fear. He said, "Boys, the Russians are coming closer. Some day in the near future - I don't know when - we may need to leave here very quickly. I probably won't be able to come with you though, because of my military duty. So you're going to have to be the men of the house. You're going to need to be strong, and courageous, and think about the needs of the rest of the family before you think about your own needs. It could get very dangerous, but always remember to put your trust in God. He will protect you. Okay?" We both nodded our heads in agreement, not quite believing or comprehending, that we could ever be separated from him, but knowing that his words were somehow ominous.

During the next few days, wounded soldiers continued to trickle into town. They would stay for the night at Daniels' or at Growes', since they had a gasthouse, and then they would move on to Pillau in the morning. That first day was the biggest influx of them for a long time, but as the fall came, they began to arrive in larger numbers. They became a slow, but steady stream, usually beginning to arrive around noontime, and continuing throughout the afternoon. Mr. Daniels started showing movies and having entertainment every night now, instead of just on the weekends. It made the evenings go by faster and helped everyone, both us and the soldiers, forget that there was a war going on.

Civilians began to be among their ranks as well. The civilians usually came by in families, with a wagon, a cow, and maybe a horse, with most of their belongings in the wagon. Some of them couldn't speak German. There were Latvians, Lithuanians, Estonians, Ukrainians, and even some Russians and Poles, but most of them were Germans that had lived in those areas. Nearly all of them were people that had lived in

Russia even before the Germans invaded. I didn't understand why they would be fleeing from the Russians, since they had already been living with them.

One day, in the midst of the refugees coming through town from the north, a few Army trucks, pulling huge search lights behind them, drove through town from the south and headed towards Grebieten. No one really noticed them, or if they did, they wouldn't have realized what the search lights might've been for. One of them pulled off the road at the top of the hill just outside of town though. Later on, Feter and I were playing up that way, and we found them, rather by accident, out in the field. The search light that they had set up was as wide as a man is tall. Anything new like that fascinated us, so we walked right up to them to get a better look. There was a big generator unit hooked up to the light, but it wasn't running right then, because it was daylight. There were several soldiers there, but all except for one of them was asleep under their truck. That one seemed to be a guard. He came over and said, "Guten Morgen," to us and talked with us for a while. He said his name was Frank and that he had been with the Flak Artillerie, which was actually a part of the Luftwaffe, for just under a year. He showed us the search light and how it worked, though he didn't turn it on or anything, and then he said that we should leave, because we might wake someone up, and he'd get in trouble. He didn't look much older than Karl.

A couple weeks later, after the weather started turning cold, just as we were about to get ready for bed, something new happened that brought the war right into our neighborhood. It started out as a faint hum, like an electrical noise, but soon it grew to a rumble and then a roar. We rushed outside to see what was happening. It was dark, so we couldn't really see anything, but we did understand what it was. Perhaps a hundred, perhaps a thousand - we couldn't tell - multi-engined bombers were flying overhead. The noise was deafening. Ursula and Gerhardt, the two youngest, started crying. Every dog in town was barking or howling. I put my hands over my ears. They droned on and on. It was terrifying, not being able to see them or really know what they were, but knowing that they were the Enemy. The Enemy that had never been there before, but that now was.

Papa said that they were probably British, since the British bombed at night; whereas, the Americans bombed during the day. He said that they were probably going to Memel or Königsberg. He would have to check with his commander the next day and find out. If it was Königsberg, he'd have to check with his sister, Tante (Aunt) Elfriede Neuendorf, who lived in town, and also with Mom's sister, Tante Gertrude, who lived in a suburb, to see if they were okay.

Suddenly a cold, blue beam of intense light stabbed into the night sky south of us, down by Pillau. A few seconds later there were other beams of light arcing up to search for the bombers. Then the light up on the hill, that Feter and I had seen, lit up, eliciting a gasp from several of the girls in our family, since they didn't know it was there. It was still dark in the corners, between the houses, but the air had become nearly as bright as day everywhere else. Next, we started hearing little popping noises, like gunfire, but a lot of it, which was soon followed by long streams of red and yellow tracers, chasing each other up through the air, weaving back and forth, crazily, like a whip, or coming together, like they had found something. When one of the search lights found a bomber though, a more serious, deeper, sound of gunfire followed, and individual red tracers raced up towards the plane.

The bombers droned on, uncaring, until all at once, a couple of them each dropped a single, dull red flare, widely separated from each other. They drifted slowly down, possibly on parachutes, and then the bombers dropped a couple more flares and then a couple more. After there were half a dozen flares angling towards the ground, I commented that they looked like a Christmas tree. And then the bombs started to drop.

We still couldn't see them, although with the flares and the search lights, we thought we could see shadows moving in the sky, but we could hear them, even over the roar of the planes. The bombs shrieked and whistled, and when they landed, there was a dull thud from the explosion. One after another after another, on and on, great rows of bombs falling and thudding until they all jumbled into one continuous ear-splitting drum roll.

Just before the bombs started to drop, the noise of the planes had been diminishing somewhat, but as each bomber got done dropping its bombs, it turned around and headed back towards us. Soon the noise of the returning bombers and the noise of those that were still dropping bombs, along with the noise from the flak grew so that it was louder than it had been when they were all directly overhead. Despite that, we all just stood there, with our hands over our ears and with our mouths open, while Ursula and Gerhardt just cried and cried. Finally, Papa broke the spell by telling us to go inside and close all the windows and turn the lights off. The young ones cried for a long time after the last sound of the bombers disappeared, and no one got any sleep that night.

As dawn broke, the townspeople wandered outside and began to mingle and swap stories. No one in the town had slept, and everyone was very shaken up. One old woman had had a heart attack and had died during the night*. Someone else's cow had a miscarriage. Several horses had broken legs or deep cuts from having run terrified through the fields in the dark. Thankfully the horses had been outside. If they had been in the stables, they could've killed themselves in their fright. A number of chickens had broken wings, and broken eggs, because they'd been flapping around in their pens, trying to get away. One family narrowly avoided having their house burn down, because one of them had been running in the dark while trying to light a kerosene lantern and had stumbled in the process. None of the storks that nested on the roofs of the buildings or in tall trees could be seen. It was all very unsettling.

The dozen or so soldiers that had passed the night in the dance hall came out and were just full of information. They told us that the Allies were beginning to bomb Memel and Königsberg now to soften them up for when the Russians came. They said that we would need to create bomb shelters in our basements and keep some food and water and a flashlight or lantern down there. They told us to keep our house lights off during the night, and to keep our windows closed, with the drapes drawn tightly over them. They said that a stray bomb or bombs could come this way, or that the Allies might even target Rothenen, just because we were there, because the Allies were using a tactic called carpet bombing, where they bombed everything in sight. One of them said that he had heard about the bombing in Dresden the year before, where the whole city was destroyed in one night and that the bombs were so intense that they'd created a firestorm that had killed nearly everyone in the city. This was the first morning that we had ever woken up afraid.

Nothing seemed to be working in town that day, except for what few emergency services we had, which Papa was mostly in charge of, and except for Daniels' store. Papa was racing around here and there, along with the men from the Fire Department and Civil Defense Unit, and a few others, making sure that everyone was okay and that there weren't any fires. No one else wanted to work or do much of anything, except talk and watch and check on things.

In the midst of all this, Feter and I noticed something new on the ground. There were small slivers of tinsel, like strings of it that you put on Christmas trees, but much finer and shorter, scattered all over town. There wasn't really enough of it to attract much attention, but to us, it was a mystery, so we started looking for more of it. Pretty soon, as we expanded our search out of town, we were rewarded by finding, not just more of it, but whole bundles of it, with thousands of strands in each bundle. This was quite a find, so we picked up as much as we could carry and ran back into town to show everyone else.

Papa was immediately interested, and he said that the bombers must've dropped it, perhaps to confuse our flak guns. He took most of it from us too, saying that he'd need to turn it over to his commander when he reported for duty that afternoon.

There weren't as many soldiers staying in the dance hall the next night. This wasn't because there were fewer of them passing through town though; it was because all of the ones that arrived earlier in the afternoon didn't stop. They just kept right on going, heading for Pillau. Perhaps they were afraid that we would be bombed too.

That night, the British bombers returned, but this time, Mom ordered us not to go outside. Papa hadn't returned yet, and she didn't want anything happening to us. We closed and covered up the windows as the soldiers had told us to do, and then we huddled in the living room, scared, listening to the drone of the bombers and the drum roll of their bombs exploding, along with the popping of the flak. Once again, we got very little sleep, though we were so excited and keyed up, we hardly even noticed.

Papa was late coming home the next day. He was very tired and went straight to bed. He'd been up for over 36 hours. Usually they were able to sleep in shifts at their little post, but since the bombing started, their officer wanted everyone to be awake and had also put a guard at their gate.

Since that was the second night of bombing though, people weren't quite as awed by it anymore, and things seemed to get back to normal a little bit. We even heard that our school teacher was back in town, so we had to go to school, though it was only for an hour or so. School was something that we didn't do very often anymore, at least that year.

The bombing continued that third night. Papa woke up as it was starting though, so Mom was more calm than she had been before. Papa didn't want any of our lights to be on, but when I asked him if I could go watch the bombers from the veranda windows, he said I could. For everyone else, he suggested that they go to bed.

The search light on the hill and the other ones scattered around the countryside, lit up the night again, but this time they started before the bombers even were directly overhead. Powerful fingers of light stabbed through the darkness, searching for the relentless enemy bombers. Here and there, they would find one, and as soon as they did, a flak battery would open fire on it, sending red tracers arching up towards the bomber. I'm not sure whether the bombers were always hit or not, but as soon as any bomber was caught in the light, it would bank hard left or right and would start a steep dive, as if it was trying to shake off the light and find the safety of darkness again. The light crews anticipated this though and followed the plane in its dive, with the flak tracers following behind as well. When the pilot saw that he was getting too close to the ground, he would try to pull up and bank away again. But this was a very dangerous moment for them, as they were much lower to the ground now, so the flak often caught up to them here, or perhaps they were going too fast and just couldn't pull out of the dive in time, but they frequently kept right on going and struck the ground, bursting into a tremendous explosion.

I was so engrossed in all of this after a while, that I didn't notice that the search light on the hill beyond us, which could actually be seen from our house, had started to arch over towards us, probably following a diving bomber to the west of town, out over the sea. All at once, the light came down and settled right on our house, catching me totally by surprise. I didn't have any time to shield my eyes or anything, so I was completely blinded by this intense beam that was aimed in my direction. I cried out in pain, quickly turning and dashing for the kitchen door, running into the wall, which I couldn't see, and having to feel my way through the door with my hands. I was terrified and thought that I had been hit by a bomb or something and was going to die. But I also didn't want any of my family to know what was going on, so I didn't go any further than the kitchen. The beam of light soon went somewhere else, leaving our house in darkness again, while I stood there, leaning against a table, panting, and hoping that my vision would return. After several minutes, it did, and I was relieved to find that none of my family had come out. After that, I went up to bed and wasn't nearly as curious about watching the bombers as before. No wonder that their pilots so frequently crashed into the ground - they couldn't see anything anymore.

Everyone started looking for the names of loved ones in the obituaries section of the newspaper. Mom and Papa had a subscription, so it came in the mail, but everything was still so confused that there weren't that many names in it at first. We thought perhaps it wasn't as bad as it looked, but really, we knew better. After the third night of bombing though, there were a lot more names. Our Aunts' names were not among them, thankfully. The British didn't return that night though, so the rescue efforts in Königsberg really got under way then. The day after that, Papa checked the obituaries again, and this time, Mom's sister, Tante Gertrude was listed among the dead.

When Papa announced this to us, he talked it over with Mom, and they decided to go to the funeral, which was being held in a couple days. Hildegaard, Karl, and I all asked if we could come, but Mom said No, because she wasn't sure if it would be safe.

The next morning, Mom and Papa walked out to the train station at Powayen and caught the train to Königsberg for the funeral. They were gone all day and didn't return until late that night.

Us kids waited up for them, or at least the three of us that were older did. When they came in, Papa had a very somber look on his face, and Mom's eyes and face were red, as if she had been crying. They said it was a mass funeral. There were over twenty people receiving obsequies there, with several hundred in attendance to pay their last respects, just at that one church. They said practically every church in the city was having one or more funeral services that day. Mom said that Tante Gertrude's casket was just a small wooden box, like what they'd give a baby that died.

She started getting teary eyed again then, so Papa explained that Gertrude and her family had been hiding in the basement of their house, when a bomb struck the building. It caved in the floor above them, and one of the great steel support beams crashed down and landed on her, pinning her to the floor. The others tried to move the beam and get her out, but it was just too heavy, and it was only a few minutes before she died. After a while, the bombs stopped falling, but the stairs and door were destroyed, so they used a basement window to get out through. They stood around for a while, wondering what to do, in shock that not only was Gertrude dead, but their whole house was destroyed too; but then someone shouted that a fire was coming. They looked, and a great wall of flames was coming their way, though it was still a few streets away. The flames leapt and danced and made the sky glow red. The fire stretched for blocks, and it was moving quickly, fed by a violent wind caused by the fire itself. The neighbor's teenage son exclaimed that he was going into the basement to see if anyone else was still in there, and before anyone could stop him, he'd already disappeared through the window. Several minutes went by, and the flames reached their street, rushing from house to house, sometimes causing explosions as it found a gas pipe or a car. Gertrude's husband shouted into the basement for him to come out, yet still he didn't, as he feverishly struggled against the steel beam holding her lifeless body down.

Finally, the fire reached their house, and Gertrude's husband ordered the boy to get out, saying that everyone was leaving to run away from the fire. Reluctantly, and with tears in his eyes and blood oozing from several scrapes, he climbed back out of the basement. Fire was everywhere, and even out on the street, it was so hot that their skin felt like it was burning. The fire sucked the breath right out of their lungs, and they struggled to run every foot of the way. There was no escaping it though, as the flames were far past them and were moving at least as fast as they could run themselves, so they headed for the river,* which was just at the next street. Jumping in over the retaining wall, they discovered dozens of their neighbors already treading water in the murky stream. The water glistened, its waves flickering golden, as it reflected the light of the fire. The flames from their houses rose dozens of meters in the air, and they watched, shivering in the river, for hours, as what little was left of their lives was consumed by the uncaring blaze. When it was over, and they got out of the water, just as dawn was breaking, there was nothing left of their neighborhood, but a field of ashes.

That afternoon, when they thought it was safe to go back into the hole that used to be their basement, all they found left of Gertrude was her charred skull and part of one leg.

Papa looked like he was in a trance, as he finished reciting what his brother-in-law had told him after the funeral. Then he bowed his head and took Mom's hand in his own and squeezed it very tightly for a long time. No one said anything.

About a week later, when Papa said that he wanted to go back to Königsberg to see if he could find Mom's other sister, Tante Lisa, I asked if I could go with him, and he said that I could. We took the train in, and

99

then we walked to the part of town where she lived. All along the way, there were bombed out buildings. There was hardly anything left standing that wasn't damaged. When we got to the street where she lived, we found her apartment easily enough, and it wasn't damaged too badly. It took us a while to find Tante Lisa though, as she was out helping someone else. We visited for a while, and she cried and went on about all the hurting people around her, and how she was so thankful that God had spared her life, as well as ours. We gave her some bread and vegetables that we'd brought with us, and then we began our journey back home.

On our way, we had to walk along a street named Luisen Alle. It was a very wide street, with tall buildings and separate lanes going each way, plus four trolley tracks going down the middle. Previously, it had been a very pleasant street to walk on, as it was flanked by sidewalks with nice shade trees planted in them, and all the apartments and shops were kept in such perfect order. There was always the smell of fresh baked bread or pastries, and everyone would say Hello to you as you passed by. Today though, it was desolate and strewn with rubble, and there was only a narrow path down one side that you could walk in. All the buildings, on either side of the street, were caved in and often black with soot, with huge gashes torn out of their walls. All the glass was gone from the windows, and they seemed to stare at you with dark, sunken eyes. This area had been spared the firestorm, as the buildings were made of brick, but the destruction was little less than in Tante Gertrude's neighborhood. People had scrawled names in chalk or charcoal, on the walls of buildings. There were a lot of names on some of them, but I couldn't tell whether these were names of people that had died in the buildings or of people that had merely been trapped there and might have been waiting to be rescued. It was too late for any of them now, if they were still in there. Even though I had seen much destruction on our way out to Lisa's, this time it was somehow worse. The impact of it left a scar on my memory that remains today.

As we were walking along, we passed an old man guiding a horse which was pulling a flatbed wagon, with short sides and a buckboard seat. The old man had a dark overcoat on, with a cap pulled low over his forehead. He was bent over, and his shoulders drooped, as if he was the epitome of grief. The horse was similarly old and drooping, and the two of them just plodded slowly along, not looking to the left or the right, as if he was attending a funeral or something. In fact, he did have a large bundle of something wrapped up in his wagon. It was big enough to be a body, so that may have been what he was doing. I remember seeing them as if it were in stop action as we passed them on that street. There they were, so old and sad, beset by resignation and despair, barely alive themselves, just walking, walking, walking in the midst of the ruin of their lives.

$\mathcal{2}$ **E 1**

Geburtsurkunde

(Standesamt M e d e n a u Nr. 10/L933)

Der Horst Herbert F l e m m i n g

ist am 11. Mai 1933

in Lindenau Ortsteil Dorotheenhof Kreis Fischhausen geboren.

Vater: Schmiedemeister Otto Flemming

Mutter: Maria Flemming geborene Helmdorf

Änderungen der Eintragung:

Medenau , den 24. Februar 19 41

Der Standesbeamte

My Birth Certificate

*My Parents'
Engagement*

*My Parents' Wedding
Picture*

*My Parents During
the War*

103

From Hitler Youth to American Soldier

*My Dad's
Training Unit
near Denmark*

*My Dad in our local
Marine Artillerie Unit*

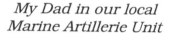

*My Dad & Gerhart,
my younger brother*

Retreat!

*Our Rothenen
house under
construction*

*The earliest picture of me
playing in Dorothenenhof*

*Our completed house in
Rothenen*

Our family in Rothenen, while we were living at the Shoemaker's house

Fisherman drying & repairing their nets at Rothenen Beach

At the beach with family and friends

*At the
Shoemaker's
house in
Rothenen*

*My older brother &
sister, Karl &
Hildegard*

*My extended family
before I was born*

From Hitler Youth to American Soldier

7

First Flight

By late December of 1944, the Russian 43rd and 39th Armies were approaching northern Samland. The latter was bound for Königsberg, but the former was bound for Pillau and would have to come right past Rothenen to get there. The number of Kurland Kampfers coming through Rothenen was increasing dramatically, so that they were practically a steady stream, as were the civilian refugees. It wasn't quite a traffic problem yet, but there was always someone, usually a group, out on the street, heading south.

One overcast night, I was surprised to look out my bedroom window to see that the sky was red. It was a dull, eerie glow that seemed to move, as if it were alive. I had this strange, sinking feeling, as though something was wrong. I watched it for a long time, unable to go to sleep, wondering what it was. In the morning, people were talking about it. Those who were in the know, said that it was the city of Memel burning, and the clouds were reflecting the glow of the flames. Memel was about 100km north of us, right on the Lithuanian border, so the fires must've been very big. The sky was still glowing red in the north that evening as well, though not as brightly. I thought of what Papa had said about Königsberg burning, and I wondered what was happening to the world.

A couple days after that, as I was walking through town on a very quiet morning, I began to hear something strange. I almost couldn't hear it at all, but it kept on coming back, just below the level where you could really hear it, as if it was a train going over a bridge, a long ways away. As I began to realize that it was real and not going away, I started looking at the sky, thinking that it might be more bombers, but they never came. And yet the noise didn't go away either. Nor did it grow any. It was just a constant low rumble.

This rumble kept up for days. People were starting to notice it, but no one seemed to want to talk about it. Maybe they were all hoping it just wasn't real. Something in the back of my mind though told me that it was real, and that it was going to get worse.

Early the next week, the noise had grown somewhat louder, and I finally asked Papa what it was. He said it was Russian artillery, pounding away at our troops, trying to soften them up for an attack. I asked where our artillery was, but he just said that he didn't know.

The week after that, the noise was definitely louder, and it was beginning to get disturbing. You couldn't go anywhere or do anything without hearing it. The refugees heard it too, and they cast furtive glances over their shoulders and hurried along a little faster, with concerned looks on their faces. Sometimes dogs would howl at it for hours.

110

It was cold now too, and there had already been snow several times. It wasn't too bad, but it made travelling more difficult. People in town had swapped out their wagons for sleds back in November, and several of the civilian refugees had sleds as well.

Papa had a customer come by about this time, a Mr. Wessel, from a nearby town. He brought two horses with him that needed shoeing. Papa and Mr. Wessel were good friends, as not only was he Papa's longtime customer, but they both served in the same military unit too. They talked for a long time, and even after Papa was finished shoeing the horses, they stood outside in the cold and talked. At one point, I noticed that they stopped talking and were just standing there, looking north, as if they were listening to the rumbling cannon fire. After a while, they talked some more, and then Mr. Wessel left. That evening, when Papa came in for supper, he announced that we were going to leave Rothenen in a few days, to get away from the Russian Army.

Suddenly everything changed about the way we lived. It was as if the low rumbling in the distance had crystallized into tangible fear. Of course, Papa was not afraid. On the contrary, he was a man of great courage, but he was also a thinker and very protective of his family, so instead of responding in fear, he responded very deliberately. The rest of us took our cue for how to behave from him. We weren't afraid, because Papa was with us, and as long as he wasn't afraid, we couldn't see any reason for being afraid either. But he did change, so we changed too.

Everything about our lives became focused on preparing to leave. Mom started putting supplies together for a long trip. She made some extra bread that Friday, and she got some hams out of storage,

111

wrapped them up, and put them in some backpacks that she made for us. Papa visited one of the farmers in town and came home with two horses and a sleigh. Mom took a day and went around to all of Papa's customers and collected any back due accounts from them, as much as she could anyway, since she was pregnant with her 9th child. Then she packed up all of our old photos, family records, the silverware, and a few other things that she wanted to keep. All of us said our good-byes to various important friends in town and packed up whatever we wanted to take with us.

Honestly, at least for us kids, I didn't feel as though we were running away at all. Rather, we were going on an adventure, so it was very exciting, and we all pitched in and helped with gusto. No one complained or got upset. Mom or Papa would give us our instructions, and we would carry them out, and everything went just fine. We couldn't do everything all at once though, as Papa still had his military duty, and we knew that once he'd taken us to Pillau, he'd have to return to his unit.

When the appointed day came, we all got ready early in the morning, but we had to wait to leave until afternoon, because Papa wasn't going to get off his duty shift at the observation post until noon. When he came home, he still had to change clothes and get ready himself, but he already had all of his stuff packed, so that took less than an hour.

So at about 2:00 in the afternoon, we were finally ready, and we all gathered in the living room and stood around the living room table, looking at each other. Papa said, "Ok, we're going to leave now. But before we do, I'd like to pray over each of you, that God would bless you and keep you safe on your journey." He hesitated for just a moment, and then, taking a deep breath, he went over to the youngest, Gerhardt, picked him up, and began to pray over him.

It was our habit in those days, when we were praying in a group like that, to hold hands, so the rest of us just automatically joined hands, while Papa was praying over Gerhardt. He held him close and prayed that God would be merciful to him, keep him warm and safe, and would see to it that he came to salvation as he grew older. Gerhardt didn't really know what was going on, but he enjoyed being held by Papa. You could see the love for him that Papa had. When Papa was done praying for Gerhardt, he handed him to Mom, who also started praying for him, while Papa went over to Ursula, picked her up, and began praying for her as well.

So Papa and Mom slowly progressed from Gerhardt to Ursula to Waltraut to Mariann, and to Ruth, who was the next younger after me. After Ursula, they didn't pick anymore of us up, but as they went down the line, we just stood there, looking at each other, bathing in the love that our parents were showing us. Papa started crying and becoming very emotional about the time he was finishing up with Ursula, as he realized that he might not see any of us for a very long time after this, and soon all the rest of us were crying too. This became a moment of tremendous family unity, as Papa entrusted each of us to the hands of the Lord. It seemed to me as though Papa and Mom were like ancient patriarchs from the Bible, as they went about bestowing blessings upon their children through the laying on of hands. As Papa began to get to us older kids, his prayers became more specific, touching every part of our lives. All of us were crying, but as soon as he reached another of us that one would just start bawling, and they would embrace and just hold each other for what seemed the longest time.

When he came to me, I looked up into his eyes and knew in my heart how much my Papa loved me. Then I was overcome with the thought that we would be separated for a long time, and once again I burst into tears, like the rest of us, and I went and hugged Papa really hard, and he gave me the biggest bear hug I'd ever gotten. Then he laid his hands on my head and prayed for my safety and health, for my salvation, and that he and I would be reunited sometime in the future. He looked me in the eyes some more, and gave me a few instructions about helping Mom and my sisters and watching out for Gerhardt, and then he went on to Karl and Hildegaard.

This was so beautiful, and it seemed to go on for such a long time. Even after Papa and Mom were done praying for us individually, we started going around to each other and hugging each other and patting each other on the shoulder and giving advice and encouraging each other. It seemed as though God Himself were in our midst, and we were sure that this was His plan, that we were in His hands. We had all been taught by our parents how that God answers prayer, and now, in the midst of the crisis of our lives, we were sure that God was going to come through for us and keep us safe and together, and that He was going to reunite us with Papa someday too. It was amazing the calming affect that this had upon us, after days of hearing the sounds of Russian artillery and weeks of seeing bedraggled refugees filing past our front yard, fleeing for their lives.

Now, all during these last two years, we had a Polish maid living with us and helping out with the housework and with us kids. This was because Mom had so many kids that the German government had given her what they called the "Wolfsangel" award, which entitled her to a free maid, which turned out to be an 18-year old Polish prisoner girl. She couldn't speak much German, and we couldn't speak any Polish, so we just called her "Nanny." Us kids got along fabulously with her, even though Mom made sure that we obeyed her, because she was barely older than we were, and so she liked to fool around and play just like we did. She had volunteered to stay and keep house for us, even after we left, so that things would be still in order for us when the war was over and we came back. Now that we were all done praying, she was standing at the door to the kitchen and said, "Oh, Papa, that was beautiful, but you really don't have to go. When the Russians get here, I will speak up for you. You haven't done anything wrong, and I will tell them that. You've treated me very well. Please let me repay you by speaking up for you when the Russians come. I will do that for you."

Papa laid his hand on her shoulder, and said with gentle determination, "Thank you, and thank you also for all the help that you've given us, but we must leave. You may stay here as long as need be, but we must leave." He gave her a hug as well, and then each of the rest of us filed past her and hugged her too. We would miss her, but now it was time for us to leave.

It was snowing when we went outside, big heavy, wet flakes, and there were several inches of it on the ground already. It was getting colder too. The snow obscured the affects of the war, which for us was limited to not being able to see or hear the stream of refugees plodding along the street in front of our house. Normally, it would also have muffled the thunder of the Russian artillery to where you couldn't hear that either, but today we noticed that they had gotten close enough that it was still easily heard as a series of dull thuds in the background. The horses and sleigh were already hitched up and were just waiting there, tied to the fence

115

between the house and the blacksmith shop. Snow had built up in the sleigh and on the horses as well, and they whinnied or snorted every now and then and shook their heads to shake the snow off.

Papa told me to grab a broom and sweep the snow out of the sleigh, while he and the others brought things out. Once I was done doing that, we put a blanket down on the floor of the sleigh, which was much like a flatbed wagon, with a buckboard seat, except it didn't have wheels, and then we set our packets of valuables, photos and so on, down on that. Then us kids clambered into the back with our rucksacks of food and clothing, and Mom and Papa arranged several more blankets around on top of us. Then they put yet another blanket on the seat for themselves and folded it over onto themselves when they got on. We all waved Good-bye to Nanny, and then Papa flicked the reins of the horses, directing them out onto the snowy street, and we were off.

The ride to the Wessels' house was like something out of a fairy tale. Going through town was a little rough, because it was muddy in a few places, and there were refugees out on the street, but once we got past the schoolhouse, it was clear sledding. There was almost no noise at all, except the soughing sound of the horses cantering through the snow. Under better circumstances, we might've had jingle bell harnesses on the horses, but today, Papa thought it best if we could run silent, so he only put the regular harnesses on them. I was laying on my side, with my head underneath the buckboard seat up front, so that I could look out between my parents' legs. I could see the horses and the vapor from their heavy breath, but beyond that, it was mostly just snow. White snow falling from a gray sky onto white ground. What few houses and trees there were appeared as mere shadows

116

in the distance. It was beautiful and exciting and hushed and mysterious. But we could still hear the rumble in the distance, and there were still refugees on the road.

Once we arrived, Mr. Wessel, who must've been waiting for us, immediately came out of his house and came over to where Papa was sitting on the sleigh. He said, "Otto, Otto, we've decided not to go. The weather is just too bad right now. I figure that if we just stay put, the Russians will pass over us, and if we stay out of trouble with them, when the war is over, they'll leave, and then everything will get back to normal."

Papa responded, "But we're all ready. Look, we've got everything all packed, and the kids are all bundled up in the back."

Mr. Wessel was concerned, "Otto, Otto, where are you going to go? Your family is going to freeze to death. They're going to die. Don't go. You didn't do anything wrong. Besides, it's not going to be that bad. The Russians will just go right on by here, and then they'll leave. The weather is getting worse, anyway."

Papa agreed, "Jah, it has been difficult to see the road. But what happens if there's fighting in our area? And what if the Russians start taking revenge on civilians?"

Mr. Wessel, who was a big, burly man, well over six feet tall, now grabbed Papa's arm, bursting into tears as he spoke, "Otto, don't go, don't go! Please! You're family's going to freeze to death. Where are you going to go? Your family is going to freeze to death. They're going to die. DON'T GO!. You didn't do anything wrong!" He begged Papa, "Look, you treated people right, the Jews, and even the prisoners that were in town. They're going to speak to the Russians. They'll defend you. You don't have anything to worry about, as long as you stay here."

It was strange to see Mr. Wessel, who was much larger than Papa, and who could be very tough, becoming so emotional and crying this way. I could see the heads of various of his family poking around the door or peeking through the window to see what was going on. Papa and Mr. Wessel had been close friends for a long time, and Papa trusted Mr. Wessel's judgment. After all, we really didn't know what dangers might lay in wait for us out there, and since we were obviously losing the war, the Russians would probably catch up to us where ever we went anyway. Perhaps it was better to face them at home than to face them in some strange place, without any food, shelter, or friends.

I couldn't see much of Mom and Papa, as I was underneath where they were sitting, but I could feel him turning to look inquiringly at her, and she responded, "Otto, you know I'm with you whatever you decide, but the children are cold, and a journey in this weather is very dangerous."

The snow continued to fall, and an eternity seemed to pass while Papa thought. Mr. Wessel looked sympathetically at him. "Look, Otto," he said gently, "God can take care of you just as well here at home, as He can somewhere else. Stay here. Please."

"Okay," Papa said. "We'll go back home and stay and let the Russians pass over us. We'll have to prepare the house for a siege though. Thanks, and I'll see you at the post."

Mr. Wessel's face immediately brightened. "Good, Otto. You've made the right decision. I'm sure you'll be grateful for it, and so will your family. I'll see you tomorrow."

Papa turned the sleigh around, and we started back home. The ride home was silent. No one said anything. Everyone was lost deep in thought, wondering how we would fare with the Russians and whether they would leave us alone. The refugees along the road looked at us like we were crazy for going in the wrong direction, though, and I wondered that myself, as the Boom, Boom sound of the Russian artillery seemed louder now than it had on the way out.

From Hitler Youth to American Soldier

8

The In-Between Time

Nanny was glad to see us, but she was curious about why we'd returned, so Mom said that Mr. Wessel had convinced Papa to change his mind. We were busy for an hour or so, unpacking and putting everything back in its place. It was strange, the way we were feeling. In some ways, we were glad at being back home, in a warm, familiar setting, relieved at not having to brave the elements of winter and war, but at the same time, despite Mr. Wessel's assurances, there was always a nagging doubt. Staying at home though was still a plan, and as soon as we were unpacked, Papa began implementing that plan, so we quickly forgot about any doubts that we may have had.

We didn't know exactly how close the Russians were right then, but we were sure that they were only a few kilometers away. Papa wanted us to be ready when they came through, so he had us change a bunch of things around the house. The biggest change was that most of us kids had to move to the basement. Only Mom and Hildegaard continued to sleep upstairs. The rest of us slept in the basement, where the ceiling consisted of steel I-beams, with brick arches between them, to hold up the main floor, as Papa thought this would keep us safe, even if the house took a direct hit from a shell. Papa himself started spending most of his time at his observation post, since the front line was very close now, and they were extremely busy because of that.

People were surprised to see us again, those that had seen us leave, and those that we'd said good-bye to, but no one criticized us for having returned. After all, they hadn't left yet either. No one really knew what to do. It was dangerous if you stayed, and it was also dangerous if you left. Travelers in the open could be attacked by Allied warplanes. They might be waylaid by thieves. Or they might be caught by some other element of the Russian Army, since most of it was bypassing Samland and heading straight for Germany. At least if you stayed, you knew what the dangers were, more or less. The Russian Army would pass over you, and if you weren't shot within the first couple weeks, you might just live to tell about it. Or that was what Mr. Wessel would have counseled, anyway.

In any event, after a few days, the Russians seemed to have stalled and weren't getting any closer. As the days dragged by, we continued to hear their artillery, but it never got appreciably louder than it had on the day we'd fled, and on some days, we even thought it had diminished somewhat.

The number of refugees continued to increase, as did the number of wounded Kurland Kampfers. Rothenen was constantly busy with them now, and there were at least as many of them as there were remaining residents. Crime became a problem in town

for the first time in living memory, as many of the
refugees were both desperate and destitute. The price of
food and many other goods was increasing rapidly too,
which made things difficult for my parents, but us kids
were mostly shielded from that sort of thing, so we
weren't nearly as concerned about it as they were.

Some of the refugees that came through town
decided to stay for a while and took up residence at the
Villa next door to us, or in some of the houses that
various townspeople had vacated in their own flight out
of Samland. Us kids thought this was a novel thing, as
it gave us the opportunity to get to know them, and
especially their children. There was nothing else to do,
and we didn't want to stay around the house, so we
would go out and play with them, especially in and
around the Villa.

The Villa had a large front porch that was raised
up off the ground and supported by wooden columns,
which also went on up to support the roof over the
porch, and which had a lattice-work of wooden slats
between them, under the porch floor, for decorative
purposes, and to keep animals, etc, out from under the
porch. However, on one side, there was a hole, and a
number of us kids, along with several refugee kids,
started using that hole to crawl under the porch, where
we would lay on the ground, looking out through the
lattice. We would talk among ourselves, fantasizing
about this or that, and we would also watch people
going by out on the street, especially the refugees. We
would wonder where they were from and where they
were going, and frequently, we would make fun of them.
Being under the porch gave us a feeling of security and
secretness, so we felt free to talk about things that we
might not have otherwise talked about.

Usually our group under the porch consisted of
Feter, Karl, and me, plus several others, including some

girls, one of which was a local named Mia, who was about Karl's age, and another of which was a refugee girl about my age, though I've forgotten what her name was. We spent quite a lot of time together, this group of ours, both under the porch and also out doing other things, so we began getting to know the newcomers quite well. And since we were beginning to get into adolescence, it was quite natural for us to become interested in these girls that were with us. We never did anything inappropriate with them, not even underneath the porch, but us boys did negotiate among ourselves which of the girls each of us would marry. I was very interested in this particular refugee girl that was my age, and I thought that Karl would like her too, so I bargained with him, convincing him to marry Mia, the local girl, so that I could marry the refugee girl. We had a lot of fun doing that sort of thing, despite what was going on all around us. We just adapted to it and kept on playing around, as any kids will do.

One of the things that happened as a result of there being so many refugees and retreating soldiers moving through town was that people that had started out carrying a lot of stuff with them eventually found it heavier than what it was worth to them, so they would drop it along the way. It got so that there were regular piles of stuff in various places, and a lot of it was military stuff, left by the soldiers passing through town, rifles, ammunition, grenades, supplies, and so on. This all probably started with one person thinking that something was just too burdensome, but then it continued as other people and soldiers would come along, see the pile, and think that it was a good place to deposit some of their stuff too. Feter, Karl, and I noticed this, so we began a sort of patrol, going from pile to pile along the refugee route, every few days or so, checking them out to see what neat stuff we could pick up and play with or take home and keep.

One particular day, Karl and I were doing this, and we were rewarded by finding an entire spool of demolition fuze. After thinking about it some, we hit upon an idea. We took it home and brought it upstairs to our bedroom window. Karl found some matches, and went outside to stand under the window, while I let down enough of the fuze for it to just about touch the ground, and then I cut it off and held it up with my hands. Then Karl lit the bottom end of it. The fuze, of course, sputtered, puffed, and sparked its way all the way up to the window, and I let go of it when it was just about up to my hands. Then I got the spool again and let down another length of fuze. We amused ourselves this way for most of the afternoon and really had a great time with it.

All the while that we were playing with the fuze, there was the usual stream of refugees and retreating soldiers filing past our house. Most of them didn't pay any attention to us. After all, we were just a couple of local kids playing around, and they didn't care whether we burned our own house down or not. Papa was at his observation post, and Mom must've been on the other side of the house, or something too, so nobody was giving us any problems with our little game. But then a very finely dressed officer, with an immaculate, perfectly pressed uniform, a wide, brightly polished black leather belt, with a pistol in a holster on it, and a long cape with warm looking fur on the inside of it flowing down his back, came riding along on a beautiful white stallion, and he noticed us. I don't know what rank he actually was, but he must've been pretty high ranking, because he was older, and he rode with a great aire of authority around him. Perhaps, being the strategic thinker that he must've been, when he saw us and the small pillar of smoke that was coming from our fuze, and how close to his column of troops we were, he thought that the Russians' attention would really be drawn to where we, and his troops, were, or perhaps he was just fooling around with us. But whatever the case, when he saw us, he waved at us and shouted, "HEY! You there! You're giving the enemy signals! You stop that!" Then he kicked his horse into a gallop and started reaching for his pistol.

We were so scared, we nearly peed our pants. We immediately dropped our fuze and the matches and ran down into the basement and hid behind the potato bin. We were down there for over an hour, but nothing ever came of it. I guess the officer figured that he'd accomplished his mission by scaring us, or maybe he and his troops had a good laugh at our expense, but we never played with the fuze again.

During mid to late January, 1945, it became very cold, and there was quite a bit of snow as well. It became so cold that not only were all of the farm ponds in town frozen over, but even the Baltic Sea froze over, out to about a mile from the beach. Most years, when this would happen, people would go ice skating far out from the beach, even going out to the edge of the ice, just to see what it was like, and a few people even did it this year. We weren't allowed to do that, but we did go out and lay along the bluff to watch them, which was something that we always did, even before all this happened. From our vantage point on the bluff, we could see out very far, so it was interesting when - probably because of the movement of the water, but it could have been from mines or submarines or Russian artillery too, I guess - there would be the sound of an explosion or something way out at the far edge of the ice, and then we could see this crack racing through the ice towards shore, with a popping sound following along with it.

126

By this time, all of Papa's blacksmith apprentices had either gone back to their own homes, or they'd been drafted into the Volkesturm, which was the rather poorly trained last reserve of the Reich, consisting of the very young, the very old, and the infirm. One of these apprentice boys though, named Heinz, who had already been in the Volkesturm, somehow managed to get away from his unit, and instead of going to his own home in another town, he came back to live with us, saying he still wanted to become a blacksmith. Heinz, who was only 15, was quite a rebellious boy, but he took a liking to me, and since he often did some very exciting stuff, I became something like his protégé. This particular time, when he arrived at our house, he carried with him a couple of rifles, a pistol, and quite a lot of ammunition, and after settling in, he immediately embarked on a program of showing me how to use these weapons, and of showing off with them too.

First, we went out to the bluff overlooking the Baltic Sea, with the ice spreading out before us, and he showed me how to shoot the rifles. We laid down on the ground, with him holding the barrel of the rifle, which was a French model, while I held onto the butt and closed my eyes while I was pulling the trigger, bracing myself against the recoil. It wasn't too bad though, because Heinz held it away from me somewhat, so after having shot it the first time, I was elated and thought I'd done something wonderful. We kept on doing that for a while, but when he would shoot, he fired down towards the ice, and the bullet would ricochet off it with a twoinging sound, and it would keep right on going.

Later that week, he grew bolder and started firing the rifle in town. This time, he shot at the ice in one of the ponds in town, and the bullet ricocheted again. Thankfully, there weren't any buildings beyond this particular pond, but there were buildings around us.

But there was so much shooting and so many people with guns wandering around, that even this was largely ignored by the adults in the area. He felt very powerful and cocky because of the guns he had, and he would brag about them and about fighting in the Volkesturm, and so on. One night, while we were waiting for bedtime, he brought me outside and was fooling around with his pistol, when the Polish milkman - the same one that had told us about the Jews being shot along the road - showed up with his wagon. Thinking he was smart or something, Heinz snuck up behind him and pointed the pistol over the Pole's head towards a tree and fired it. We were right outside our house, and the milkman was right there with us, in the front yard. So the poor milkman, who'd already seen more than his share of fighting and people being killed, practically jumped out of his skin and then fell on the ground in front of us, crying hysterically and begging us not to shoot him. Thankfully, Mom came out and yelled at Heinz and took the gun away from him.

I was already beginning to get uneasy with the way Heinz was behaving with his guns, but this really shook me up, so I stopped hanging around him altogether. It was only another day or two after that before Heinz left and went somewhere else.

Not too long after he left, Mom's uncle, whom I'd never seen in my life, showed up at the house with a sled and a horse. He was at least sixty years old, and he had become a refugee, fleeing from his home out east somewhere. He said he was tired of running though, and he just wanted a place to stay until his days were over. I don't remember what his name was or much else about him, but I do remember that he stayed at our house even after we finally left, saying he would take care of it for us. Later on though, after the war, we heard that he had been executed by the Russians after a storm had uncovered all those bodies of the Jews that the Gestapo had shot out on the beach, near Papa's observation post. The Russians wanted to retaliate on the local populace for this, so they counted out a number of people equivalent to the number of bodies that had been exposed, and they executed all of them, including Mom's uncle.

It was very near the end of January by this time, and the Russians had gotten closer to us again. They were so close, and their artillery was so loud now, that there were times when you had to raise your voice just to be heard in normal conversation. We could hear other, smaller, guns too, like the sharp reports from tank cannon and the popping rattle from machine guns. We could even see the Russian artillery shells, as by this time, they were firing over our heads, towards Pillau. It was overcast most of the time, so the shells appeared as small, dark shadows rushing through the clouds, sometimes creating a wake effect, and making a whistling noise with a flapping, corkscrewing kind of sound along with it, I guess, because the shells were tumbling or fishtailing as they flew. And there were also all sorts of airplanes flying around, fighters and bombers and spotter planes. Most of them were Russian, so they attracted a lot of flak from the German side. When the fighters came down to strafe something, their guns made a heavy ripping noise, much louder than regular machine guns on the ground.

Karl and I thought all this was exciting and fascinating. It was like something right out of a Karl Mai adventure novel - he was a popular German author who wrote stories about the American Wild West. We didn't realize how much danger we were really in.

On the evening of January 30th, we huddled in our basement, knowing that the Russians would probably be in town the next day. Papa was still at his post, and by this time, we weren't sure how we were ever going to make contact with him again. The stream of refugees had become a torrent, and our street was packed with them, fleeing in every imaginable conveyance, cars, trucks, farm tractors, horse-drawn flatbed wagons, buggies, sleighs, and even conestoga wagons, and many, many of them were simply fleeing on foot. Our main street had become about the only remaining route into Pillau, as the Russians had come so close now that only a narrow strip of land separated them from the Baltic Sea.

There was something very powerful and reassuring about being in that basement that night, with Mom and my brothers and sisters. We were together, as a family, and this was our house. Every part of that basement became very real and meaningful to me, from the shelves on the wall of the front room, with all the jars of preserves, pickled pigs knuckles, and pork chops, to Papa's wine still, made from a glass jar and some spiral glass tubing, with which he made his cherry wine, to the potato, onion, and turnip bins in the back room, where we had laid our straw mattresses that we'd been sleeping on since our return to Rothenen, several weeks earlier. We were there together, and we knew that God would preserve us together, even though we knew that the next day would bring a tremendous change in our lives.

The morning of January 31st, brought a renewed Russian artillery barrage, closer than ever now. This time, we could even hear the sounds of rifle fire, popping like the sound of boiling water in a coffee pot, along with the more ominous sounds of machine guns and tanks firing. It seemed like it was all around us. Mom didn't even have to tell us kids to stay indoors that day. We just did.

Sometime around noon, the sound of the rifle fire changed. It became much clearer and crisper. It was as if it had come over the horizon and was coming nearer to us by the minute.

I rushed up to my bedroom and climbed into the rafters above my bed, so that I could see out of the small triangular window that was at the highest part of our house. It faced north, out of town, along the road and up the hill towards where Nodems and Grebieten lay. There, coming down the hill and moving westward towards the coast, were soldiers running. They were running and falling and shooting and running and falling and shooting. They were shooting at each other. I couldn't really make out the colors of their uniforms, as they were all dark, but I could tell which side was which. The Germans were running away, being chased by the Russians. But there were times when the Germans would make a stand and would turn and run back towards the Russians, and then the Russians would run back up the hill until more of them came over the top, and then they would turn around and chase the Germans back down the hill. There were a lot of them, but they were still far enough away that I couldn't really tell which of them were getting hit. They would run a ways and then dive to the ground and start shooting, and then they would get up and run a bit further. This went on and on, as they gradually worked their way down the hill towards us.

I was mesmerized by watching them, oblivious to the danger, until Mom called to me from downstairs and told me to get into the basement with the rest of the family. We sat around for what seemed like hours that afternoon, waiting for the inevitable.

It came just before dusk. The volume of shooting outside suddenly grew to enormous proportions, with a lot of it seeming like it was right outside our house, rattling every window pane and glass plate or cup in the house. Ignoring Mom's pleas for me to stay put, I rushed up to my bedroom to peek out the triangular window in the gable to see what was happening. Dozens and dozens of German soldiers were running through town. Many of them were going from house to house, using the buildings as cover, while a rear guard just above town was firing at some Russians back up the hill north of our house. There were also German vehicles, armored half tracks, trucks, and a tank or two, all of them firing, with their guns pointed up the hill in back of our house, or over the Villa to the east, while they fled south. The noise was deafening, and I was awestruck.

Incredibly, our house wasn't hit, not even once, and I thank God for that. The Russians didn't seem to be chasing the Germans anymore, and they certainly didn't pursue them through town, nor did they even seem to be firing at them while they passed through. The German unit passed through and soon were gone, yet Rothenen was unscathed.

After that, it grew quiet, oddly enough, except for the continual artillery shelling, though after the clamor that had just passed by our front door, the artillery seemed insignificant. The town itself was deserted. No one was on the streets at all, not the locals, not even the refugees. That was the last of either the refugees or the German soldiers that we saw in town. They were all gone. Now we were just waiting for the Russians to come. So I went back down to the basement.

It didn't occur to me then that the German front line had just passed through town, going in the wrong direction, and that we were now in No Man's Land.

9

Final Flight

Meanwhile, Papa's squad at the observation post were packing their bags, getting ready to retreat too. The battery had observation posts scattered all the way up the Samland coast to the Lithuanian border, and as the Russians came down that way, the various squads occupying those posts had retreated down to the next one further south, and so on, until they began arriving at his post too. None of the squads operating these posts had any vehicles, since they weren't designed to go anywhere; they were only supposed to stay in that one spot and report on what they saw. So when it became imperative that they retreat or be captured by the Russians, their soldiers used whatever personal vehicles they had, usually horse-drawn wagons or sleds, and they loaded their guns, grenades, ammunition, food, and supplies into these and joined the hordes of refugees fleeing south. When they arrived at the next station, they would stay there and rest for a while, somewhat bolstering the post's own defenses - though none of them desired to see real combat at all, as they weren't designed for this either - and when the Russians got close enough, the officer in charge of that station would order them all to retreat to the next station south of there. This process continued on down the coast, and soon Papa's station was ordered to leave as well.

Along the way, one of the other squads picked up some German soldiers from another unit. These men had been taken prisoner by the Russians days earlier, and then, while they were being transported from the local POW collection area to one of the large processing camps far to the rear of the Russian Army, they escaped. Then they hid and slowly made their way back towards the front, mostly traveling at night and sometimes aided by the local populace. Finally, they crossed back into German lines during one of the Germans' frequent counterattacks, and now they were trying to make it down to Pillau to rejoin an operational unit there.

What was significant about these escaped soldiers though, was that they had a story to tell, and that story spread like wildfire through the German ranks, especially those of the Marine Artillerie, who were considered reservists.

Their story was of what the Russians would do after they had captured an area. They had seen with their own eyes how the Russians would go into a town, round up whatever men were there, frequently finding some excuse to execute many of them, and then march them off to labor camps in Russia. Then they saw the Russians go into the houses and rape and torture the women, often killing them when they were done, right in front of their children. Many of the children were also raped, tortured, and killed. And finally, the Russians would raze the town, burning or bulldozing the houses to the ground. They told tales of utter horror and depravity and of atrocities that were simply unspeakable. They said that the Russians were driven by absolute hatred of the Germans, and not just of the German Army, but of all Germans. They said that the Russians reveled in killing German civilians and thought of it as quite a sport, even a patriotic duty, as if their ultimate goal was to annihilate the entire German race from the face of the earth. And they made a point to say that the Russians simply had no respect for human life at all, often killing their own men if they showed any signs of cowardice or hesitation in obeying the orders of their officers.

This story sent shock waves through the Marine Artillerie, and it galvanized them to stand and fight for their families and homes, most of which had been left behind. No wonder the beleaguered German Army fought so hard during this time, as that same story was repeated by hundreds of others in similar situations all up and down the Eastern Front, as I found out years later.

In Papa's particular situation, their story changed his mind about the whether to leave his family in Rothenen. After all, at least in his case, even though they had retreated south of Rothenen, the Russians had not followed them, and in fact, the Russians' attack had even begun to falter by the night of February 1st, as the Germans' defense was now being aided by the arrival of the pocket battleship Admiral Scheer, which was sending huge 11-inch shells crashing into the Russian lines, tearing great craters in the ground and making so much rubble of their armored formations and headquarters areas*. So there was a chance, and where there was a chance, there was hope.

Immediately, Papa talked with a farmer friend of his from the same squad, who was also from Rothenen, Oskar Audehm, and he persuaded him to join Papa in a foray back to Rothenen to rescue their families. Together, they went to their battery commander, and he gave them permission to do this, so they rounded up a wagon and a couple of horses and headed off into the night, not knowing what they would find and being armed only with their rifles, but being totally prepared to give their lives to save their families.

Late that night, long after we had barred the door, closed the curtains, and all gone to bed on our straw mattresses in the basement, there was a loud knocking on our front door.

Mom, who was sleeping in her bedroom with Hildegaard, sat straight up in bed, jolted fully awake in an instant at the one sound she most dreaded to hear. In a loud whisper, with the hairs standing on edge on her back and arms, she gasped, "The Russians are here!" Mom was very pregnant with her 9th child, but she and Hildegaard rocketed out of bed and rushed downstairs to wake us and tell us to hide. Some of the rest of us had heard it too, and we were already awake by the time they got down with us, so we quickly hid. Karl and I were behind the potato bin as Ruth rushed in carrying Gerhardt, and followed by my other sisters, all of them clambering over each other in their haste and fear, the younger ones whimpering and crying just a little.

But the sound of the door being crashed through never came. Instead, there was only silence. Then, there came a faint tapping noise on the kitchen window. It kept up for a while, and eventually we heard someone calling from the outside, in a muffled yell, with their hands cupped between their mouth and the window, "Maria! Maria! Karl! Come quickly! Open up! Open the door!"

It was Papa!

Ursula giggled gleefully, "It's Papa, it's Papa!"

Ecstatic, everyone rushed out of the potato room and up the stairs to let Papa in. We crowded around him in the dark and peppered him with so many questions that he couldn't get a word in. Finally, he held up his hands and said in a stern yet hushed voice, "All right! Enough! Listen, the Russians are just at the top of the hill. They could be here any minute, so we must leave immediately. Let's get ready, now, go!"

Mom quickly took control then, having already thought out what everyone should do. She gave orders to each of us, and then we began scurrying around, trying to find things in the dark, without causing a ruckus by running into anything and knocking it over. Karl and I both put on a couple extra layers of our own clothing, and then we put on about three layers of Papa's clothing too, to give us something to grow into, and also for when Papa finally would return to us. I had to roll the sleeves and pant cuffs way up on Papa's suits, so I must've been quite a sight. Mom and Hildegaard got our backpacks and put a ham into one and a huge loaf of bread into the other and then gave them to Karl and me. Each of the rest of us put on extra clothing and gathered what few necessities that could be stuffed into a bag. Papa retrieved a few important legal documents, such as our birth certificates and their marriage certificate, and gave them to Mom, but that was all we took. We didn't even get our photo albums. We were done in just thirty minutes, by midnight, and then we were out the door and getting into the milk wagon that Papa had borrowed.

The horses were alert and tense, their breath forming billowing clouds in the night air. As Papa flicked their reins and guided them out onto the snowy street, they seemed to know that we were fleeing for our lives, and they joined us in trying to be quiet and fast, pulling hard when we got stuck in some mud or slipped on the icy cobblestones, but never whinnying, not even once.

The night was clear and chilly, but we hardly noticed it. No one said a word, as we crouched together for warmth and security in the back of the wagon. This time, the ride was not a fantasy at all. Russian artillery pieces thundered salvo after salvo from somewhere very nearby, their flashes lighting up the sky like lightening and reflecting off the clouds of their smoke like the fires of Hades, their shells glowing dull red and scudding away like demons. More ominous though, was the sound of armored vehicles maneuvering and churning up the dirt just at the top of the hill behind our house. I imagined that I could even hear the sounds of voices, as the unit commanders ordered their tank crews into some kind of formation just above our little village. I could even see some of this going on, in the glow from the artillery flashes, as I turned to look back towards our house.

Down by the schoolhouse, we met up with the other wagon and Oskar Audehm's family. He and Papa exchanged a few words, and then they continued down the road, south, towards Pillau, with our wagon in the lead.

The time passed agonizing by, as the horses trotted on and on, as fast as they could reasonably go in the snow, yet nowhere near fast enough. Soon we found out where that battery of Russian artillery was, that seemed to be firing from a position so close to town. They were between us and the next town, but they were up on a hill, overlooking the road. Papa and Oskar just kept right on going, grimly determined to pass them or die trying, while Mom whispered "Thank You Jesus, thank You Jesus," over and over again. Over a dozen heavy Russian guns were lined up on top of this hill, just a couple hundred meters away. They fired one

right after another, from one end of the line all the way
to the other end of the line, and then they would start
over again. Each shot was so loud that we could feel
the shock waves hitting us, taking our breath away and
causing Ursula and Gerhardt to whimper and cry,
putting their hands over their ears. The flashes of the
guns filled the sky and reflected brilliantly on the snow,
lighting the entire area around us and exposing us for
all who cared to see. The soldiers manning the cannon
were in plain sight, silhouettes, also exposed by the
flashes, moving like small robots, back and forth and
back and forth, carrying shell after shell to the fire
breathing dragons that they served and fed. It was a
wonder and a miracle that they didn't see us, for we
certainly would have been short work for them if they
had cared to notice us.

    Passing from there, we drove on, mile after mile,
passing several towns, and not seeing anyone on the
road. It was eerily silent, except for the constant
barrage of artillery in the background, and we were
praying constantly. It seemed as though perhaps two or
three hours had passed, when suddenly there was a
brilliant flash of light on the road, right up ahead of us,
by about a kilometer. This was immediately followed by
another flash of light, an explosion, just a couple
hundred meters in front of us, and a little to our left.
The nearly simultaneous twin booms coming from those
bursts hit us like thunderclaps and we all screamed,
because of how scared we were. Then more flashes of
light and explosions, one, two, three, four, until a total
of five sets of boom - swish - boom, with their paired
flashes, had turned the landscape in front of us into a
burning cauldron of twisted metal and smoldering junk.

    We were terrified and crouched low in the wagon,
but Papa and Oskar continued to press forward, despite
having to rein in the horses, which had reared up in

fright at the first explosions. The fires left over from the explosions acted like beacons, guiding our way in the dark, and making us easy targets for whoever had done all this shooting. Yet as we drew near the fires, we could see that they belonged to a column of now-burned out Russian tanks, probably a recon element, pressing deep into German lines, trying to find where the German defenses lay. Well, they had found them, all right, and soon we passed them too, a single German anti-tank gun, poking out from behind a berm near the road. We could see the shadows of the German soldiers, hunkering down over their weapon, the vapor of their panting breath making little white puffs of cotton in the now waning firelight of the burning tanks. We could feel their eyes following us, and without making a sound, we whispered, "Thank you," as we passed them by.

Time passed slowly as we rode silently on, quietly praying and thanking God for His deliverance. None of us really thought much about our having just left home for the last time. We were too keyed up, too afraid for our lives and afraid of what the Russians might do to us if they captured us. Yet for us kids, it was also like an adventure. We didn't really understand about the things that might happen to us, so although we were afraid, we were only afraid of the immediate dangers from the gunfire that was close to us. Beyond that, in the quiet time that we spent riding in the wagon, our thoughts, or at least my thoughts, drifted into imagining that we were on some great adventure, making a heroic escape during the night, sneaking away from the enemy right under their noses. After a while, the road got closer to the beach, so we were able to look out over the ice and see the moon reflecting silver off the frozen sea. It was beautiful and yet out of place in its beauty, because of what we were doing. It made me think we were going on a midnight cruise on the ocean, but perhaps on a ghost ship, or something, because it certainly wasn't a fun cruise.

Just before dawn broke, those of us in the back of the wagon were rudely awakened as we lurched to a stop. Someone shouted, "Halt! Wer it Da?", which means, "Halt! Who goes there?" In back of us, along the side of the road, was a long line of refugee wagons and people milling about or laying on the ground, sleeping. They had obviously spent the night there, and some even looked like they'd been camping there for quite a while. But right in front of us was a German Military Police roadblock. They had a large truck parked sideways across the street, with an armored half-track up on one side of the road, with its machine gun pointing in our direction. Two soldiers stood in front of our wagon, one with his rifle in the ready position, pointing it at us, and the other with his hand up in the air, as he was the one that had spoken. A third soldier was standing behind their truck, off to the side, covering the first two with a sub-machine gun.

Papa and Oskar, still in their uniforms and carrying their rifles, got out of the wagons and went to speak with the MPs. When they came back a few minutes later, they said that the MPs were only allowing people with official business in Pillau to pass by, since the city was already too crowded with refugees. Papa and Oskar could have gotten through, because their unit was now in Pillau, but the rest of us wouldn't be allowed to pass.

Oskar, however, was a farmer, and he was friends with several of the farmers that lived in this area, so he knew the lay of the land. He now said, "Otto, let's turn the wagons around and go back a ways, so the MPs can't see us. Then we'll turn off and go across the field, as I know another way into the city."

So with that, we turned around, and Oskar led the way off the road and across the fields of the north end of the Frishe Nehrung isthmus, through the little town of Lochstadt on the Frisches Haff side of the isthmus and south along the other beach road there. There were quite a number of refugees on this road too, and soon we came to another roadblock. This time, Oskar led us up a narrow dirt track, between farmers fields, and then back and forth in an almost zigzag pattern through or between various fields, or along the single rail road track that went through some woods as we approached Pillau. There were a few houses and outlying villages, but there weren't many people around right then, so we were able to make it without any further encounters with the MPs.

There was an ancient wall that formed the city limits, dating back to the days when the Swedes landed there and built a fort as part of their war with the Poles. It was about five meters high and one meter thick, and in many places, the woods came right up to it, though the MPs had cleared the woods from around where the two main roads came into the city, so that they could set up their roadblocks there. The rail road tracks came into the city only about 200 meters inland from the road on the Baltic Sea side of the isthmus, which was less than two kilometers wide at that point, and they didn't have a roadblock, even though the guards could see them from their position on the road. We found though, that by getting off the tracks and driving along the edge of their inland side, between their berm and the woodline, so that the berm that they were built on shielded us from the view of the guards, we could get to where the tracks passed into the city, mount the berm with some extra effort and pushing, and then go along the tracks into the city. As soon as we did this though, dozens of other refugees that were on the road, waiting at the MPs' roadblock saw us and began rushing across the small open space between the wall and the woods to get on the railroad tracks as well.

Once we had made it past the city wall, we had to stay on the tracks for a while longer, as they passed through the old fort, and there was a moat between the inner and outer walls. This was a tricky feat, because the wagons weren't much narrower than the gauge of the tracks on the bridge, and the horses really had to watch their step to keep from falling between the ties. Papa even got out and guided the horses by hand. After making it through the inner wall though, we were able to switch back over to the road.

Papa and Oskar knew how to get to their battery headquarters, which was where we now headed. It was on the Baltic coast, about a kilometer past the inner wall along the main road, so it was quite close to where we came into the city. Their headquarters was a small compound* with a few aging 150mm coastal artillery guns in revetments built into the old city wall, 30 meters from the beach. They had a headquarters building with a fire control tower on top of it and a barracks building, supply shed, and ammo bunker behind that. Their area behind the old city wall was surrounded by a smaller, more recent (but still old), and more decorative wall that now had barbed wire installed on top of it. Nearly the entire complement of the battery's soldiers was now present. Most of them were setting up fighting positions on top of the buildings, at the front gate, and in places where the ground was high enough that they could see over the back wall. Others of them were trying to figure out how to take their cannons out of their casements and turn them around to fire at the land behind them, up the peninsula, as the casements had been built so that they could fire only out over the water, giving about a 180 degree zone of coverage, which was totally inadequate for their current situation. They didn't look like they were making much progress.

Papa brought us into the headquarters building and had us wait in the hall while he went to find his commander. After about half an hour, he returned with his commander, their first sergeant, and a couple of soldiers, one of whom had a bundle in his hands. Papa introduced us to his commander, though I don't remember now what his name was. He greeted us and introduced us to the first sergeant and the other soldiers, Kurt and Markus. He complemented us on our having such a fine man as Otto as our Papa, saying that Otto had served the unit and the Papaland well during his five years with them. He said that he would've liked to have had the opportunity to show us around the base, but of course, because of the current preparations, he couldn't do that. However, he did give us Kurt and Markus for the rest of our time in Pillau. Kurt, the one with the bundle, knew his way around Pillau, and Markus would be able to help carry things. He also offered Kurt's bundle, which had a few military food rations in it, as a token of his appreciation for us letting him keep our Papa.

Then he said what we really wanted to hear. The German Navy had started a mass evacuation of the entire Samland pocket. Every available ship was being called into service for this, at Admiral Dönitz's personal command. Right now, although there were several ships boarding passengers, our best bet would be the General Von Steuben, a converted hospital ship. It was going to leave soon, so we should probably make haste to get down to the docks. Kurt would be able to help us do that. He said that a lot of refugees were trying to cross the Frisches Haff (sound) on the pack ice, or on the Frische Nehrung isthmus, but he strongly advised us against this, as the Russian artillery was targeting all the routes that the refugees were taking, which was why Pillau itself wasn't getting hit by artillery right then. He said that thousands of people had already been caught out in the open by the shelling and were simply slaughtered, or they had fallen into the frigid waters when the shells ripped up the ice and made it unstable. The Russians weren't very good at artillery spotting though, and they had a hard time at hitting specific targets, like ships, so it would be better for us to take one of the ships out. The Russian Navy also hadn't done very much against German shipping, though there were reports of their submarines prowling around now and then. There was one ship that had been sunk just the day before, the Wilhelm Gustloff, another converted hospital ship, but it had sailed out of Gotenhafen, a long ways from Pillau.

His words weren't very encouraging at this point, but they gave us our only way out, so we grasped at that straw and believed that God would take care of us and get us out of Pillau alive and together. He then took us into their small kitchen and let us rest and eat the rations he'd given us. Papa was anxious for us to be on our way though, so he soon had us organized and on our way again.

On our way out of the headquarters compound, we ran into some other friends of ours from Rothenen, the Schaack family. Rudy Schaack was Karl's age, and his father was a fisherman who was also a member of a different reserve unit where they would be on duty for several weeks and then off duty for several weeks. Rudy's father was in civilian clothes, which we felt was rather odd, but they said he was taking Rudy's mother and two younger sisters down to get on a ship too, so Papa asked them to join us, which they were glad for.

145

The roads in Pillau were jammed. Wagon after wagon lined the streets, with an occasional sled, automobile, or Army truck mixed in between them. The wagons were piled high with people's belongings. It wasn't just clothes and furniture in the wagons, either. It was valuable stuff, like expensive paintings and boxes of jewels. But it was all abandoned by the side of the road. The people who owned this treasure had fled towards the harbor. More people constantly passed by too, but they just ignored what was in the wagons, completely focused, as they were, upon making it to the docks.

We hadn't gone far after making it back onto the main road before we had to leave our wagon by the road and go forward on foot too. It was completely impassable. Up ahead, someone's wagon had overturned in the middle of the road, and the father and older son of that family were trying to get their horse under control. It kept on rearing up, terrified at being confined and not understanding what was going on. Finally, they just cut the traces and let the horse go free. Dozens of other horses were roaming around as well, their owners already having done that. Papa and Oskar did this with their horses now too.

We then joined the throng of people streaming down to the harbor. It wasn't a panic, at least not just yet. But no one was wasting any time either. The sky was bright with sunshine this morning, but no one was laughing or standing out enjoying the sunshine. It was completely different from how I remembered it coming back from my cruise with the Rothenen fishermen. No one was selling fish or bread or anything else. No one was talking in pleasant tones, and what was said was hushed and urgent. In the distance, the whistling scream and reverberating thuds of the Russian artillery shells still drove us on.

146

The street that we were on was so packed with wagons, horses, and people, that it was very difficult to make progress, and Papa was growing frustrated. We constantly had to pick our way back and forth between the wagons, and even keeping our footing was difficult, since the cobblestones were covered with ice, and the street was bowed in the middle, so that water would run off into the gutters on the side of the road. Several of the wagons had crashed into each other, creating roadblocks in places, and sometimes you'd even see horses falling down, because their hooves had slid out from under them on the ice. Finally, Papa asked Kurt if he knew a better way to get to the harbor. Kurt said he did and motioned for us to follow him.

We cut off to the left, taking a narrow side street, all twenty of us, trudging on and on, for nearly an hour. We took first one street and then another, going first left and then right through alleyways and around dark corners. When we came out onto a main street, Kurt admitted that he didn't know where we were, but after a while, Papa looked around and saw that we were on the same street that we started on, just downhill from where we had been by about 200 meters.

Papa got angry with Kurt now, but he was in too much of a hurry to do anything about it right then, so we plunged back into the crowd heading down hill towards the harbor.

It took us another hour of slipping and sliding down the crowded street before we reached the dockyards. There before us, lay mountains of suitcases and bags and boxes that people had thrown away, since there wasn't any room for them on the ships. Long lines of people snaked between piles of discarded luggage, abandoned wagons, wandering horses, a bombed out freight car on a rail road siding, and several warehouses and fish factories, most of which also had considerable bomb damage. There were heaps of rubbish, rotting food, and feces, whose smells overpowered the faintly pleasant smells of fish and seawater. Oddly, there were even some shade trees lining the water's edge and along some of the streets, as the waterfront district in Pillau had once been a well-designed and manicured place of beauty, but they seemed out of place in this mayhem.

The lines of people went down to the water, where a great white ship was docked along the stone quay. It looked like a big passenger liner, and it had a gangplank going steeply up the side of it onto the deck, where people were fanning out, trying to find a place to spend their imminent sea journey. I could see the name, General von Steuben, under the bow of the ship, and it occurred to me that this was the same ship we'd passed next to in the fishing boat, when the fishermen from Rothenen took Karl, Feter, and me to Pillau to deliver their fish a couple summers ago. It made me wonder where Feter and the fishermen were and how they were making it through this time. Thinking about them made me miss Feter too and wish that he was with us. Already, the entire deck seemed to be covered with people, and not just the main deck, but also the decks on the superstructure, all the way up to the top. The ship seemed to be very full, riding so low in the water that you couldn't even see the waterline painted on the hull.

"Over here. This is the way," said Kurt, as he headed off towards one of the lines of people. As we obediently followed him, we noticed that people in the other lines seemed to queue up tighter as we passed, as if to keep us from cutting in front of them. Many of them still carried heavy suitcases and other belongings, in some vain hope that they'd be allowed to keep them once they boarded the ship. We saw that there were many other ships in the harbor too. Some of them were military. Some were freighters or fishing boats. But all of them had a line of people leading up to them and piles of discarded belongings at various places along that line.

Once we were in the proper line, Papa said to Kurt, "You will stay with us until we board the ship. I want you to help Maria with little Gerhardt, since she is pregnant with our ninth child and is nearly due." It was another hour of waiting in line before we neared the ship. We spent the time talking with the Schaacks, swapping our stories of how we each made it out of Rothenen and past the police cordon around Pillau. It was comforting having them with us, even though we weren't really friends. They were encouraging for us, just having someone else from our hometown along with us.

We were starting to get excited, the closer we got to the ship. It would be such a relief to be on board finally, and to get underway and escape from the Russians. But just as we were nearly there, with only another ten or twenty people between us and the entrance to the gangplank, someone called down from the ship, yelling, "No more! No more! The ship is full! The ship is full! Nobody can get in here anymore!" And then they pulled the gangplank up and began throwing off the big mooring ropes, so that they could move out into the channel.

We all just stood there at first, too shocked to do anything. This was our last chance to escape from the Russians, and a sense of despair and dismay began spreading through the crowd. We could hear the artillery shells crashing in the distance, and we all wondered whatever would happen to us, now that we were trapped in Pillau, with the 39th Guards Army bearing down on us.

At first, we all just stood there, too stunned to respond to what had just happened. But after the shock had worn off a little, Papa became lividly angry with Kurt. He put down his pack and shoved Kurt, saying, "This is all your fault! You said you knew how to get us here, but you were just showing off, you stupid fool. Didn't you know that my family's safety depended on them getting on board that ship? Even if we had stayed on the main street, we would've made it here in time to get on board, but no, you had to take us on that stupid detour, and you got us lost!" Kurt was terrified, not just because Papa was so much bigger and older than he was, but also because he was a Master Sergeant, and this could have a lot of impact on him once he got back to the unit.

Mom tried to intervene, "Otto, Otto, please, stop this," but he kept on shouting and berating Kurt, just ignoring the rest of us. Finally, Oskar stood between them and said, "Look, Otto, this isn't helping anything. We need to find another ship, and we must do it quickly. Come now. Let's start looking."

Papa calmed down then, though he had to walk away for a while to do that, but when he returned, he and Oskar agreed that they would split up. Oskar would take Kurt, while we would take Markus and the Schaacks, and they would try to find another ship that way. After talking about it a while longer, Papa decided that he would take us over towards the naval pier on the other side of the harbor, while Oskar took the rest towards the marina in the center of the harbor.

So we started off on another long walk. This time, we were cutting across and through the lines of refugees waiting for boats. There were a lot of people milling about now, doing the same thing we were doing, after having been turned away from the Von Steuben. We followed the cobblestone and granite quay inland to where it made a right turn, dodging the piles of refuse and luggage as we had before, but this time, we weren't nearly as excited as we were earlier. With no immediate prospect of finding a decent ship, and since us kids didn't really know where the naval pier was, we became bored and irritable. Papa was focussing on getting us there, and perhaps because of his earlier spat with Kurt, he wasn't saying much to anyone, so it was up to Mom, Markus, and Mr. Schaack to hold us together and keep us from getting separated and lost.

It turned out that the naval pier was a couple of kilometers away by foot, even though it was only half that by water, as we had to make a great U-turn along the harbor's edge. Since we weren't in the best of spirits right then, it seemed like it took forever to get there, and we were tired and sore as well, but as soon as I saw the four or five naval ships there, my curiosity quickly got the best of me. There weren't any large navy ships, but there were a couple of destroyer-like vessels, a tender of some sort, and some smaller ships*. There were also more military personnel walking around, but no one seemed to be in charge here anymore than they were on the other side. Long lines of people still snaked around towards whatever ships were present, passing near their attendant piles of discarded stuff.

As Karl and I gawked at the naval ships, we were only partially aware that Papa had left us standing in the middle of the wharf, between boarding lines for a destroyer and the tender, while he wandered off in search of someone to talk to. I was fascinated by all the machinery, the cranes, guns, torpedo tubes, and so on that was on the navy ships, plus their raked lattice masts, with their radars and radio antennas all crowding each other. And off in the distance, now in the middle of the harbor, was the long, white form of the General Von Steuben, riding very low and sluggish in

151

the water, slowly making its way past various other boats and a couple of tugs, towards the channel.

Papa was gone for a long time, and since we had nothing else to do, we did what kids everywhere would do and started fooling around, or at least Karl, Rudy, and I did. Mom and the girls just sat dejectedly on the ground, or on their suitcases. Markus and Mr. Schaack stood politely next to each other without really saying anything. As the sun was getting ready to go down, one of the destroyers blew its horn, and someone on it announced that it was full and that they were leaving, much like what happened to us in the line to the Von Steuben. People began milling around, some rather stunned, some angry, but most just depressed at having to start looking for yet another ship to leave on. There were lots of ships and boats loading people, but there were just so many people, thousands upon thousands, that the ships couldn't load them fast enough to make even a dent in the crowd.

Just then, Papa showed up with a smile on his face. He gathered us together and said, "Come, follow me, quickly." With that, he forged out towards the end of the naval pier, where there weren't any ships docked at all. Confused, but obedient, we followed him, only to see him stop and stand near the water's edge. He turned to us, grinning from ear to ear, and said, "Just wait here. There's another ship, an ex-French minesweeper, about to arrive from Denmark, and we can get on that one. It's already got its supplies and everything, so there won't even be any waiting for it."

A few more minutes went by, and it started to get dusk. Normally, the harbor lights would've come on by now, and there would be musicians playing nearby at some café, making a soft, romantic scene. This evening, however, there would be no lights, only the teaming thousands of scared people and the incessant whine of

Russian artillery shells passing overhead and heading towards the hapless refugees out on the ice pack of the Frische Haff. As the sun glided beneath the horizon at the mouth of the channel, it started to grow colder too, and a hush fell on the harbor. No one seemed to want to speak or make any noise at all. People just huddled closer together for warmth and protection and hoped that the night would be a short one.

All at once, two loud horn blasts came from out in the harbor, but quite nearby. Turning, we saw a rather smallish naval escort vessel of some type approaching us from the channel. It was gray, with several machine gun tubs, two at either end, and two more in the middle, and it had some funny-looking rails on its after deck. Several sailors now appeared next to us and waved to the pilot, who guided the boat expertly to a stop right in front of us. Its diesel engines still throbbing, the crew let down its gang plank to allow an officer to get off. This man stopped to talk with another officer on the quay next to us, and then both of them turned and got back on the boat. The one that was part of the crew reached up to a box on the bulkhead next to him, opened it, and pulled out a microphone. Turning it on, he announced over their loudspeakers, "Attention! The minesweeper Lotringen will begin boarding refugees immediately. Please form a line in front of the gangplank for checking in."

Like a stampeding herd, people from all over rushed towards us. They came from the backs of other lines. They came from far down the pier, near the marina. And they came from all around the buildings and streets in back of us. Anyone who wasn't already committed to another line dropped what they were doing and ran to get in line for the Lotringen. The sailors who had helped tie up the Lotringen now directed these newcomers where they should stand, and as we looked, to our great amazement, we found ourselves standing right at the head of the line, without having to go anywhere.

Papa just grinned, looked skyward, and whispered, "Thank You, Jesus!"

10

The Lotringen

As soon as one of the sailors motioned to us,
Rudy Schaack grabbed up little Gerhardt, who'd been
sleeping in Mom's arms, and rushed up the gangplank.
Ruth, Karl, and I were quick to follow him, but Mr.
Schaack was next, scooping up Ursula in his arms and
acting like he was one of the family too, while Mom -
who as you will remember, was very pregnant and about
to burst - brought up the rear, herding the other girls
and trying to keep the rest of the people at bay long
enough for all of us to get on board. When we got to the
top of the gangplank, we were met by several of the
crew, but hordes of other people swarmed up from
behind us and began rushing this way and that,
everyone looking for a corner or someplace to plop down
and call their own. Since we were trying to be all
orderly and polite, we were simply overwhelmed by
everyone else, and soon people were jostling us, moving
between us, and beginning to separate us from each
other.

It didn't take long before Hildegaard realized that
Mom and Papa were nowhere to be found, so she
ordered us to hold hands while we figured out what to
do. It took quite a bit of effort for us just to link up like
that. Markus and the Schaacks were also gone, and
Gerhardt was gone with them, so it was just the seven
of us, wondering what to do, lost in a sea of people, on a
ship that we knew nothing about. More and more
people crowded up the gangplank in back of us, and
they were now covering every part of the ship that we
could see from where we were. Ursula, who'd been set
down by Mr. Schaack at the top of the gang plank, was
crying and whimpering, clinging desperately to
Hildegaard's skirt, not content with just holding her
hand, while the rest of us slowly closed the distance
between us until we were all huddled in a small group
near the middle of the ship. This allowed us to talk
among ourselves, and it gave us some protection from
the swarms of refugees roving around.

All of us began asking each other were Mom was
and when we'd last seen her. Mariann and Waltraut
sensed our fear and confusion, and they began
whimpering as well, which just drove Ursula to cry even
more, sobbing, "Where's Mommy? I want Mommy!"
Mom and the others just seemed to disappear, and even
the older ones of us were really starting to get worried
about it.

After what seemed like forever, we heard over the
loud speaker, "The Flemming family stay where you are.
Stay where you are. The Flemming family, stay where
you are. Your mother is okay. We'll come and get you."
Karl, Hildegaard, Ruth, and I all looked at each other in
amazement, making comments like, "What the...?" and
"What's going on?" The younger girls looked up at us
with hopeful expressions on their faces, Mariann
asking, "What does that mean? Where's Mommy?"

while Ursula raised her hands towards Hildegaard to
ask to be picked up and held.

Soon, Karl noticed a couple sailors on an upper
deck, leaning over the railing and looking down over the
midships at the throng of refugees milling around on
the deck, like they were looking for someone, so he
waved his hands and shouted, "Jah, the Flemming
family is over here! We're over here!" One of the sailors
pointed to him and then waved back, shouting
something that we couldn't hear, and then they both
came down the stairs and headed for us.

When the sailors finally arrived where we were,
one of them said, "Don't worry, kids, your mother is ok.
Captain Lieutenant Sehlbach has given her his quarters
and has asked us to find you and bring you there too.
Get your things now, and come with us. Thank you."
So with that, we picked up what few things we had with
us and trotted off after the two sailors.

The sailors led us around to the starboard side of
the ship, a little forward of where we got on, up
underneath the superstructure, along an open
passageway on the main deck, to the executive officer's
stateroom, dodging or stepping over dozens of refugees
and their belongings along the way. Karl and I were the
first ones into the cabin, as we were a little bolder than
the girls. The first thing that struck me about the room
was how small it was. There was only one small bed,
and it took up half the room, on the left as we came in.
Then over on the right side of the room was a small
sink, a table and chair, a mirror, and a small chest of
drawers with a wardrobe attached. It seemed crowded
in there even without any people in it, and now the
seven of us were pouring in, so I could see that it was
going to be so tight that it would be hard to even turn
around without bumping into someone.

We found Mom sitting in the chair by the table, holding Gerhardt and trying to recuperate. Mom looked really tired, but as soon as we saw her, we all ran up to her, shouting "Here's Mom!" "Mommy!" "Where have you been, Mom?" "What happened to you, Mom?" "We were so worried about you, Mom!" and so on. The girls were hugging on her and talking on and on, with Ursula jumping up and down and trying to crawl into her lap with Gerhardt. It took quite a while for our joyous hubbub to quiet down, what with all the questions and exclamations we had, so we didn't even notice when the sailors left.

When Mom finally got a chance to speak, she told us that she'd fainted and fallen to the deck after having to climb up the gang plank. The ship's executive officer, Captain Lieutenant Lloyd Sehlbach, had found her and had gotten some sailors to bring her to his cabin and to see after her needs. Papa and Markus weren't allowed to board the ship, since they were able-bodied fighting men - and in uniform, and they'd been met at the bottom of the gang plank by an officer who had told them so. They had to return to their unit anyway, so they left as soon we all got on the ship. We fell silent upon hearing that, as we knew that it would be a long, long time before we could ever see him again, and the chances that we would never see him again were very high. But this was war, and things like that happened all the time, so we just accepted it. Besides, he'd prepared us for this, and he'd said his good-byes weeks in advance, the first time we started to flee. As for the Schaacks, well, they'd just disappeared after Rudy dropped Gerhardt off, probably so no one would tell them to stay and fight too, like had happened with Papa and Markus. We never did see them again, though I've spoken to Rudy in recent times and found that they did finish the voyage with us.

We spent the rest of the evening there in the cabin with Mom, content just to be with her in a quiet, secure place, while outside, crowds of people jostled each other in the hallways and on the decks for a place they could call their own for the journey. The only time we ventured out was to go to the bathroom, which we discovered was downstairs on the first "inside" deck. It was very crowded and smelly there, and there was a line of people that stretched nearly the whole length of the hallway where it was. Other than that, the only people we saw was when a sailor knocked on the door to deliver supper to us, "Compliments of Captain Lieutenant Sehlbach, and with his best wishes." I was very impressed with this Captain Lieutenant Sehlbach, though I never did see him, because of the kindness and consideration that he showed us even during this time of confusion and war.

After several hours, we heard an announcement over the loudspeaker system, saying that the ship was full, and a few minutes after that, we heard the diesel engines starting and felt a bump and then some movement, as we pulled away from the dock. We didn't go far though. Just a few minutes after getting started, we stopped, I guess at the entrance to the harbor, and dropped anchor. It was late at night by this time, so we just went to bed after that, with us older kids sleeping on the floor, the younger ones on the bed, and Mom staying in her chair. It was another whole day before we left that spot, as we were apparently waiting for an escort ship.

The next morning, despite the crowds thronging all over the ship, our curiosity got the best of us, and we asked Mom if we could go exploring. Confident that we couldn't wander too far away on board a ship at sea, and that the crew - who had already proven themselves competent and courteous - would look after us, Mom agreed to let us go, though she decided that Ursula and Gerhardt would have to stay with her. So in wide-eyed wonder we dashed out of our cabin and immediately set out on a quest to explore every inch of the ship.

We started by turning left and going up to the forecastle, where the anchors were hanging, suspended in the water by their chains. Then we went up on the fore gun tub, which we discovered was a dual-purpose 88mm anti-aircraft cannon. It was really big, and Karl and I at least, were in awe of it. There was a young sailor there, just a couple years older than Karl, who explained how everything worked, how the gun was elevated and turned and so on, but he didn't let us touch anything. After seeing his demonstration, Karl and I had a little disagreement with Hildegaard over what to do next. We were eager to push on and see the rest of the ship, but she wanted to take a more leisurely tour, so that she could see more of these sailors and maybe get to talk with some of them. Karl and I just laughed at her and forged ahead, leaving Hildegaard to shepherd Ruth, Mariann, and Waltraut around at their own pace.

So Karl and I, now freed of our sisterly fetters, ran up the steps onto the bridge and walked around, inspecting everything. The crew didn't let us go into the enclosed bridge, but they did show us around on the flying bridge above that, so we saw the gyrocompass, signal lights, and helm, etc. Then we went back down to the quarterdeck and saw where the life boats were, where the smoke stack was, and the 37mm gun tubs amidships, and the fire direction boxes, and all that. And finally, we ran back down to the main deck, towards the stern, and explored where the aft gun tub was, which was also an 88mm, and the mine rails, which went along the sides of the deck past our cabin, where there was a storage room for them, and all that, before heading down inside the ship, to explore the wards, galley, sleeping areas, and all the other places that there wasn't some crewmember stopping us from getting into. We spent practically the entire day exploring the ship, and we still hadn't even really left port yet. Along the way, we also met some other boys our age, though I don't remember any of their names, so now we had a gang to pal around with. By the time we were done with all of this activity, it was getting dark again, and we were exhausted and terribly hungry. That night, and for the rest of our time on the ship, Karl and I decided that it would be better for us just to sleep outside the door to our cabin, on a blanket, and let the girls have the crowded room to themselves.

That night, about midnight, the ship's diesel engines fired up all at once. A couple minutes later, there was a long series of heavy rattling noises, and then with a lurch, we were suddenly under way. Out on the hard cold steel deck of the side passageway next to our cabin, a breath of icy sea spray made me shiver, but I didn't mind. The sudden movement and noise may have interrupted my sleep, but it also meant that we were finally leaving Pillau and the menace of the Russian Army. It gave me hope. And after a few more minutes of continual throbbing and the gentle undulations of the waves, it also gave me sleep.

The next morning, it was as cold as ever. I woke up groggy and stiff, and I had no idea where I was. The sky was a dark bluish black towards the bow, while towards the stern, it was gradually becoming a light gray and then a light blue, with yellow streaks pointing towards where the sun was promising to come up. The sea stretched bluish gray as far as the eye could see. Half a dozen sea gulls glided along, parallel to our course, probably hoping that someone would drop something good to eat in the water.

I groaned and slowly managed to get up. I had to pee, and very badly at that, so I stepped over Karl and headed for the stairway down to the bathroom, or head, as the sailors called it. The passageway was littered with people, laying all over the place, mostly still sleeping, but some trying to wake up. A few were walking towards the bathroom ahead of me. My short journey down the passageway, down the stairs, and then back up the inside hall towards the bow, where the bathroom was, took much longer than it should have, as I ended up hopping most of the way, rather than walking, to avoid stepping on people.

About 30 meters short of the bathroom door, I had to stop, because that's where the line ended. The passageway was crowded with people waiting in line for the bathroom. I'd hoped that there wouldn't be as many people as yesterday, since I'd gotten up so early, but I was wrong. There were at least as many, if not more, in line this time. And it was everybody, men, women, children; it made no difference. This was a Navy ship, and there simply weren't any separate facilities for the women, since there weren't supposed to be any women on board anyway, so everyone had to use the same bathroom. But no one really cared either, since we were all just glad to be there alive.

Now, since Rothenen was just a small town, a village really, and since we only barely had electricity, let alone running water, my family didn't have modern toiletry. We had an outhouse. And even though I'd already been to places like Königsberg and Pillau, and even though I'd ridden for several hours on a train, somehow, I'd never managed to use a modern, flushing toilet, though I had seen them before and had some idea of what to do with them. So after forty-five minutes of very uncomfortable, impatient waiting in line, when it was finally my turn at the front of the line, I was

fascinated to discover that the stall that I was in had a
flushing toilet.

Of course, I had been in the bathroom yesterday
and the evening before, but so far, I'd only used the
urinal, a skill that came rather naturally to me. The
urinal though, did not flush. It was simply a trough
with a drain pipe at the bottom and a drip pipe at the
top. I guess all the excitement of being in a strange
environment had sort of stopped me up, but now that
my plumbing was working again, I just had to use this
opportunity to find out how flushing toilets really
worked.

This particular toilet, like many in Europe even
today, had its tank mounted on the wall behind the
bowl. There was a large pipe running into the bowl, and
there was a pull chain hanging off of the tank so that
you could flush it. The height of the tank was just a
little higher than I was tall, so after I was done using it,
I climbed up on the toilet seat to look into the tank
while I pulled on the flush chain. The flush went off
beautifully, and I studied every moving part, noting the
stopper, the float, the fill tap, and how they all worked
together. After that, having satisfied my curiosity, I
turned around to get off the seat, when CRACK!

My feet flew out from under me, and my arms
went flying above me, managing to catch the rim of the
tank and the top of the stall divider just in time to keep
myself from falling to the floor. Still, I hit the divider
with a thud and a grunt, knocking the wind out of me.
After letting myself down, I checked to see what had
happened, and I was mortified to discover that the side
of the toilet seat that I'd been standing on had split
clean in half, with the outer half now laying on the floor
next to the toilet. It had landed there with a loud
clattering noise, explaining to everyone in the room
what the cause of the thudding noise moments earlier

was. Already, there was a chorus of groans and curses from outside my stall.

"Uh oh," I thought. "I'd better get out of here, and fast." So I opened the stall door and made a beeline for the hallway. The next person in line though, an older gentleman, nearly bowled me over and made an ugly face at me, muttering, "Stupid kid." Then everyone else joined in with, "Aw, you've ruined it for us!" "Hey, kid, what'd you have to do that for?" "Couldn't you see how many people are out here waiting? Now there's one less stall for us to use," and those were just the polite ones. The word of what I'd done reached the end of the line before I could, so I had to endure this humiliation all the way down the hall. And Karl was just arriving in line, so he greeted me with, "So, Horst, I hear you're going to be a plumber, and not a blacksmith, after all. Wait 'til Papa hears about that!" as he laughed at me until I disappeared up the stairway.

After that little incident, and not wanting to face my Mom and sisters right then, I headed for the gym, where they were serving breakfast from huge kettles that they'd brought out from the kitchen. It turned out to be pea soup, which was what they'd served yesterday evening too. Well, we Germans liked our pea soup for sure, but having it for breakfast too was pushing it. I was hungry though, so I ate what they gave me.

With nothing to do for the rest of the day then, I started wandering around the ship again, taking about the same route as I'd taken yesterday, but much slower, so that I could look at things more closely. I'd noticed these "railroad tracks" running along the passageway past our cabin before, but this time, I followed them forward to where they stopped at a large sliding door with a warning sign on it, saying something about watching out for the mines. "So this is where they store them," I thought. Then I noticed that they were only a few meters forward of our cabin, so I thought, "I wonder how many mines are in there and whether they can explode if they bump into something in a storm." The door was locked though, so it was pointless to stay there.

Then, going around to the port side for my trip towards the stern, I stopped in my tracks when I saw some real Navy stuff going on. Several of the sailors were operating a boom or crane from amidships and were lowering something that looked like a small torpedo with stubby wings on it into the water. They had another teardrop shaped thing, with a large scissors apparatus on the front of it, laying on the deck, as if it was going to be next into the water. I stood there for a long time, watching them as they let the torpedo thing out on its cable, as if they were trolling for fish or something. Finally, I approached one of the crew and asked him what they were doing, and he said that they were searching for mines, which the scissors thing would cut the cables of, and that this was why the ship was going so slowly. I hadn't really noticed, but I took his word for it.

That occupied my time for about an hour, and then I continued on my journey down the port side of the ship. I hadn't gone far though, when I heard muffled laughter and talking above me. I looked up and saw some of the boys that I'd met yesterday peeking out from under a large metal hood of some kind on the deck above me, watching the sailors with the torpedo thing. Running a little further on until I came to some stairs, I went up and asked if I could join them, and they said that I could.

Ducking under the hood thing, which was rectangular, about three meters long, and in the center of the ship, up on the quarterdeck, behind the stack, I quickly discovered why they were hiding up there. It was warm. The hood was an air vent for the ship's diesel engines, which were fully visible through a large opening under it. There was a shelf or step up, which was where they were all standing or kneeling, and then there was a metal wall going up to the lip of the opening, but it was up inside the hood, so you couldn't see what it was from the outside.

Volumes of warm, humid air poured up from within the engine room, along with the greasy smell of diesel fuel. It was a welcome relief from the frigid air and icy spray, and I knew right away that this was going to be our base of operations for the entire trip. Not only did the hood provide warmth and protection from the elements, but it also provided protection from our parents, since unless you knew where to look, you'd never even know we were there, though on the other hand, by stooping down and peering from under the hood, we could see most of the ship.

The engines themselves turned out to be the best part of this hood that my newfound friends had discovered. Over a dozen pistons, the size of barrels, were visible through the vent, their cams and rotating shaft moving constantly up and down and side to side, gleaming bronze yellow, with oily blue streaks running along their smooth, polished sides. There were also many small pipes and gauges running along or into the engine, and we spent forever trying to figure out what everything did and how it all worked.

It took us a long time to get bored with the engines, but eventually we did, so we jumped down and started a game of hide and seek. One time, as I was running along searching for a good place to hide from the It person, while dodging the adult refugees standing or laying all over the deck, I happened to spy about five life boats stacked up neatly on a slanted skid next to the gunwales. Thinking that perhaps I could hide in them, I ran over and ducked underneath them. That wasn't good enough though, so I squirmed up between the gunwale and the first life boat, briefly hanging my buttocks over the side of the ship, and slithered into the crack between the first and second boats, or rather rafts, as they were really rather squarish and made of cork, with canvass bottoms. This was a marvelous hiding place, as the It person passed right by me three times without seeing me.

Unfortunately, it was a little too good of a hiding place. When I saw the It person start running after someone else near the stern of the ship, and I started trying to climb out of the boat so that I could dash for the goal, I made the mistake of coming down on the inboard side of the life boats, right in front of one of the crew's officers. He shouted, "Hey, you! Get out of there! You can't be in there! Come here so that I can bring you to your mother! You shouldn't be running around like this." When I hit the deck though, my feet were already going, and although he tried to catch me, I was too fast for him, dancing between dawdling refugees, shimmying down a set of stairs into the main deck cabin, and racing right out the opposite door. Thankfully, he didn't call for help from anyone, but I made sure I didn't go near the life boats again.

Later that afternoon, after we'd become bored of playing games on the deck and we'd again congregated under the ventilation hood, one of the younger boys in our group rushed up to the rest of us after being gone for a while and panted, "Hey guys, come quick! You gotta look at this! I saw this really huge fat guy sitting down in the hall on the way to the bathroom. You gotta see him!" We all responded, "So what?" But he persisted, "No, really! He was so fat he took up TWO WHOLE CHAIRS! He can hardly even move, he's so fat!"

Curious now, we all ran down below deck with him, but as we came around the corner and into the hall where this fat person was, the ones in front were so surprised that they stopped short, and the rest of us plowed into them. Everyone waiting in the line for the latrine turned around to see what the commotion was, including the fat guy. He was dressed like a farmer, with coveralls and an old white shirt, but they were so big and baggy that all of us boys could've fit into them at once. And sure enough, as he sat there with both his head and his hands resting on a cane, he was hanging off of the outside edges of two chairs. We couldn't believe it. We'd never seen anyone so fat before. For several moments, we just stood there, staring at him, until we realized that everyone else was staring at us, and then our embarrassment got the best of us and we ran off through another passageway, laughing and making rude jokes about Old Two Chairs as we went.

All during the rest of the trip, whenever our whole group got together, one or the other of us would dare the rest of us to go and look at Old Two Chairs. So we'd sneak down in twos or threes and peek around the corner into the passageway. After seeing him, our mouths would inevitably drop wide open, we'd look astonished at each other, and then we'd run away, snickering and telling more rude jokes. It was quite a thing with us. I'm not excusing what we did. It was rude. But we were just boys back then, and we didn't know any better. After the war was over, we discovered Old Two Chairs living a rather miserable life in a town near ours. He'd lost an incredible amount of weight, so that his skin and clothes hung all over him in huge baggy folds. I guess that wasn't too healthy for him though, because we heard that he died shortly after that. I hope that what we did to him on the Lotringen, poking fun at him like that, didn't have anything to do

with that, but how could we know. Not everything that
we did was right, you know.

That night, and the next morning too, we had
more pea soup served to us in the gym. We were really
starting to get tired of it by this time, but we didn't want
to complain too much, because we could see how
ravenously some of the refugees, who were almost all
women, children, and old men, ate the soup. So many
of them were so scrawny, and we realized that they
hadn't eaten this well in a long, long time. My family
hadn't even begun to feel the effects of the war like that
yet, as we'd just left home a few days before, and we still
had the big ham and loaf of bread with us.

Those first couple of days at sea passed fairly
quickly, because of all the new things there were to see
on the ship, and because of our new friends and all the
games and adventures we had together. But by this
time, we were getting very bored. Everything was the
same, even the diesel engine in our air vent. The sea
was the same. The food was the same (pea soup). The
sailors lowering their torpedo thing in the water were
the same. All our games were the same. Everything
was just the same, so we were bored.

Some of us started getting irritated with each
other because of this, so there were some small fights
that broke out, and more than a few arguments. But
me and another guy, Hugo, started hanging around
together and just talking. We talked about everything,
our lives back home, what our families were like, how
the war had affected us, and what we thought things
were going to be like when we landed. Sometimes we
walked around, and other times, we just stood at the
gunwales and watched the sea go by, or stood under our
vent hood and watched the engine run. Hugo and I
became really good friends during those few days
together, but once we landed and got off the ship, we

never saw each other again.

It was during one of those talks that Hugo and I were having, while we were standing on the starboard bridge wing, looking back up towards the quad-20mm machine guns mounted in a tub or crow's nest on the main mast, that the announcement came, about 1:00 on that second day at sea. "Achtung, Achtung! Luftangriff! Zewiel personal unter Deck - Miletaer personal auf Posten!" which means, "Attention, Attention! Air Attack! Civilian personnel below deck. Military personnel, battle stations."

Before we could even figure out what to do, every sailor on that ship had sprung into action and was running this way or that way. None of them were getting in each other's way either, as they seemed to have a system all worked out for this sort of emergency. But then all of us civilians figured out that we were in danger, and it would be a good idea for us to get below deck, like the loud speaker had said. So all of a sudden all the civilians on deck, who easily outnumbered the crew by five or six to one, started running around in a confused mess, everyone heading for the nearest door into the cabins or below deck, creating traffic jams and bottlenecks, with people bumping into each other and tripping and running over each other. This was terrifying, and wherever these bottlenecks occurred, people were screaming and shouting and jumping up and down, pushing and shoving, trying to get under cover. Thankfully, I only had to race down two flights of stairs, because our cabin was right on the main deck and fairly close by, but I did have to throw myself against the railing coming down as sailors bounded up, trying to get to their positions. Then, just before I ran in through our cabin door, I happened to look over my shoulder, and I saw four specks, high up in the sky, but diving rapidly towards us. My blood ran cold at the sight.

And just after I'd gotten into our cabin and shut the door behind me, the anti-aircraft guns opened fire. Two 88mm, two sets of 37mm, and at least four 20mm guns began firing all together. The smaller ones fired continuously, while the larger ones let off ear splitting single bursts, all of which reverberated throughout the ship like a million hammers pounding at our ears. Mom, my sisters, Gerhardt, Karl, and I crouched frantically together on the floor of the cabin, Ursula and Gerhardt screaming at the top of their lungs, while we covered our ears with our hands in a futile attempt to protect them from the thundering din of the cannon fire. As each second passed in slow motion, we thought it would be our last. The firing went on for what seemed an eternity, as we huddled like mice caught in a trap. Finally, Karl shouted over the clamor, "Mom! Let's pray!"

So Mom prayed, "Lord, keep us safe, and let everything turn out all right for us, in Jesus Name, amen."

And the shooting stopped, just like that. Silence.

We looked at each other in thankful amazement. Then we just fell into each other, our arms and legs shaking like gelatin, as we hugged each other again and again, so thankful to God that we were alive, and that He had answered our prayer like that.

After a while, when we dared to venture out again, we didn't see any signs of damage to the ship at all. There was not one single bullet hole or bomb crater in the entire ship, and I went looking for them too. Everyone was buzzing around in a daze now, telling and retelling how they'd weathered the attack, but I just kept thinking to myself that God had answered Mom's prayer. He respected her and loved us enough to answer our prayer immediately like that. I hadn't yet accepted Jesus as my Savior either, so this made a big impression on me. Wow. The love of God seemed to overwhelm me, and I realized that we would make it through this war alive, and Papa would too, and if God was big enough to send those enemy planes away like that, perhaps He could even bring Papa back together with us when this whole thing was over with.

We spent another two days on the Lotringen, slowly making our way westward, searching constantly for mines as we went. If they found any mines though, I don't know what they did with them, because there were never any explosions or any shooting or anything like that, beyond that one air attack. The sea was calm the whole time, and no one even got sea sick, at least to my knowledge. It did rain on the third day, and it was cold the whole time, but it wasn't anything out of the ordinary. We just kept on with our routine, running around, playing games, looking at the engine under the ventilation hood, making fun of Old Two Chairs, and eating pea soup in the gym. By the end of the third day, I got dysentery from the pea soup, and I imagine some other people must've too, but I survived that.

Sometime on our last day on board, someone noticed that they could see land again, and word quickly spread throughout the refugee community, so everyone started standing near the gunwales, watching the shore as it slowly got closer to us. Someone among the crew must've mentioned that we were coming into the port of Swinemünde too, which today is the Polish port of Swinoujscie, because after awhile, that got passed around too. When I heard about this, I was filled with curiosity, because I'd heard that this was where Dr. Von Braun, the inventor of the V-rockets, had his laboratory and testing grounds, but I ended up being disappointed, because they anchored far off shore and waited out the rest of the day there. When we did go into port, it was late at night, and there were guards that kept us from wandering away from the group.

From Hitler Youth to American Soldier

11

The Train Ride

There were no lights, of course, because of the threat of air raids, so coming into port at Swinemünde was probably a treacherous feat for the crew. Standing out on deck, it was difficult for me to tell how close to shore we were, and it took a long time, but eventually we landed safely.

Getting off the Lotringen was much more orderly and efficient than getting on it, in spite of the darkness. Everyone was very helpful and patient and just queued up and waited their turn to go down the gang plank. There were guides, as well as guards, to meet us on shore, and they led us on foot across the shipyard to the railyard, which was perhaps a kilometer of walking.

It was all very strange and mystical. You couldn't see much more than the people right in front of you, and even they were just shadowy forms in the dark. Somewhere, out there, I knew there was a rocket testing grounds - Dr. Von Braun's - but being unable to see anything, I had no idea where it really was or what it looked like. We just trudged on and on, quietly, in the cold darkness, for nearly an hour, until we got to the rail yard, where there was more darkness.

Somehow, the guides managed to bring us to the correct train, in a maze of track, switches, standing stock, and warehouses, all of which were just shadows. Every now and then, someone would trip and fall on a rail tie or pot hole or something; or someone would drop what they were carrying, out of pure fatigue; and sometimes people would run into each other or trip over each other, when this happened. But no one got angry or anything, and when people dropped stuff, the people behind them would help them pick it up and would give them a hand in getting up too. It was very gratifying to see everyone helping each other like that.

When we got to the train, I was surprised to find that it was just a cattle train. At first, I didn't think it was for us, because I was expecting a passenger train, like those we'd ridden in Samland, but the guides herded us alongside the dozens of cattle cars at the loading dock and then directed us to go into them. There were so many refugees that our car, and probably all the others too, was pretty well packed, so even though there was straw scattered on the floor, no one could sit on it. So we just stood there in the dark, not wanting to breath or move because of how close we were packed together.

It took a long time for everyone to get into the train, I guess because the line of refugees walking over from the shipyard was so long, so it was getting light out, and everyone was very tired, groggy, and achy by the time the train finally got going. There were a couple of blasts from the whistle up front, and a huge plume of smoke and loud growling noise from the engine, and then with a bang and a clank and a jerk that threw us into the other refugees standing in the back of our car, we were finally moving again on the next leg of our escape from the Russians.

Most of the people in our car were women or children, though there were a few old men too. The light of the day and the rush of the cold air through the slats in the walls served to wake us up and make us take notice of our surroundings. Mom and all of us kids had managed to stay together, and we were all clumped together in the midst of the crowd of refugees standing in our car. After just a couple hours, our legs hurt so bad that we were all leaning on each other and on the walls whenever we could. A few children managed to sit in the straw at their mother's feet. In spite of there being slats in the walls, we couldn't really see out, or at least I couldn't, because of how many other people were around us. Eventually, despite the cold air, the cinders from the engine's smoke, and the discomfort of standing up, the clickety-clack of the railroad tracks lulled many of us to sleep.

At the time, it didn't occur to me that these very same cattle cars might also have been used to transport prisoners, either POWs or Jews or others, to concentration camps and prisons scattered around Germany and its satellite countries. Being in the cattle cars was a new and not very pleasant experience for us, and I'm sure that there might've been some of us that might've been a little offended at having been treated this way. But now that I know who else may have been in those same cars, I think that we probably had it pretty good, compared to them. At least none of us were beaten or wounded or killed.

We did have to go to the bathroom though. The old men and the boys just shuffled to the sliding door, opened it, and let it go. There was no shame or modesty. We couldn't afford to have modesty under

177

those conditions. The women and girls had a more difficult time with this though, and many of them simply chose to hold it and suffer. Some of them ended up doing what I did though.

I had dysentery, as I'd mentioned before. All during our walk to the train and then the hours of standing in the car, I was in incredible discomfort with gas pains and with desperately trying to hold it in. Finally though, something had to be done, or I was going to make a mess. So after talking with Mom, we hit upon an idea. We shuffled over to the sliding door and enlisted a couple other women to help. I had quite a struggle getting the several layers of my Papa's pants off, but I was highly motivated, so no obstacle was too great. Once that was taken care of, Mom and the other women held onto my arms while I swung my butt out the door and over the edge, and then I let'er go. Oh, what a relief that was, despite the cold and the embarrassment. We found something or other to wipe myself up with, and then I put my Papa's pants back on. That was an experience I shall never forget!

Now, as you can imagine, that was a pretty smelly experience too, and I had to share it with everyone in the car, and in all the cars behind ours as well. And I wasn't the only one either. With so many hundreds, or even thousands, of people crammed into those cars, after nearly a week of eating nothing but pea soup, there were a lot of us that had dysentery, or that just had to go, even if it wasn't due to dysentery. It'd been at least a week since anyone had bathed or changed clothes or washed their mouths out too, so everyone was dirty and crusty with sweat and reeked of body odor. We didn't notice it so much on the Lotringen, because you had more room, and because you could spend your days up on the deck, where there was plenty of fresh air and sea breeze, but in this cattle

car, with everyone packed in so tightly, you couldn't
avoid the smell, and the stench of old cow manure and
urine that had soaked into the cars over the years just
made it worse. It was a wonder that we didn't vomit too.

After several hours of enduring this, we slowed
down and pulled into a train station. We already had
the sliding door open, so at least some of us could see
where we were going, and they passed the word back
that we were coming into Rostock, which is about
150km west of Swinemünde. As we stopped, there were
guards and some people from some kind of aid society
or something setting up some huge kettles of soup on
the loading platform, for us to eat for lunch. We were
pretty excited about this, because we hadn't eaten
anything since the day before, when we were still on the
ship. There was also someone talking on a loud speaker
about where the bathrooms were and where we should
queue up for the food and so on. Once the train had
stopped, we poured out of the double doors, rushed
across the platform, and mobbed the restrooms. As
people got done with that, they came back out to line up
by the soup kettles. Feeling much better and in higher
spirits now, everyone was talking and carrying on and
thinking that things were about to get better. People
commented on how much better it would be to be
captured by the Americans, rather than the Russians,
and how they were looking forward to having a new
home and to living at peace again once the war was
over.

Then, just as the aid society staff were about
done setting up, and some people had even managed to
get served their food, we were interrupted by a loud
whining siren that rose and fell and seemed to permeate
the entire atmosphere. People looked knowingly and
fearfully at each other, and a loud speaker announced,
"Air Raid! Everyone to the air raid shelter, except the

refugee train." The guards and the aid society people scattered, dropping their soup kettles and utensils where they were and running towards one of the buildings nearby. The rest of us just stood there, gazing wistfully after them and wondering why we couldn't go down into the nice, safe air raid shelter too. Seeing that, the loudspeaker repeated its warning, telling us refugees to get back in the train and leave while we still could. Now the train's engineer poured on the steam to the engine, sending a huge cloud of black smoke into the sky, and as one person, the whole crowd of refugees turned and ran for the train, praying that it wouldn't leave without us. There were so many of us though that the train was moving well before the last of us got on. People were slammed into the back of the car by the rush of more people behind them, and many people got separated from their families. Thankfully all of my family managed to stay together, and none of us got hurt. Mom was panting very hard though, and her face was as white as a sheet.

Inside the cattle car again, people were shaking and crying, angry that they'd been deprived of their food, angrier still that they couldn't use the air raid shelter, and now very afraid of what would certainly happen in the next few seconds. I happened to be standing just ahead and to the right of the sliding door, on the side of the train towards the station, so I could see out back the way that we'd come. We kept the door open too, in spite of the air raid, so that we could get more air in the car and so that we had a better chance of jumping out if we were being attacked by one of the bombers. This gave me a ringside seat, so to speak, to watch the air raid with.

As we pulled out of the station, the tracks curved around in a wide swath to the left, allowing me to keep the station in view for quite a while. I saw perhaps a couple dozen fighter bombers circling around the city, dodging flak bursts, looking for targets, and several of them dove at the train station. I saw them releasing their bombs and heard the scream of the bombs as they fell, along with the ripping noise of their machine guns firing as they strafed the station. When the bombs landed, they caused tremendous explosions that flashed bright red and yellow and sent debris and shards of buildings flying in all directions. Some of the bombs fell on the railroad tracks where we'd been, just a couple minutes before. The impact of how close an escape we had touched me deeply. I don't know why the planes didn't chase us down and attack us as well. Surely they could see us from the air. Then I thought of how God had delivered us from the air attack on the Lotringen, just three days before, and I realized that He must have done it again, and that He was still doing it too. Still, for me, it was exciting, like being part of my very own adventure. I had no idea the kind of danger we were really in. I wasn't nearly as afraid as everyone else was.

The rest of the trip was uneventful, but we were all nonetheless painfully aware that we were no safer in the western part of Germany than we were in the eastern part. I continued having dysentery and stomach cramps. We had one other rest stop where we got some sandwiches, but that was all, so people began to eat whatever they'd brought with them, which for us was the big loaf of bread and the ham. A lot of people just went hungry.

By this time, we were just south of Denmark, where the Elbe Rive crosses over to the North Sea, and the countryside had mostly turned to fruit orchards, windmills, and irrigation canals. We stopped at Bucholz for a while, after coming through Lübeck, and then we went back up to Lübeck to go to Hamburg. As we went through Hamburg, it was plain to see that the city had already been bombed very heavily, again reminding us of Königsberg, Pillau, and Samland, which we'd just left a few days before. After crossing the Elbe River, we went to Buxtehude and then to Stade, and then went back and forth between Buxtehude and Stade several times. We began to get the idea that either no one wanted us, or no one knew what to do with us. We finally disembarked from the train at Buxtehude, and after waiting a while longer, they loaded us into some trucks and buses and took us to a small town west of Hamburg, called Jork ("York").

12

Jork

Jork was just a short distance from the western banks of the Elbe River, downstream from Hamburg, on the part of the river which was subject to the ebb and flow of the tides from the North Sea. Years before I was there, Dutch prisoners, criminals working their way free from jail, had built dikes there, along the Elbe River, so that local farmers could reclaim some of the land from the tidal flats, and now there were orchards of apple, plum, and cherry trees along the banks of the river, interlaced with drainage canals and old windmills, making a patchwork of agrarian beauty. It was still cold and raw, and the trees were bare, but there wasn't any snow, and the grass was green, so to those of us in the backs of the refugee trucks, it was almost like going to Heaven.

The trucks stopped in downtown Jork, across the street from the town blacksmith shop, on Borsteler Reihe, which was the only main road there, and which continued up to Borstel, a small port town on the Elbe River. There was a stream that ran along the east side of the road, through town, which was to our right in the convoy. The banks of the stream were of brick, to keep it in the channel, and there were iron railings along the side by the road, to keep people and cars from falling into the stream. The other side of the road was lined with shops, such as the blacksmith, a dentist, a tavern, and a gasthouse, going back the way we'd come through town. There was also a Lutheran church on the far bank of the stream, opposite where we stopped, but you had to take a side road and a bridge over the stream to get there.

Our guides told everyone to get out of the trucks, that we would be staying here. While we were doing that, one of them wandered off in search of some local officials, and before long, he returned with several people in tow, including some that turned out to be from the German government, from the Housing Authority, and from a group in charge of refugees. They set up a couple of desks, right there on the street, and they had us line up and file past them, saying what our names were and showing our internal passports. They wrote the information down and then assigned us to a local person that would take us to where we would be staying. Because of the huge numbers of refugees coming into central Germany from all directions, the government was requiring literally everyone that had any extra rooms at all to take people in. So before long, we found ourselves being escorted to the back of our convoy, to the house just past the gasthouse, where a certain old lady named Oma Moje ("Moya") lived.

Oma Moje greeted us at the door in a bubbly, grandmotherly fashion, apologizing for the dirt on the floor, even though there wasn't any, and leading us through her central hallway and then off to the left,

184

where she had an available bedroom. Her hallway was rather large, with a couple bedrooms and a kitchen off to the right, and a couple larger bedrooms on the left, with ours being the second one. At the far end of our bedroom, there was a walk-in closet, or perhaps a pantry, where she'd set up a folding bed for one of us, and then she also gave us another small room just off and two steps up from the kitchen. It was separated from our other rooms by a storage room and the hallway though. There were some steps that went upstairs to a couple more bedrooms from our room by the kitchen too.

Everything in Oma Moje's house spoke of quiet, but pleasant, oldness. There were old pictures of her family on the walls and old knickknacks, dolls, and decorations on the tables and shelves. There were also some old lamps and a couple of old paintings, and the house had a warm, musty smell to it. There wasn't any dirt or dust anywhere to be found though, and all her dishes and utensils were put away in cupboards. The one thing that was missing from this quaint scene of grandmotherhood was the smell of baking bread.

The harsh reality was that there was no food. Constant Allied bombing, the need to feed what was left of the German Army, and the tremendous influx of refugees had stripped the entire area of any type of foodstock. The shops in town were empty, and the local farms had mostly already been picked over. Whenever there was a shipment of food from somewhere else, a line immediately developed, and it was soon gone.

The new refugees would make things even more difficult too. There were already two ex-German soldiers living, or hiding, in the bedrooms upstairs, and there was another, Russian, family living in the first bedroom on the left too. And Oma Moje's sister, Tante Trina, and her daughter lived with her too, in the other bedroom next to the kitchen.

We were just glad finally to be somewhere that we could call home again though, and we were confident that God would provide the food and other things as we needed them. Just how much He provided became evident the next day.

We arrived at Oma Moje's house on February 9th, 1945, with only what was left of the food that we'd brought with us remaining and none to be found in the house or the surrounding area. Since he was now the man of the house, on the morning of the 10th, instead of helping the rest of us get better settled in, Karl headed out to find a job somewhere, either in town or at a local farm. When he returned by the end of the day, he was jubilant, having secured a job at the blacksmith's shop up the street, for a few pfennigs per day. It was amazing, because there was so little work in general, since the war had wrecked the economy, but he was a strong young man, and he knew some about smithing, having been taught by Papa, and people like that were in very short supply, as most had joined the Army already. So at least when there was food available, we would have the money to buy it.

As for the rest of us, Hildegaard and my other sisters helped clean house or took care of Mom. Mom was just about ready to give birth now, so she had a very difficult time moving around and doing things. On those few occasions when we had food to cook, Mom or Hildegaard would take turns with Oma Moje in the kitchen, as there was only room for one person to use the stove. I became the official gopher and scavenger. It was my job to run errands and to wait in the food lines at stores or farms when they had food. This gave me lots of opportunity to explore and to develop friendships with other boys in the neighborhood, so that was fun for me.

Just a couple of days into this new routine, on perhaps the 13th or 14th of February, we were in Oma's kitchen, listening to the radio news that evening, when a piece about Russian barbarism was announced. It was nothing new, since there were many examples of it every day in the news, but when they announced that a Russian submarine had sunk the refugee ship General Von Steuben, on her way from Pillau to Kiel with over 5000 refugees on board, on February 10th, Mom, Karl, Hildegaard, and I all froze. Mom said, "Wasn't that the ship that we were supposed to get on in Pillau?" Karl said, "Jah, it was." We stopped what we were doing and turned the radio off right then and prayed, thanking God for His protection and even for having used that young soldier, Kurt, whom Papa had gotten so mad at, to delay us, since if it hadn't have been for Kurt getting us lost in the back alleys of Pillau, we would've arrived at the ship on time, and we would've boarded it.

About a week after that, Mom and Hildegaard were in the kitchen, when Mom turned to look at Hildegaard and said, "It's time for me to go." Hildegaard immediately turned and ran to tell Oma Moje, and the soldiers upstairs, "Uncle" Hans and "Uncle" Karl, that Mom was going into labor and had to go to the hospital. Oma Moje had already informed us that the cooking school up the street had been turned into a maternity ward, and Mom had arranged with Hans and Karl look after us kids while she was gone. Hildegaard and Oma both offered to go with Mom, but Mom felt that she could make it on her own, and she didn't want them to be burdened with her, so she headed up the street under her own power.

Mom got to the school in time, and the staff there took care of her after that. By morning, she'd given birth to a very small baby boy, whose skin was a pale bluish tint with some darker areas. Mom named him Ulrich. She stayed there for another night, but after that, they asked her to return home, to make room for other mothers. Unfortunately, Ulrich had to stay at the maternity ward, since he was so small, and since he was sickly. A lot of babies were being born that way, they said, because there was so little food for the mothers to eat.

Mom went to visit Ulrich every day after that, to feed him and hold him and take care of him, but the staff said that he was too weak to return home. Hildegaard brought each of us other kids in turn up to see him, one at a time, until all of us had visited, but then we had other things to do, so only Mom went to visit him. On about the third day of that, Mom came home and said that the staff had diagnosed Ulrich with pneumonia, so he'd have to stay there until he got better. She didn't like that though, because the cooking school, despite being turned into a maternity ward, didn't have any heat. It was cold and damp in there as a result, and she doubted whether he could get better in a place like that, especially since medicines were also in such short supply, because of the war.

Life and the war kept right on going though in spite of our small personal situations. The Allied offensive was in full swing again after having paused for the winter and Operation Autumn Mist (the Battle of the Bulge), and we began to hear that there was an English army headed our way. Contrary to how everyone felt back in Rothenen and Pillau with the Russians bearing down on them, this actually inspired hope in people, and there was a rather optimistic, upbeat mood in town because of it, even with all the hardships that we still had to bear.

Among other things that we dealt with were the Allied bombing raids. Most of the time, they just passed us by, but one time, I counted seventy-two bombers in a raid on Hamburg, just fifteen kilometers from us. On an earlier raid, a single bomb had gone astray and had fallen in Jork. This was the only bomb ever to fall on Jork itself, from what I saw, and from what my local friends told me. This one bomb fell in an open lot and blew the Spanish roofing tiles off of the corner of a house. The people that lived were friends of mine though, so on this particular day, during the current raid, their son and I climbed up through the hole in their roof, using the open rafters as a ladder, to watch the bombers.

As they approached, we could see that they had four engines each, with little bubbles poking out at various angles from their fuselages. There were dozens of them, grouped roughly in fours, with a lead plane, one at either side of that one, but at an angle, and then another one behind and a little above them, forming a kind of diamond. There were also smaller, single-engine planes, which we guessed were fighter planes, flying between them to protect them from our Luftwaffe, even though we couldn't see any German planes around at all. They flew directly overhead, creating a tremendous roar that shook the air, just like back in Rothenen.

The planes dropped their bombs, which emitted an ear splitting scream as they fell, followed by the usual thudding noise of the explosions, and then the planes turned around and headed back the way they'd come. Unlike at Rothenen though, there wasn't much opposition at all, and what little there was came from light anti-aircraft fire on the ground.

After the war, our Uncle Henry, who had been in Hamburg during the bombing there, told us that he'd been manning a 37mm flak gun position, set up on the highest building in the city, the Hochhaus. They'd been hoping to have a better shot at the Allied bombers from there, but what they got was a ring-side seat for what felt like the Battle of Armageddon. Bombs were falling and exploding all around them. It was utter chaos. Death and destruction were everywhere. A bomb would hit and go into a building, and then the building would seem to rise up off its foundation, only to collapse into a heap of rubble, moments later. Once one bomb fell, there were dozens of others, right behind it, and they would land in a row, going up a street, for instance, but they would be so close together that it all seemed like one big, long explosion. It went on and on for what seemed like hours, and when it was over, he was completely exhausted and practically deaf, despite the earplugs that he'd been given. He wanted to cry after that first time, because the once great city of Hamburg now lay in ruins, in just the space of an afternoon, but he couldn't, because he was so drained and tired. He said it was a miracle that he'd survived.

For us boys though, it was exciting. We didn't understand, even after all this time, how dangerous it was. We were living in our own adventure book, and every day seemed to bring something new. With no school at the time, and with very few men around to enforce discipline, we pretty much did whatever we wanted to do.

Things went on like this for several weeks. Mom was going back and forth to the maternity ward at the cooking school. Karl was working nearly all the time at the blacksmith's, and at a farm too. Hildegaard helped Oma Moje clean house and also watched the rest of us kids. And I stood in lines, waiting for food to be handed out, or I was out playing with my friends.

One day in mid March though, we got some news. It was good news, but in a sense, it was also bad news. It came in the form of a check in the mail, from the German government. It was for Papa's military pay, which was good news indeed. But there wasn't any news of how he was doing or where he was. Mom was quiet for a long while after opening it, but then she put the check away and went back about her duties. We were all trusting God to bring Papa back to us, so we couldn't let our imaginations interfere with that. Besides, getting his paycheck was a definite turn for the better, even though there wasn't much in the stores that we could buy with it.

After that, word of where we were seemed to get around, without our doing anything to announce it. The first sign of that was when Papa's sister, Martha Wentzel, showed up on our doorstep, with her daughter, Marianna. Tante Martha lived in Masuren, an area of East Prussia southeast of Königsberg, near the Polish border, where they had a series of lakes and boat portages that were a big tourist attraction. They went to our house in Rothenen during mid-February, looking for us, but since we'd already left, they just stayed there with Mom's uncle that I mentioned before. Tante Martha was the one who told us about his execution. When the Russians came back through later on, an entire squad of Russian soldiers gang raped Tante Martha while Marianna slept by her side. Somehow they managed to escape and get into central Germany. They didn't have anyplace else to go, and they were unfamiliar with this part of Germany, so we let them move in with us, in the room next to the kitchen. This brought the number of people living in Oma Moje's house to nineteen. I guess someone at the Housing Authority told them where we were.

A few days later, about the first of spring, which was quite a warm day, we had a group of about 200 American POWs come marching through town, past our house, probably going to another prison camp, because of the advancing Allied armies. They all had flight jackets on, so I guessed that they were from the American Air Force, probably bomber crews that had been shot down. They were in good spirits and good health too, though quite a number of them had wounds. There were some on crutches, with one or both legs in casts, and others had bandages around various parts of their bodies. But they were all happy, and they waved to us as they ambled slowly by.

Mom told me to run and get a bucket of water for them, with some cups, and when I came back with it, they were overjoyed to see it. They fairly mobbed us, and I had to go fill up the bucket several times before all of them had enough. In return, some of them gave us candy bars or cookies and so on. I'd never had a Hershey's Chocolate Bar before, so this was quite a treat. I guess they got them from the Red Cross, in care packages. They actually looked better fed than we were. So they crowded around and talked as best they could for quite a while, and then they moved on. There must've been some German guards around somewhere, but they never interfered, and I didn't see them.

Mom made me share my candy stash with the rest of our family, which I was happy to do, since there was so much of it. That was the best we'd eaten in a long time.

Our quest for food was now the single greatest concern on our minds. I was always out looking for it, and what it was or how I got it became secondary issues. One thing that helped with this was that people that had supplies of food were afraid that when the

English got here, they would confiscate it from them, so they often distributed it to people around town to keep the Allies from getting it. So when we heard that a farmer was passing out lard or something, I ran over to where his farm was and got in line. I ended up being the last one before his supply ran out, and he gave me the entire box and whatever was left in it, which was between 1-2 kilograms. Then I put it on my shoulder and headed home.

By this time though, near the first of April, the British were just a short distance away, and they were advancing steadily. They weren't coming too quickly though, because of all the bridges and canals that crisscrossed this area. There weren't any large units of German forces in our area either, so as the front approached, the fighting was minimal. There also weren't any of the massive artillery shelling or running engagements that we saw around Rothenen as the Russians approached. Instead, there were a lot of airplanes flying around, and there were a lot of small unit engagements, with occasional booms from tank or cannon fire. It wasn't really enough to disrupt our daily lives, in other words.

And that's how I got caught out in the open by a British machine gun crew on my way home from that farm, carrying the box of lard. I was just about to turn into the gate of the picket fence that Oma Moje had surrounding her front yard, when I heard this "tap tap tap" noise from far down the street, towards the next town. I didn't think anything of that, since noises like that had been around for a while, but when I heard these whooshing, crackling noises right near my head and realized that they were bullets from the machine gun down the street, I ran through the gate and rushed into the house. I don't know how close the bullets actually came to me, but the crew stopped shooting after that, probably because they couldn't see me anymore.

Things got interesting after that, but I continued going out on my foraging trips, despite both Mom and Oma telling me to be careful.

A squad of German soldiers passed by, heading for the English lines, laden with carts of dynamite and detonators. They stopped at a house down the street from us and asked if they knew where the lead English units were, as they were planning on blowing one of the bridges between Jork and the English, to slow them down. In a strange turn of events though, the people in the house, and some others that gathered around, warned the soldiers away, saying that if the soldiers tried to blow any bridges, that these guys would shoot them. The soldiers said, "Wir ferteidigen Deutchland bis zum letzten tropfen Blut." ("We'll defend Germany to the last drop of blood.") But the civilians wouldn't have any of it, because they didn't want any more damage to their town than what was absolutely necessary. They knew that winning against the English was impossible now, so they stood the soldiers down and made them go back the way they'd come.

Then a couple of teenagers in civilian clothes came by in a truck that had been converted to run on wood, with a steam engine. They only had no weapons with them, but they were waving their hands around and whooping and hollering, saying, "Wir fahren gegen dem Tommics!" ("We're going to fight the English!" "Tommy" was a nickname that the Germans gave the English soldiers.). I have no idea what they thought they were doing. Soon after that, we heard some firing down towards the next town, and about an hour after that, these guys came sneaking back past our house, with their faces white as sheets. One of them, the driver of the truck, had blood running down his arm where he'd been hit. When I asked them what'd happened, they said that the British fired at them, hitting the one guy in the arm, which made them swerve off the road and into a ditch. The British continued firing at them, so they slid out of the truck and crawled or dodged between hiding places, the whole way back to Jork. Now they were tired, dirty, and ready to go home.

Later on, while I was out wandering around town, I had another close call, this time with a British fighter plane. Their fighter planes were all over the place, but they flew so fast and so low to the ground that most of the time, you didn't even know they were there until they were past you. They fired at practically anything too, but you hardly ever had a chance to dodge them, so you just tried to walk along the sides of the streets and stay away from big open places. I was walking past the blacksmith's shop right then, and I just happened to see the fighter come out over the trees down the street. He immediately started shooting at me, but I ran into the blacksmith's open carport, which had Spanish roofing tiles on it, and that saved me once again. The roofing tiles exploded into small bits and showered down on my head under the impact of the bullets, but I was spared, thank God.

In spite of all that going on though, Mom still went up to the cooking school to feed Ulrich. The weather had warmed up considerably by this time, but she said it was still cold and dank in the maternity ward. This time, when she came home she seemed rather moapy, and she had a blank stare on her face. When someone asked her what was wrong, she said simply, "Ulrich has died." The next morning, the town undertaker made a small wooden casket for Ulrich, and we all walked out to the cemetery just outside of town, to bury him. The undertaker was dressed in black and wore a black silk top hat We all walked behind him. All I could think of was that scene in Königsberg, when Papa and I were coming back from visiting Tante Lisa after the bombing, and we saw that old man with his horse and wagon, so sad, and carrying what was probably his wife out to be buried. I felt as though I was that old man, and even though I'd only seen Ulrich once, I felt as though a part of me died along with him.

The next day, the English came into town.

13

The English

There wasn't much opposition, and what there was melted away as soon as the British started advancing. There was some firing and some artillery shelling. One shell exploded less than a hundred meters from Oma Moje's house, in a vegetable garden across the street, but it didn't do any damage to any buildings. Their attack started pretty early in the morning, in that first week of April, so we hadn't yet gone out of the house for anything. Soon the firing died down somewhat, and then we heard the roar of diesel engines and a great clanking noise, as several British Chieftain tanks rolled past the house, followed quickly by quite a number of armored personnel carriers and infantry on foot.

There was a little more shooting, as the British cleared away a few German snipers and leave-behinds, and then we heard more shooting out beyond town, probably up by Borstel near the river, but that was all.

Jork wasn't along any of the major approaches to Hamburg, which the Germans did try to defend, so this British unit got up to the river and then just stopped. A little while later, the majority of them came back into town and started setting up camp there, so to speak. They had a lot of patrols going around, with armored cars and armored personnel carriers (APCs), and an occasional tank, but most of them busied themselves with occupying some buildings that they wanted for this or that.

By that afternoon, since things seemed quieter, Karl and I begged Mom to let us go outside, and after promising her that we'd be careful, she agreed to let us out. We'd stayed indoors nearly all day, and although everyone was very apprehensive about what the British would do, Karl and I were also very excited and curious about them. There were already a bunch of other kids out there, and we wanted to join them too. As soon as we found the other kids, we roamed around town, watching what the British were doing, noticing where they set stuff up, and trying to stay out of their way so we wouldn't get shot at.

Being boys, we were fascinated by all their machinery. Their tanks were simply monstrous. They were long, wide, and squat, with flat, boxy turrets, armored skirting around their tracks, and gun barrels that were as long as the entire tank body. They were also so heavy that they left furrows in the cobblestone paving of our streets as if our streets were made of nothing but mud. Our streets were so chopped up by all the tanks that ordinary cars couldn't drive over them at all, if anybody had wanted to try it.

One of the tanks got itself in trouble, because of how heavy it was. We didn't see this happen, but we heard the noise and the commotion, so we ran in the direction that the noise was coming from and soon

found a tank lodged perfectly in a brick-lined canal.
This was on Borsteler Reihe, just north of town. It had
been crossing the bridge over the canal, but as soon as
it got square in the middle of the bridge, which was only
a little longer than the tank itself, the bridge gave way,
and the tank fell into the stream, plugging it. The turret
was just a little higher than road level. The crew were
trying to get out of the tank, and they looked pretty
shook up. Seeing this caused a howl of laughter from
us, and we started poking fun at the British crew. But
there were some infantry in an APC behind the tank,
and they got out and ran in our direction, waving their
arms and telling us to go away.

A couple days later, we came back to see if the
tank was still there. It was, but they'd removed the
turret and used the tank chassis as a support to build a
temporary bridge with. We had fun with that too and
called it the Tank Bridge.

The English armored personnel carriers were
interesting too. They looked the same in the back as
they did in the front, and they could go backwards just
as fast and as nimbly as they could go forwards. This
was so striking to us that we imagined them being like
monkeys that could swing from the trees in either
direction, so we called them Monkey Swings. They had
open tops, which allowed their infantry to get in or out
quickly or to fire in any direction from inside them, and
they were fully tracked, unlike the German APCs, which
were half-tracks. We started following them around,
just to see how they moved and what they would do.
Sometimes, when a bridge was out over a stream or
canal, they would even go right through the water, so we
got the idea that they were amphibious too.

The English also had armored cars. These had
four big rubber wheels, which gave them a lot of ground
clearance. They had long, sloping back ends, where

their engines were, and they had a small turret on top, with a machine gun poking out from a slot. These were the main vehicles used in patrols and so on, and they often had several infantry troops sitting on their backs while they were patrolling around.

By evening of that first day, a column of trucks came into town too, bringing a lot more soldiers, along with their supplies, furniture, and the higher officers. They set up their headquarters in a public school down beyond the horse riding school on Osterminnenweg, and they turned the horse riding school itself into a garage for their Monkey Swings, since it had a large stables attached to it. They also took several private homes as quarters for their officers, and they took part of the cooking school and used it for a field hospital. It definitely looked like they'd come to stay.

The next day, I was up bright and early to go out with the gang of boys I was friends with so that we could watch what the British were doing. They grouped up by squads, and then each squad met up with one of the armored cars. These teams then separated and each headed out to different parts of town on patrol.

At first, we didn't think much of this, but when the team we were following stopped at the last house on our street and banged on the door, we began to wonder. It was still early, and the woman that answered the door was in her nightclothes. The soldiers pushed past her into the house and something of a commotion ensued. We couldn't hear all of what was going on, but soon the soldiers came back out, carrying several rifles and an expensive-looking camera. They threw the camera into the armored car and laid the rifles on its sloping back, tying them down with some cables.

The patrol moved on to the next house, while a second patrol began tackling the house across the street, on the far bank of the stream. Now things were becoming clear to us, and several of the boys in our group peeled off to run to their houses and alert their families to what was coming. I ran back to our house and shouted that the British were going from house to house looking for guns and cameras.

When I came back to where the patrol was, it had advanced to the fourth house on the street. This time they found a match set of chrome-plated tournament pistols, an old mahogany flint lock rifle, and a couple of shotguns with fancy carving on their stocks. On and on they went, going from house to house, retrieving a stack of very impressive firearms, quite a number of cameras, and a variety of other things that interested them, such as radios, binoculars, maps, a compass, and several old swords. At one house they dragged out a young man with a military haircut who was probably a soldier in hiding. Across the street, they captured several other young men, and they marched them all away towards their headquarters. Every so often, you could hear shots from various places in town too, as diehard Nazis or fugitive soldiers tried to avoid capture. This was turning into a very scary day, and there was a deep sense of apprehension and fear spreading across town.

As the British patrol our group was following finally got to our house, I ran in through the door before them and shouted that the Tommies were here. The soldiers gathered in Oma's large hallway, their faces ashen with fear, sweat pouring down their foreheads, and a rifle pointed at each door. This was the first time I'd gotten to see them up so close. I hadn't thought that the soldiers might be afraid of us. I'd just thought that we were afraid of them.

My whole family, minus Karl, who was at work, filed out of our bedroom. Oma Moje and everyone else came out as well, making a crowd in the hallway. At first, the soldiers backed up together as a defense, but when they saw so many young girls, several mothers, and some old ladies, they realized that we were just refugees, and they began to relax a little. One of them, a sergeant, asked in broken German, "Soldat, und Kamera, und Pistole, und Gewehr," which we took to mean that they wanted any soldiers, cameras, pistols, and rifles. The sergeant also motioned that he and his troops were going to search the house, so as they moved forward, we backed away, allowing them into our rooms. With so many people packed into Oma's small house though, the place was a total mess, and there wasn't anything laying out in the open for them to find. After just a cursory look in each room off the main hallway, the soldiers regrouped in the hallway and backed their way out the front door. They never did try to go upstairs, where Hans and Karl, our "uncles," were hiding, and they didn't find Papa's gold watch or our camera, both of which Mom had hidden under her bed.

It took the soldiers nearly all day to go through the entire town, but when they were done, their armored car was piled high with rifles and shotguns on its back and overflowing with cameras and other paraphernalia inside. When they got done with this search, the patrol we were following, as well as all the others throughout town, gathered in the center of town, between the blacksmith shop and the stream, which we called the Flet, and unloaded their cache of guns and other loot onto the cobblestone street. A couple dozen children from all over town joined us to watch them, and many adults showed up as well, prompting the British to post a squad of soldiers around their activity as a guard.

From their half dozen armored cars, they amassed an unbelievable quantity of guns, hundreds of them. None of us ever imagined that there were so many guns owned in such a small town as Jork. There were very few military guns among them too. Most of them were hunting rifles or heirlooms from generations ago. Many of them looked like they cost thousands of Deutschmarks and amounted to a significant part of the family treasure.

As we watched, the twenty or so British soldiers that weren't guarding us spread out around those piles of guns, and each one of them picked up a gun and began to take it apart. Sometimes they stripped out the bolt and threw the firing pin and other mechanisms in the stream. Other times they took the gun by the barrel and smashed it over the iron railing on the edge of the stream. The stock would splinter, and then they would take apart the bolt and so on too. All of this then got thrown in the stream. They would dissemble pistols the same way, taking each little piece out and throwing them in different directions in the stream.

It was heartbreaking, watching all that. Some of the old men among the onlookers broke down and cried. None of us thought that any of this was necessary, since we'd mostly been looking forward to having the English come and end the war. No one that I knew of anyway, had been planning on resisting the British occupation, so we saw this merely as a senseless act. On the other hand, there was real fear in the eyes of the British soldiers as they were collecting the guns, so I guess they must've thought that they were protecting themselves by doing that. That evening, we went to bed with a great sense of loss and vulnerability, even though the soldiers hadn't taken anything from our house.

The next morning at dawn, I was jolted awake by the thunderous sound of a formation of planes flying low over our house. Confused and groggy, I wasn't really sure what had caused the noise, and I thought that maybe the Rapture had come, and all my family had gone to be with Jesus, but I'd been left behind. I

203

panicked for a moment, until I saw Karl still sleeping next to me. Then I heard their engine noise trailing off in the distance, and I calmed down. Every morning for the next couple weeks, those planes kept on coming back though, going somewhere.

The British were a lot more at ease around town beginning that third day. They still had their patrols, but there were fewer of them, and they also allowed individual soldiers to walk around. Most of them were very friendly and tried to make us more comfortable with them by giving us candy bars or by smiling and waving. We had a sense that everything was going to be all right, now that they were here.

That wasn't completely true though, as I found out later on that day. I was walking around, trying to survey where all the British were in town when I happened to pass a particular jewelry store that had its door smashed in. Curious, I looked inside, only to see a British soldier there stuffing his pockets with gold rings that he was taking from some drawers. Not wanting him to see me, since he had his rifle with him, I hurriedly kept on walking. We had this idea that the British and Americans wouldn't do things like that, I guess because of the image that their propaganda had created, and by and large, that was true, but obviously there were some bad ones among them too.

Whenever we'd come upon a group of British soldiers doing something, they would always smile and wave at us, since they couldn't speak German, so we would smile and wave back at them. I was only twelve years old at the time, having just had my birthday, and I was one of the older boys in our group, so we didn't really know of anything else to do. Pretty soon, the British got used to us hanging around watching them, and they began to invite us in closer to them so that we could see what they were really doing. They liked to show off to us, and those that knew any German tried to impress us with that. We just laughed, and then we laughed at them some more once we were by ourselves again. We enjoyed their attention though, since our own Papas weren't anywhere to be found, and soon we found ourselves becoming friends with them.

The place where I hung out the most with the British was at the horse riding school on Osterminnenweg, which they had turned into their motor pool and garage. There were a lot of trucks and Monkey Swings there, which I liked to look at, and the men there were more relaxed and friendly than most of the other British. There was always a lot going on too, with trucks coming and going and equipment and supplies constantly being unloaded and distributed out to the troops in town. I could understand that sort of thing without having to speak English, so it was fun.

There was one particular soldier, a truck driver on what I later learned was a Deuce and a Half, who befriended me. He gave me candy bars and let me help him unload his truck sometimes. That was really exciting for me, since it gave me something constructive to do, and I felt like I was doing something important. After unloading the truck, I'd even help him sweep it out or wash it off.

My official job, according to Mom, was still to forage for food and to wait in lines though. The British motor pool was a good place to do this from, since a lot of news as well as food passed through there, and since they sometimes handed stuff out to us too. It was also located close enough to the center of town that I could get to most stores in pretty good time if I heard that they had food there. Nonetheless, there were many times that I stood in line for a couple hours or more, only to find out that they'd run out of whatever food they had before I got to the head of the line. That was frustrating, and it wore on our nerves. All of us were pretty skinny back then because there wasn't much to eat, though I have to admit that God always provided us with something. Usually though, it was yellow turnips, and although Mom fixed them in every way imaginable, it was always patently obvious what we were eating. We grew to hate those turnips.

One time, I was in the kitchen when Mom was cooking some more turnips, and I complained, "Mom, don't you have anything else to eat." She turned around and started to say, "Son, I wish..." but then she choked up and turned away from me. I heard her sniffle and start to cry, and I realized that I'd said something terribly wrong. I felt ashamed for having asked such a stupid question, when I knew that if she had anything else, she would've gladly given it to us. I went away from there determined to find something better for us to eat, so that Mom could be proud of giving it to us again, as she was always such a good cook back in Rothenen.

A few days later, my truck driver friend brought in a load of food, and I helped him unload it. We swept up, and I helped him fold up the canvass cover that went over the arched aluminum struts forming the frame over the bed of his truck. We laid that behind the cab, and then I wandered off to find something else to do. All of that was pretty normal. But after walking a ways, I happened to turn around and looked back towards his truck, and I spied him acting rather suspiciously.

He was glancing furtively around, trying to see if anyone was watching him, and he had what looked like a couple of loaves of bread in his hands. I'd gone behind another truck by this time, so he didn't see me. He was standing in the bed of his truck right then, and I saw him bend down and hide these loaves of bread under the canvass tarp that we'd folded up behind his cab. I don't know what he was doing with them, since he was obviously very well fed being a soldier, but it seemed to me that he had stolen them. I thought perhaps he had a German girlfriend and was going to give them to her after he got off duty. Well, I had a German girlfriend who needed them too, my mother, and I figured that if he had stolen them already that they were fair game for me as well.

I circled back around the motor pool and came in from the side at the end of the row of trucks where his was parked. I crept closer, moving between or underneath the trucks and then hiding between the two trucks nearest his until I was sure that no one else was around. Then I slipped up beside his truck, lifted the canvass tarp just enough to see the bread, drew it slowly towards me, and hid it beneath my overcoat. I let the tarp back down and walked as nonchalantly as I could out of the motor pool, holding the bottom of my coat tight so that the bread wouldn't fall out of it.

Once I was away from the motor pool, I broke into a run until I got home. Still running, I burst into the kitchen where Mom was working and exclaimed, "Mom, Mom! Guess what my truck driver friend gave me at the motor pool today!? He gave me two loaves of WHITE bread!" I'd never had white bread before, so this was going to be quite a wonderful meal that evening. Mom was very thankful and said to be sure to thank my soldier friend at the motor pool. I said I would, but I had no intention of doing it, because I'd stolen the bread, and I'd just told my mother a lie. I came up with all kinds of rationalizations as to why it was okay, but I still felt guilty about it, and I know today that I shouldn't have done it.

Everyone enjoyed eating the white bread that evening, since it was the first white bread we'd ever had, and since it was a great break from the routine of yellow turnips. The rye sourdough bread that Mom used to make back in Rothenen was much better tasting, but all we had since coming to Jork was cornmeal bread, which was very dry and hard. There was a rumor going around that they even put sawdust in the cornmeal to make people think they were eating more than they really were. I thought this bread tasted good, and I enjoyed all the popularity and acclaim I received in my family for having gotten it, but my enjoyment of it was hollow, since I still had this gnawing guilty feeling in the pit of my stomach. By morning, I realized it wasn't worth it, and I decided not to do anything like that anymore.

I said I wasn't sure what my truck driver friend was planning on doing with the bread, and I wasn't sure when he was planning on retrieving it either. After taking it, I stayed away from the motor pool for the rest of the day, thinking that he would come back for the bread that evening, and by morning, it would've mostly blown over. I was wrong about that though.

He didn't come back for the bread until I was on my way in to the motor pool the next day. I saw him standing on the truck bed again, looking under the tarp. He lifted the tarp and looked all around under it and then cursed and threw the tarp down. I didn't know English, so I'm not really sure what he was saying, but I'd been around the British soldiers long enough by that time to recognize what their favorite swear words were. I guess he assumed that someone else from the motor pool had taken it though, since he didn't say anything to me about it when I got there. He probably couldn't really do anything about it anyway, since he'd stolen it himself to begin with. He continued to let me help him unload his truck, and he was still friendly towards me, but he never hid any more bread where I could find it.

About the first of May, things took a definite turn for the better. The cherry harvest began. The British were being quite relaxed with people by this time, so they didn't mind when nearly everyone in town turned out to help the local farmers pick cherries. The area around Jork was filled with fruit orchards, and cherries were one of the main crops. Hildegaard, Ruth, Waltraut, and Marianna all came with me to a farm nearby, and the blacksmith even let Karl off work to help out.

For the next several weeks, we practically did nothing but harvest cherries. These were large trees too, and we had to use ladders to get up into them. We had baskets that had a hook on them so that you could hang them either from the top rung of the ladder or from a branch of the tree you were working on. It was hard work, but it was a pleasant break from not having anything to do. We were paid in cherries too, and for a long while, we had all kinds of cherries to eat. This was okay though, since it wasn't yellow turnips.

From up on those ladders, we also had a beautiful view of the surrounding countryside. There were apple and plum trees growing there too, and the farmers had cows grazing in the grass between the trees. They'd put iron shackles on the cows' forelegs, with chains running to a halter around their head to keep them from eating the lower leaves and fruit off the trees. Some of the cows were smarter than that though and would raise up on their hind legs to eat from the trees.

Everyone was happy to be there though. It was the beginning of the recovery time from the war, and we were all optimistic, despite having to endure continuing hardships and lack of food. The war ended on May 14th, and things began to get somewhat easier. The British unit that was occupying the town soon packed up and left too. With them went one of our sources of food, but other sources would take their place in time.

Mom sent off a letter to Tante Lisa, Papa's sister in the USA, not the one from Königsberg, but the one that had emigrated there in the 1920s, asking her if she could send us anything, so we were expecting something from there too. We got her first response from that towards the end of June. Tante Lisa sent us a large care package, wrapped in a 100 lb flour bag made of duck cloth. Inside the package were a variety of foods and sundries, like flour, sugar, cookies, crackers, bathroom items, and even some clothing, like sweaters. There were also things that Lisa must've known we wouldn't use, such as cartons of cigarettes, but Mom traded these for things that we did need, like potatoes, fruit, and meat. Mom even used the packing materials for things, like small tables, drawers, and shelves, and she made short pants for Karl and me out of the duck cloth. Tante Lisa kept on periodically sending us those care packages for several years, and it was always a big occasion when we received one of them.

While we were still waiting for Tante Lisa's first package though, another letter arrived from someone we didn't know. It was from the town of Soholmbrueck, near the Danish border. We didn't know anybody from that area, and the handwriting on the envelop was a mystery to us. Most of us happened to be there when it arrived, so we all gathered close around as Mom cautiously opened the letter.

There were actually a couple different letters in it, and a photograph. The photo was of us, which was perplexing, but one of the letters was in Papa's handwriting. As soon as Mom saw that, she gasped, "Papa hat geschrieben!" which means, "Papa has written!" When she started reading it though, she found that it wasn't addressed to her at all, but to someone named Frau Schmidt, so she said, "No, it's not him. Let me see what's here."

Upon reading it in more detail, she discovered that it was one of several letters that Papa had written soon after he'd bid us farewell and sent us away on the Lotringen. He'd sent these letters to various people that he'd met throughout Germany, telling them that we were refugees and asking them to help us if we ended up in their area. This particular one was to the wife of his training unit commander when he'd been training at the base near Denmark, soon after the start of the war. It was an invitation to her to take one or more of us in to help her on her farm, in exchange for room and board. The picture of us was enclosed so that she could see what we were like. Frau Schmidt had found our names on one of the many refugee locator bulletin boards which every town had at least one of, and she had enclosed both Papa's letter and the picture to introduce herself and to explain why she was writing. She said that she wasn't able to take all of us in, but she would take the one she'd put an X over in the picture, and she'd give him all his room and board. She'd chosen the biggest one of all of us in the picture. Me.

Mom was livid. She said, "No. Absolutely not. You are part of this family, and you shall stay here and continue to be a part of our family. I'm not having my twelve-year old son going off to live with some strange woman doing who knows what and possibly getting hurt or getting into some kind of trouble. I'm not going to allow it."

I didn't argue with her right away. Instead, I waited a couple days until she cooled off a bit, and then I reasoned with her. I knew that I had the biggest appetite of any of us, even bigger than Karl's, so my leaving would relieve Mom of one very significant mouth to feed. I said, "Mom, please, let me go. You have enough to do here. You have the other kids."

211

She immediately responded with, "No, no, no. You're not going. You'll be away from home. You're too small. You can't go yet. You're only twelve years old. You can't go."

I kept at her though and said, "Yeah, but Mom, this will help. That way, you won't have to worry about me. She promised to give me food and clothing and so on. Why don't you let me go?" This went on for several days. Food was tight though, and eventually, she agreed to let me go, but only after making me promise that as soon as I got homesick, I would come home.

Frau Schmidt had enclosed her phone number, so Mom walked up town to where there was a public phone and called her. She agreed to send us the train fare for me to come stay with her. Now it was just a matter of time.

14

Frau Schmidt

About the third week of June, 1945, we received yet another exciting letter. This time it was from the International Committee of the Red Cross. It was just a single, short, typed paragraph, but it was the best news we'd had in months. It said, "Frau Flemming, This is to inform you that your husband, Otto Flemming, has been taken prisoner by the armed services of the Union of Soviet Socialist Republics. He is being held near Smolensk, the Ukraine. According to the Geneva Conventions, he has the right to send and receive mail, although national authorities have the right to restrict what can be said in his correspondence." And then it gave his address. It didn't say how he was doing or anything, but we now knew he was alive, so we were jubilant.

A week later, we received the package from Tante Lisa, and then a couple days after that, Frau Schmidt sent me a train ticket and my itinerary to go live with her. Mom had just enough time to make my shorts for me before I had to leave. Packing wasn't a problem, because I had so few things to take with me. I had the clothes on my back, some toiletry articles, my official papers, a couple pairs of underwear, and maybe one other change of clothes, besides the shorts that Mom made.

The itinerary had me leaving from Buxtehude on July 2nd, so Mom accompanied me to the train station. She cried and said that she'd miss me and would write to me. I said I would too, but I was wishing that the train would hurry up and come so that I could get on with this adventure. I was a little apprehensive about living with someone else, but the thought of forging out on my own and contributing to the family's efforts and being able to take care of myself made me excited. And I was a little proud too, because although I was only the third oldest, I was the largest of us children, so Frau Schmidt had picked me, even over Karl, who had a regular job. In some ways, this was my way of showing Karl that I could help take care of the family too.

Soholmbrueck was a tiny village with only five or six houses near Bredstedt, in the state of Schleswig Holstein, up on the Danish border. It was only 160km from Jork, but it took all day, because of the many stops that we made along the way. Frau Schmidt's cousin, Lowenz, met me at the train station and drove me back to their farm in his truck.

Their house was built in 1700, which was announced by large black iron numbers in the gables attached to the system of bolts anchoring the bricks that the walls were made of, and it had a heavy thatched roof. The heavy thatch was really an amazingly efficient insulator, as it kept the house quite warm in the winter but cool during the summer. Back it those days, thatch was still pretty common in roofs.

214

The house itself was fairly large, and it was in the shape of an L, with one leg being the house and the other leg being the barn. That way, if it was raining or snowing out, you could still get to the barn to do your chores without getting wet. As I mentioned before, there was at least one house in Rothenen like that too.

Their farm wasn't very big, as most farms aren't in Europe, but they did have about seven cows, fifteen heifers, four horses, and maybe a dozen chickens, plus perhaps five acres of fields surrounding the house. They grew wheat, hay for the animals, and a variety of vegetables, including the hated yellow turnips.

Frau Schmidt was a thin lady in her mid-forties. She was quite pretty too, and she wore her hair up in a bun. Her husband, who had been Papa's commander while he was in training, was killed during the war, so she had to run the farm by herself. She'd brought Lowenz in to help her, but even though he was several years younger than her, there was still too much work for the two of them. Then she hired a maid to live with them and help with the cooking, cleaning, and light farm chores, but even that wasn't enough, so now they'd hired me.

True to her word, Frau Schmidt brought me into town and bought two sets of good work clothes for me, plus some work shoes and a hat. Boy, was I proud. I'd never had clothes this nice before, and they fit just right too. And the first meal that I had at their house was scrumptious too. I had meat and potatoes and vegetables and a big glass of milk. I had forgotten what good food was like in the months since we'd left Rothenen. And then she served dessert. She made a vanilla pudding and poured beaten egg white into the mix just before it cooled. It made these spongy white places in the pudding as she finished stirring it. Then just before she served it to us, she poured red raspberry

215

syrup over the pudding. Oh, that was so good, it's making my mouth water now just remembering it.

The room that she assigned me wasn't very big. It was just a cubby hole without any windows, in the middle of the house, but it was all mine, and there was a locking door too. The furniture was old, but it was nice. There was a dresser, a chair, and the bed, and although the bed wasn't any bigger or better than what I was used to, it was all mine. No one else was going to sleep in it with me. I'd never had it so good in my entire life, not even back in Rothenen. So that night, I slept better than I had in months and dreamed dreams of good food and nice clothes and a good life.

Those were just dreams of course. The reality was that I had to get up at 6 o'clock and help Lowenz milk the cows and clean the manure out of the stalls before breakfast, which was usually just coldcuts, rye bread, milk, and maybe boiled eggs. Sometimes on the weekends, Frau Schmidt would make wintbeutel, which was buckwheat, boiled in a covered bundt pan floating inside a kettle and then served sliced with syrup or butter. That was really good, but there wasn't time for it on school days, since I had to leave by 7 o'clock and walk two miles to get there on time. School was a challenge, as it'd been over two years since I had any kind of regular classes, so my mind wasn't used to it anymore. Then when I got back home, there was more farmwork to do before dark, and after dark, I had to do my homework. Now and then I'd get letters from Mom, but I couldn't read them until after everything else was done.

This went on for a year and a half. Of course, there were days when I had some time to myself. Frau Schmidt let us more or less take Sundays off, but there was still work to do. I asked to be allowed to go to church in town, and she said that I could do that.

However, I still had to take care of the animals, and when she and Lowenz were done eating lunch, I had to be there to clean up. Then I also had to wash the floors that afternoon and wash the dishes again after supper. She and Lowenz both slept in on Sundays and didn't go to church. The cleaning girl wanted to go out dancing on Saturday night, which she was allowed to do, and then she was also allowed to sleep in on Sunday morning. So I started feeling like I was being taken advantage of after a while. I was encouraged by how much my being away must've been helping Mom though, so I kept it up, month after month.

I did get some time off on Sundays though, and once in a while, I'd get done with my after-school chores early enough to have some time off then too. During those times I used to hang out with three other boys my age, and we'd go swimming off a particular bridge over the Treene River, or we'd go exploring together and so on.

Most of the swimming that I did there was that first summer. This bridge over the Treene River was made of concrete, and it was arched. At either end, the abutments were about four feet above the river, while in the middle, it rose about fifteen feet high. Being boys, we wanted to make an adventure of our swimming, so we began diving off the bridge into the water, starting at the low end of the bridge and daring each other to go up higher on the next dive. When I finally made it to the top of the bridge and dove off, it suddenly occurred to me that I was so high up that I might hit the bottom of the river with my head when I landed. By that time though, I was nearly in the water, so I jerked my body up, intending to alter my course of flight into a shallower dive. It didn't alter my trajectory though, just the angle at which I hit the water. In other words, I belly flopped.

When my hands hit the water, instead of slicing cleanly through it and breaking it for my head, the water threw them up behind my head, wrenching my shoulder muscles. When my head hit the water, it hit full force, snapping back hard and giving me a minor case of whiplash. Water powered up into my nose and ripped open my mouth, ramming down my throat and into my stomach and lungs. As the top part of my torso followed my head and arms into the water, the water accelerated the arching motion that I had started in my back, compressing my spine and causing some very intense, sharp pain in the small of my back. Once my whole body was in the water, I reacted violently, leaping up and thrashing around, coughing and sputtering and finally flailing my way to shore, while the other guys stood there laughing at me. After that, I refused to jump off the top of the bridge any more.

We found other things to do in the water though, that didn't require jumping off the bridge. There was an abandoned Luftwaffe base nearby, just outside of Bredstedt, and since this was one of our favorite places to explore, we thought we might find something useful to play with there. The Luftwaffe had left in a hurry, less than a year earlier, and they tried to destroy what was left of their planes and facilities on their way out, but they didn't get everything. There was a lot of equipment and pieces of airplanes just laying around, so we scrounged around looking for stuff that we could use. What we found were some boats. Well, they weren't really boats, but that's what we used them for. The first type of boat that we found consisted of the fuel tanks in the wings of several of their aircraft. The wings and fuselages of their planes were pretty well ripped apart, so we spent a lot of time looking inside these as we clambered around on and in the various junked airplanes. As we were doing this, one of us noticed the size of the wing tanks, which were made of sheet metal with a lining. With a little ingenuity and effort, and a few tools from the farm, we managed to disconnect several of these tanks and pry them out of their aircraft. Then we turned them over and cut the side with the holes out with some metal shears, creating some rather odd-shaped boats, which were neither streamlined nor symmetrical, and had curves in funny places.

We found our second type of boat at an air defense post at one end of the air base, where there were some abandoned search lights. This boat, a coracle actually, was made of the lens cover from a searchlight. It was wider than I was tall, and it was about a foot deep and surprisingly lightweight. We just removed its hinges and clips, and presto, we had another boat. We were quite proud of our little flotilla, even though they foundered easily if you leaned too far over the side and even though the coracle spun around whenever you tried to paddle it. We spent a lot of time either racing or chasing each other up and down the river in them.

There were lots of adventures and opportunities to have fun there on the farm too. Frau Schmidt had sort of inherited this gray German Shepherd dog from an Army unit where he served as a messenger dog. His foot got run over by a truck, so he was given a "medical discharge," which is how she got him. After he recovered from his injury, he became a great farm dog, and he and I loved to play together. I'd tell him to Stay, and then I'd run into the barn or under a haystack or something to hide. When I was good and hidden, I'd whistle for him, and he come running. He'd sniff around for a while, but he always found me, and then he'd grab me by the back of the neck, which he was trained to do for recovering people from injuries. He never hurt me though.

Frau Schmidt also sent me to Milking School in Bredstedt to learn how to milk cows correctly. They taught me how to massage the cow's udder and nipples before milking her and how to clean her udder and keep foreign objects out of the milk bucket. After milking, they showed me how to put salve on the nipples to keep them soft. We had a cow while we were living in Rothenen, and I'd helped milk her before, but I never really learned how to do it correctly like they were showing me in the school. The best part about milking the cows though was squirting milk at the cats that hung around the barn and trying to hit them in the face or mouth with it.

Working with the horses was fun too, and it reminded me a lot of Rothenen as well. One time though, Lowenz asked me to fetch this particular mare that had foaled in the spring of '46. She was out in the corral with her foal, and she was feeling rather chipper that day, so I had to chase her around with the bridle for a long time. Finally, I cornered her and just as I was about to put the bridle over her head, she whirled around and kicked at me with both her hind legs. One hoof went on one side of my head, and the other hoof went on the other side of my head. If her hooves were a couple inches closer together, she would've kicked my head in and killed me right there. I nearly wet my pants, I was so scared. I left her in the corral and gave the bridle back to Lowenz, telling him to get her himself. Of course he went back and had the bridle on her in under two minutes, much to my embarrassment.

In those days, right after the war, there were a lot of unique things that people did to cope, since the economy wasn't really functioning yet. One situation that we had to deal with on the farm was not having any coal. The mines weren't yet operating, or at least the distribution system wasn't operating, so we didn't have any coal to heat the house with that winter. The answer to that was in something we called brown coal, or torf. It was actually peat. Down near the banks of the rivers, there would be these large mossy areas, and if you dug under them and removed their top soil, down to twelve to eighteen inches or so, you would find this layer of peat that was perhaps five or six feet deep. We had these special knives, with a two-foot long shovel handle on them and a foot-and-a-half long double-edged blade, to cut through the peat with. We'd cut it into tile squares, and we'd lay them out to dry. It would burn fairly quickly, but there was a lot of it, so it didn't matter.

The hole that we dug for that peat was a good twenty meters long, so everyone felt that we should fill it back up when we were done digging out the peat. There was a hill of sand about 200 meters away from there, so someone hit upon the idea of filling our hole with sand from that hill, thus flattening out the whole area so that it could be used for crops. Of course, we were going to put the top soil back in place after filling the hole with sand. Two hundred meters is a long ways to carry what amounted to several tons of sand though, so someone else came up with the idea of creating a railroad system with tilting buckets of sand sitting on carts or dollies and rolling down the hill on these rails that they made. After dumping several cartfuls of sand at one spot, the sand would pile up, and we'd have to move the rails. It became my job to stand in our hole and push the sand around as they dumped it in, so that they wouldn't have to move the rails so often.

While I was standing knee-deep in the sand, pushing it around like that, I suddenly felt little pins and needles all over my legs and moving up under my pants and onto my body. At first, I just ignored it, but it quickly got worse, to the point that it was burning. I looked down then, and my legs were covered with fire ants. There were hundreds of them, and they were biting and stinging me all over. Frantic, I leaped out of the hole and ran screaming down the bank and jumped into the river. I swam around for a while and rubbed my body down, making sure that all the ants were gone. Everyone else had a good laugh, and after that, I found a different way to push the sand around. It took several days before all the welts had disappeared from my legs.

Life and work with Frau Schmidt was generally pleasant enough, and the knowledge that I was helping my family allowed me to overcome most of the obstacles that I encountered. As time went on though, there started to be a lot of little things that went wrong, and after I'd been there about a year, it seemed that Frau Schmidt and Lowenz were conspiring to make life difficult for me.

I mentioned the situation on Sundays already. There was also a period of about two weeks, during my second September there, in 1946, when both Frau Schmidt and Lowenz caught pneumonia and were confined to their beds. During those two weeks, I had to get up at 4 o'clock instead of 6 o'clock. I had to milk the cows, feed them and all the other animals, and clean out their stalls before leaving for school at 7 o'clock. Then when I got home, I had to take a wagon and a team of horses and go collect the turnip and beet harvests, and after that, I had to wash the dishes too, plus everything else I was already doing. Basically I had to do most of both Frau Schmidt's and Lowenz's jobs as well as my own. It was hard work, and I was exhausted at the end of every day, but I was willing to do it because they were so sick.

Shortly after their sickness though, I accidentally walked in on them doing things together that cousins shouldn't be doing. I exited immediately, and I never

222

mentioned the incident to them or anyone else, but I could tell that their attitude towards me was changing. They gave me more and more work to do, and when Lowenz and I would be working together in the barn, he would outdo himself to overwhelm me with work. It was as if he was competing with me to see who was the hardest worker, except that he was in his late twenties, while I was merely thirteen, so he was much bigger and stronger than I was. There were times during the hay harvest when we'd be bringing the hay into the barn, with Lowenz on the wagon, passing hay up to me in the hay loft of the barn, where I would use a pitchfork to move the hay further back into the barn, that he would throw hay up to me so fast that I would be up to my shoulders in it. They would also exclude me from conversations and show favoritism to their maid and talk down to me and criticize and ridicule me at every opportunity. Finally, after enduring about three months of this, and having been reduced to tears more than once, I asked to go home.

They agreed to this, as if they'd been wondering how long it would take me to arrive at this conclusion. So a few days later, I boarded a train and went home to Jork again.

From Hitler Youth to American Soldier

Oma Moje

*Oma Moje's
house in Jork*

*The place in Jork
where the British
soldiers broke the
rifles into pieces*

224

The picture we sent to my Dad while he was in the Russian prison. He brought it back when he got out

In front of Oma Moje's house

The Baptist Youth Group in Jork

My sisters, Mariane, Ursula, Hildegard, & Waltraut

My youngest brother, Ulrich's death announcement

Mom with my brother Gerhart

Frau Schmidt

Elim Church, in Hamburg, where I received Jesus Christ as my Savior

Aribert Krause, Me, & Werner Zopke in front of the Jork Baptist Church

My Blacksmith's Journeyman Papers, with my teacher, Peter Mahnke's signature

The day before we embarked for the U.S., our Uncle Balsahm and his family came to see us off

My Parent's Immunization Papers

Our last family photo before embarking, taken at the Immigration Camp

A ship I helped build while I was working at the Krantz Shipyard

Me, in my galley apron, on the U.S.S. General Taylor

The U.S.S. General Taylor, the Liberty Ship we sailed to the U.S. on

M. S. „General M. B. Stewart"

15

Jork Again

When I arrived in Jork in December, 1946, eighteen months after leaving, it was like coming to a completely new town. Everything seemed to have changed. Money from the Marshall Plan had been pouring into Germany as a whole, and since Jork was a suburb of Hamburg, it received its share of that. Many of the buildings had been cleaned up, and most of the rubble from the war had been cleared away. The bridges over the canals had been repaired or rebuilt, and the roads were paved or at least had new cobblestones put in. There was little evidence left that we were still an occupied country, and everyone seemed to have a positive, upbeat mood. The British and Americans were now being regarded as our friends, and there was talk about Russia being a new threat.

I was now nearly fourteen, and I was much taller and more confident than when I had left. I had several new sets of clothes that Frau Schmidt had bought me, and I was strong and healthy from all the hard work and good food on the farm. I had become used to going to school again, and I was used to working too.   I was looking forward to life with my family and to finding out what new opportunities that might hold for me, such as starting trade school with a blacksmith specialty.

Karl was already doing that and had become a full apprentice at the blacksmith shop in Jork. Typically as a child became an adolescent, he or she was required to take a test, roughly near the end of elementary school. The results of that test determined whether they were eligible for middle school, which was rather like high school in the US. If you didn't go to middle school, you went to trade school, but trade school in Germany in those days was the opposite of what it's considered in the US now. It was a prestigious thing. It practically guaranteed that you would have a good income and a place in the community, and it could only be taught by men who had gone through certain required levels of education, been tested successfully at each level, and achieved a measure of success actually doing that trade. These men were called masters, and they had a great deal of power and prestige within their trade. No apprentice would dare challenge his trade master, and a prospective apprentice's parents had to apply for their son to get accepted by a master. There was a lot of competition between families to get their sons accepted by the best masters, and many times if a family didn't have connections or a good reputation, their sons might have to wait several years before getting apprenticed.

In my situation, I was never able to take this test, due to the war, and I had lost nearly a year's worth of school time too. So I had to make up a year of elementary school before being allowed to attend trade school, and then I would have to apply for the

blacksmith specialty. Karl had heard of a certain Mr.
Mahnke, who was a master smith in Hedendorf, a town
about twenty minutes away by bus, near Buxtehude.
Mr. Mahnke, at age seventy-three, was one of the very
best master smiths in the entire area, but he also had a
reputation of being tyrannical and cruel to his
apprentices, sometimes physically beating them.
Consequently, although many boys considered applying
with him, only the hardiest ever did, and few of them
ever stayed with him long enough to graduate and
become a journeyman. In fact, by the time I was ready
to be apprenticed, the local Innung (trade guild, which
would be like a blacksmith's union in the US) had
banned Mr. Mahnke from having any more apprentices.
I didn't have much choice though, if I wanted to be
apprenticed to one of the better master smiths, because
we were refugees from the other side of the country, so
no one in the area knew us very well or knew of Papa's
reputation either. In any event, I couldn't even apply
until I was about to graduate from grade school.

Life had gotten better for my family while I was
away. Hildegaard had gotten a job, and with Papa's
military pay still coming in, they were able to make ends
meet and keep everyone in food and clothing. Mom
spent her time helping Oma Moje clean house, and she
finally felt that she was getting a handle on things. So
when I came back, not only did she make sure I went
right back to school, so I would be ready for trade school
when the time came, but she also made sure I went to
church with them on Sundays.

I had gone to church in Soholmbrueck too, but
not every Sunday. I'd become rather lax in my attitude
towards it as well, because it wasn't the kind of church
that I'd grown up with, and because I was alone and
didn't have anyone to hold me spiritually accountable.
So there were times when I didn't appreciate Mom's

233

edict that we attend a church all the way into Hamburg, about a two-hour journey, just because of what brand of theology they taught, especially since there was a Lutheran church just up the street from us in Jork.

Mom insisted that I go with them though, and despite my size, strength, and budding feelings of independence, I'd been well trained by Papa to obey everything that Mom told me to do. So I went with them. We got up at 6 o'clock on Sunday morning so that we could leave at seven and arrive by nine. We walked to Borstel, the small river port town about two kilometers north of us, where we took a steam ferry from there to Blankenese, a subdivision of Hamburg. From the ferry dock there, we had to hike about a hundred stair steps up the bank of the Elbe River to get to street level, and then we caught a subway train to Barmbek, another subdivision of Hamburg, where we walked the last six blocks to the church.

All the churches were full in those post-war days, and missionaries were arriving from England and the US in droves. People were hungry spiritually, because of the shock of freedom after having spent nearly a generation under Hitler and having realized that part of the reason for Hitler's success was the German people's spiritual apathy. They felt a sense of guilt and responsibility for having allowed Hitler to do what he did. People also felt desperate financially and personally. The economy was in a shambles, because people's businesses and places of work had been destroyed, and everyone was closely related to someone who had died during the war, causing a sense of grief and personal loss. But despite that, a two-hour journey into Hamburg was still way beyond what most Germans were willing to put up with to attend church, and if it wasn't for my Mom telling me to go, I'd be no exception.

The church that Mom had us go to was called
Elim Assembly, although it had no connection at the
time with the Assemblies of God. It was Pentecostal
though, and it was an Evangelical Free Church, like the
ones that Papa used to preach at while we were living in
Rothenen. Elim Assembly was actually meeting in a
Seventh Day Adventist church nearby then, because
their own church at No. 8 Bach Strasse had been
bombed out during the war. The Adventists didn't mind
of course, because they met on Saturday.

Elim Assembly was pastored by a friend of
Papa's, Rev. Paul Rabe, who had gotten saved at the
same time Papa did. They had a congregation of several
hundred, and church was always packed. They had
meetings going on almost constantly, nearly every day of
the week, and when the Adventists were using the
church building, Elim would hold their meetings in the
street or at someone's house. People were getting saved
every week, and you could see the congregation literally
swell with new people from month to month. The Holy
Spirit was moving powerfully among them, and there
were prophecies and healings and the gifts of the Spirit.
People flocked there to see what God was doing, and
they were eager to attend as many meetings as possible,
often arriving early so that they wouldn't miss anything.

Their main Sunday morning service started at 10
o'clock, but we usually arrived around nine, while they
were still having their holiness prayer meeting, which
started an hour or two earlier than that. You could hear
them outside the church, from as much as a block
away, as they were praying. There would be a sort of
hum, and as we got closer, we could hear one or more
people praying or singing loudly, and then there would
be a chorus of Amens or someone following with another
message after that. To look at them from inside the
sanctuary, there didn't appear to be any organization or

leadership at all during these meetings. Many of them were up walking around, while others were prostrated in the aisles or at the altar. Some would be weeping and crying out to God, while others prayed loudly, invoking the Blood of Jesus and binding the devil from being able to influence some situation. Still others had messages or prophecies in foreign or angelic tongues that someone else interpreted. Some people had songs to sing in the Spirit, while others gave testimonies of what God had done for them that week. Often there would be spontaneous congregational singing, followed by a great hush and a sense of awe as the presence of the Holy Spirit filled the room. It was beautiful, and although it had the outward appearance of disorganization, it was obviously well-orchestrated by the Holy Spirit, as no one ever created a scene or got out of line, and everything worked out in perfect order.

I think if the ferry across the Elbe ran any earlier than it did, Mom would've had us come to the holiness service too. As it was, we got there in time for Sunday School. My class was the adolescent class, which was taught by a woman in her mid forties. I don't remember what her name was, but she had a way with us. It was as if she knew exactly what we were going through as young teens, even though she was far older than we were. She went through all the issues that we were dealing with in those days, as well as explaining Bible stories, and she told us in no uncertain terms that we needed to give our lives to Jesus Christ. I had heard all the Bible stories and the message of salvation throughout my entire childhood, growing up as I did, the son of a lay preacher. I'd always known that I needed to accept Jesus as my Savior, but somehow it never got through to me how that would really happen. This Sunday School teacher explained it in ways that did get through to me and made an impression on me though. Throughout 1947 and into 1948, I felt an aching desperation about my spiritual condition, and I knew that I needed to do something about it. How that happened later on utterly changed the course of my life.

After Sunday School, of course, they held the regular church service, which was more geared towards people who might walk in off the street. There was more organization and a formal order to the service, even though they still had some spontaneity and freedom in the Spirit. They usually got done between noon and one, and then everyone would go home for lunch.

Around 3 o'clock though, many people got back together at the subway station near the church for an evangelistic street meeting. They had a Posaunen Kohr (brass band) and a guitar choir that would perform, and people would stand up on a wooden box and give their testimonies in between songs. Then one of the pastors would give a short message on salvation, ending up with an altar call and an invitation to come to church that evening or next Sunday morning.

They did have another regular service on Sunday evening, at six, which we attended too. This one featured more in-depth study of the Bible, and it tended to be less formal than the main service. There was also more time for people to give their testimonies and to ask for prayer for specific needs than there was in the other services. Sometimes these services lasted until late at night, and we'd have to leave early to be able to catch the last ferry across the Elbe.

Mom found Elim Assembly by talking to Papa's sister, Elfriede, and her husband Henry, who had managed to escape from Königsberg as refugees about the same time as we escaped from Rothenen. They had settled in Hamburg after locating us in Jork, and since they had kept in touch with Pastor Rabe, as he had attended their church as a young man, it was only

237

natural for them to start attending Elim too. Once we started attending there, we needed a place to go to eat lunch and to pass the time between services, so we would go over to Tante Elfriede's house. This was our big socializing time of the week too, as we'd spend the afternoon swapping war stories and catching up on what other relatives were doing. I learned a lot about life, the war, God, our relatives, and even about myself by listening to them.

One Sunday in early March, 1948, after being back in Jork for over a year, I was having an especially bad attitude on the way to church. I didn't want to go, and I was making that very clear to Mom and everyone else by my body language, my eyes, my tone of voice, and so on. Mom made it just as clear through her own determined attitude that I was going with them. Just before we left, she turned and told me, "Horst, you're going." So I whirled and turned my back to her and sarcastically repeated, "Okay, I'm going," as I stomped off towards the bathroom. Once we got to church, we walked into the holiness meeting, and everyone was praising God, and the Spirit was moving powerfully as usual. Someone cried out in a loud voice, pleading with God to have mercy and to heal a disease that a loved one of theirs had, and I thought, "Now what're they praying about." And just about that fast, things grew suddenly awkward and clunky in the spirit. Suddenly, no one seemed to want to pray or praise or sing or do anything, and those people that continued doing those things seemed to have to force themselves to do it.

Later that afternoon, while we were eating dinner with Tante Elfriede and Onkel Henry, Tante Elfriede commented about the service that morning. She said, "How strange it was at this morning's prayer meeting. It was such a beautiful prayer time, and then all of a sudden, something happened, and the Holy Spirit pulled back. It was as if someone had quenched the Spirit." The adults continued talking, speculating about what could've happened, but my jaw dropped, because I knew what had happened. I realized it was me she was talking about. I was the one that had quenched the Spirit, because of my attitude that morning. I watched it happen. We walked into the service, the Holy Spirit saw my attitude and that I was unwilling to change, and He walked out.

After that, something clicked in my mind. I'd grown up knowing about God, but this was the first time I'd ever seen God responding like a real person to something that I had done. That realization shook me. He was a real person, so He could be offended or could love just like other people, except that He was God. I'd been taking Him for granted up until then, but now I knew that I had to do something about Him, to make sure that He knew that I loved Him. I understood this meant accepting Jesus Christ as my personal Savior, but despite having grown up in a Christian home, somehow I'd missed how you actually did that. So I determined that I had to find out how to do that and soon.

The week after that, our school had its spring vacation. This just happened to be the same week that Elim Assembly's church rebuilding program got into full swing. A couple of weeks earlier, they'd received a donated prefabricated church building from a large Pentecostal church in Stockholm, Sweden. This church had already donated large quantities of food and clothing, both to Elim and to many other churches in Germany. I even got my first suit jacket from them, a white wool jacket that I looked very good in, just the month before this. Then they sent us an entire church building, of all things. It was shipped in sections that they assembled on the site of Elim's original church

239

building, which as I said had been bombed out during the war. The building, which they called a "Sweden Kirche," was basically just the main sanctuary, so Elim had to come up with any other rooms or features that they wanted their building to have. There were still heaps of bricks and rubble from the original building laying around, so they decided that the best way to get construction materials was to renovate and reuse as much as possible from the old building. As a result, most of the other kids in my Sunday School class and I spent our spring vacation in the church yard, knocking old mortar off old bricks with a hammer and then brushing them clean before passing them to the men that were mixing the new mortar so that they could use them to build the rest of the church. By doing that, we built an office, a small conference room, an overflow room, and a foyer onto the front of the church, with an apartment for the pastor and his family on a second story. It went up very quickly, as it had nearly the entire congregation working on it, and they were able to move into it by the first Sunday in April.

Spending that week working at the church helped me to work out in my mind some of the issues that had been bothering me with my spiritual life. It also gave me opportunities to see the pastor, the church elders, and my Sunday School teacher at work in a more ordinary environment than Sunday meetings, and I got to know the other kids in my class better too. So when the next Sunday, Palm Sunday, March 21st, 1948, arrived, I was ready to see God do something in my life.

The church was packed that Sunday morning, and so was our Sunday School class. I showed up determined to find out how to get saved, and that was exactly what our teacher spoke about. She told the whole story of how Jesus submitted Himself to being crucified and how that fulfilled the requirement for a perfect sacrifice for our sins. Then she explained step by step how we could receive Jesus into our hearts and ask Him to forgive our sins. I had always thought that getting saved would require some big ceremony, celebration, or miracle, but the way she described it, everything made sense, and I knew that I could do it.

She said all you had to do was confess with your mouth that Jesus is Lord and believe with your heart that God raised Him from the dead, since it was with your heart that you believed, resulting in righteousness, and it was with your mouth that you confessed, resulting in salvation. She quoted from Romans 10:9-10 for that. And then she also said that we needed to ask God to forgive our sins, based on I John 1:9. She said if we did those simple things, that we would receive Jesus into our hearts as our Savior, whether we felt like anything had happened or not.

After the class, Pastor Rabe came into our room to explain some things to us about that morning's service. It was a graduation service of sorts for our class. Many of us, including me, were starting trade school the Monday after Easter, so the pastor had arranged for us to go up front during the service and be recognized and prayed over. He talked to us about where we needed to sit and what the signal would be for us to go up front. When he got done, he asked us to gather around the table to pray before going out. There weren't any chairs in our room that morning, since the ushers had taken them out to the overflow room because of the size of the crowd, so we had to kneel on the floor around the table. He prayed, and then he asked if any of us would like to pray too.

Well, the Holy Spirit had been dealing with me for weeks now, and after that morning's class, I just had to do something. So I spoke up and prayed, "Lord forgive me of my sins," and my heart just erupted with grief and remorse. I started crying and confessing all of my sins that I could think of. Then I asked Jesus to come into my heart and be my Lord and Savior, and there were several other things that I added in there as well. When I got done, a girl named Erika started up, but I hardly even heard her, because I was still crying. Inside me, I was arguing with myself, condemning myself and begging God to really forgive me.

We couldn't stay there and continue for long though, because the service was starting. We filed out of the room and made our way up to the first row of chairs to sit down, and all the while, I was bawling and blubbering over my sudden realization of what a miserable, wretched, sinful person I was. As soon as the pastor got up on stage, he announced to the crowd, "I've got some good news for you. Herb and Erika already gave their hearts to the Lord this morning!" The congregation broke into applause, and people were congratulating me and patting me on the back and saying how they'd been praying for me. I was miserable though. I thought, "He doesn't know what he was talking about." I was expecting some big miracle or some fantastic feelings of rapture, but nothing like that had happened, and all I felt was guilt and anguish. I didn't realize that you didn't need feelings or miracles to get saved.

The pastor's sermon concentrated on Jesus' triumphal ride into Jerusalem on a donkey, with His subsequent encounters with the Pharisees, and hints at His later betrayal and crucifixion, and that just made matters worse for me. I could see it all graphically with my mind's eye, and although I knew He had done all that especially for me, I felt like I wasn't worthy of that kind of love and mercy. I cried through the whole service, and I was gloomy and melancholy all that afternoon and evening as we went over to Tante

Elfriede's, went to the other services, and finally took the train and ferry home.

The next day though, I woke up singing. I sang "No, Never Alone. He promised never to leave me, never to leave me alone." I had a strong witness in my spirit that I had indeed gotten saved the day before, and I was excited and joyful. So I sang, loudly. I didn't care who heard me, even with a house full of people, only about half of which were in my family. I sang despite the first curious and then irritated looks that Karl gave me as he woke up on the other side of our bed. And I continued singing as I got ready and came out of our bedroom, in spite of my younger sisters making fun of me.

I kept on singing that whole day and even for days afterwards, as my comprehension of what Jesus had just done in my life grew in my mind and spirit. I threw myself into Bible study, reading at least a chapter a day and often many more than that, and I would pray for long times after finishing with my reading. For the first time in my life, I had met Jesus Christ in a personal way, and as the days went by that week between Palm Sunday and Easter, I discovered a growing hunger and thirst, even a desperation, for spending time in God's presence. By the end of that week nothing mattered to me anymore, except getting to know Him better. And then I had to start trade school, the Monday after Easter.

The agreement was that I would go to live with the Mahnkes, who had two other families living with them too, in Hedendorf during the week, and I would come home on weekends. I slept in a small room near the entrance of his house and worked in his blacksmith shop Mondays through Wednesdays. Then I went to school on Thursdays and worked in the shop some more on Fridays and often on Saturdays too. In fact, Mr. Mahnke even wanted me to work on Sundays, cleaning up in the shop, but when I started complaining about it, he let me go home, so that I could go to church.

This was a time of great contrast in my life, between my newfound love of Jesus Christ and my newfound work with Mr. Mahnke, who cared nothing for God and little more for people. Mr. Mahnke was a very serious man who demanded nothing short of perfection, gave little praise if you achieved it, and heaped on criticism if you failed in any way. He was also a very large and powerful man, having been a machinist on a battleship in the German Navy during WWI. I could understand why his earlier apprentices could be so afraid of him.

I didn't care though. I sang, hummed, or whistled all I could while I was working for him, at least while he wasn't right nearby. When he'd hear me, he would come over and say, "There is no singing here, only work." Sometimes he would yell at me or criticize me. I think my very happiness irritated him. One time when he did that, I responded, "What? I'm not doing anything. What did I do wrong?" That must've really set him off though, because he took a swing at me. This was the only time he ever tried to hit me. Thankfully, I ducked, and he only hit my hat off my head. We had an uneasy relationship that way, but I think he was grateful that the Innung allowed me to come and help him, so he was trying to be very careful with me. I too was grateful, because he was very knowledgeable, and he was probably the only master smith in the area who would take me.

An odd result of these two contrasting paths in my life was that only a few weeks after getting saved, I began to lose interest in living. Now don't get me wrong. I wasn't suicidal at all. Rather I had discovered such a better, more powerful, more exciting life with Jesus Christ that compared with my life in Jork and

Hedendorf, I simply was more captivated by what life would be like when I went home to be with Jesus. Learning the blacksmith trade was interesting, but it wasn't what I dreamed about doing.

Practically my every waking thought was about Jesus, and I spent all my free time reading the Word and praying. If I was doing something else, I was also singing. I went to bed singing. I would continue singing until I fell asleep, pulling the covers over my head so that people walking by my room wouldn't hear me, and then I'd be singing when I woke up too. I rode my bicycle back and forth to Jork from Hedendorf, a good 45-minute ride, singing all the way, just so that I could be sure of being able to go to church at Elim. So although I had a good time building my smithing skills, I was really only doing it because I had to.

But then I began being obsessed with wanting to leave this world. I started praying that I would have an accident or get run over by a car or something, so that I could die and go to be with Jesus. I prayed, often crying too, "Lord take me away from this world, because I want to be with You. Lord, Lord, take me away, and let me go. Let me come home to be with You." One of the reasons I wanted to go to heaven so badly was because of people's sin and the possibility that I might fall into temptation and do something that was displeasing to God. I stopped wanting to be around other people, unless it was at church, and I lost interest in doing just about everything else as well. I dreamed of going to heaven. I felt homesick for it. All I wanted to do was to be close to the Lord, and it was so wonderful, how close we really were.

I actually began looking for something to happen that would kill me. One time I was working outside, in our shop yard, building a piece to go on a wagon. There were some very large trees on the other side of Mr.

Mahnke's fence, and they overhung the entire yard, blocking out both sun and rain. I had to heat up this iron rod which I was going to run through a hole that I had drilled out in a piece of wood. I had to make the hole wider so that I could put a particular bolt into the hole, and pushing the hot iron rod through the hole would do that. Then I needed to fetch something from inside the shop, and when I came back out, I picked up the electric drill again to drill another hole. What I didn't realize was that while I was inside, it had started to rain. The trees blocked the rain from coming to the ground until I got back outside and picked up the drill. Then some wind blew, and a whole bunch of water fell out of the trees. Some of it got into the drill that I was holding, shorting it out and delivering a massive 220-volt shock through my body. The current caused my hand to tighten around the grip of the drill, preventing me from letting it go, so I couldn't do anything but stand there and shake violently while I was being electrocuted. I was only barely able to call for help, but Mr. Mahnke heard me and came over. He didn't know what to do though, so he just stood there feeling helpless. Finally, I shook so much that the drill broke free from my hand on its own, falling to the ground and releasing me from the electrical current. He apologized, saying, "Oh, no, I should've unplugged the cord. I just didn't know what to do. I'd never seen anything like that before." But I was disappointed that the shock didn't kill me.

It was almost like being infatuated with the Lord, and as I can see now, it was growing into somewhat of a fantasy for me. Life on the outside was hard, but now I'd found a way to escape from that hardship, or so I thought. Being such a young Christian, I didn't realize that God had ordained for His children to go through hardships and trials, to help them mature into spiritual adults, like His own Son, so that they could spread the

Gospel and change the world, like Jesus did. In His love for me though, He was merciful in how He revealed that His grace had to be sufficient for me too, as it had been for the Apostle Paul before me.

One night in late summer, 1948, the Lord gave me a dream. I dreamed that I died. My body was laying on my bed, and my family was standing around it in a horseshoe shape, with Mom near the head of my body and my brothers and sisters on either side of it. No one was at the feet, because my Papa was still a prisoner in Russia. I myself was floating where the ceiling should've been, but there wasn't any ceiling, and if I looked up, I could see beautiful green fields and an awesome spring day about me. I didn't see God or Jesus or angels, but I felt magnificent, and I was excited, because I knew that I was on my way to be with Jesus in Paradise. But Mom, Karl, Hildegaard, and the others were all crying. They were bent over my body and were touching it and caressing its face, weeping as if the end of the world had come. I told them not to worry about me and not to cry over me, because I was happy and everything was just fine where I was going. They didn't hear me though, so I said it louder, "Please don't cry for me. I'm happy. I'm where I want to be." They still didn't respond. It was as if they didn't even know I was there. Then I realized that I hadn't said anything at all, and in fact, I couldn't say anything, at least not that they could hear. I tried hitting the wall or tapping them on the back, but to no avail. They couldn't hear me or see me, and there was nothing that I could do to change that. There was no way for me to communicate to them that I loved them and that I was happier now than before. I was utterly impotent and helpless to comfort them in their sorrow. I burst into tears and cried and cried and cried.

In the morning, when I awoke, my pillow was soaking wet, apparently because I really had been crying. Feeling the wetness on my face jarred me into alertness, and I sat up in bed. I remembered the dream vividly, as if it had really happened. Obviously, I wasn't dead, and I wasn't in Paradise either, so I thought about the dream and what it meant. I realized that I had been selfish to want to go to heaven so badly that I would be willing to forsake the life, responsibilities, and people that God had given me right where I was. That desire left me right then and never came back, though I continued to press on into the Spirit and presence of God in the days and years that followed. I knew then that God had, with life and salvation, given me a mission to accomplish, so I set about finding out what it was.

That experience gave me a new sense of reality and determination in my life. My daily routine with Mr. Mahnke was no longer so onerous to me, and I didn't see any more conflict between my life in Jesus and my life in Jork. I enjoyed my work and studies as a blacksmith apprentice, and I began to realize that God had called me to do this work. I enjoyed working with iron and steel and other metals and even wood. I enjoyed the feel of them in my hands and being able to turn them into a usable product. I also enjoyed helping people. There were farmers who would bring their horses to be hoofed or their wagons to be repaired. There were carpenters who needed a new tool of some sort. There were homeowners who had a problem with their plumbing. Yes, I even learned plumbing as a blacksmith. And there were so many other kinds of people needing other kinds of work, on furnaces, trucks, farm equipment, sheet metal, door hinges, fence gates, and all sorts of machinery. There was always something new to do, and there were always new people to meet.

In the mornings, I would wake up singing and praying, even though I had to go directly from bed out to the shop to start the fire in the forge. I would take a piece of iron and stick it in the fire to heat it up while I drew a bucket of water from the big hand pump in the yard. Once the iron stave was hot enough, I'd stick it in the water, which would fizzle and steam, so that it would be hot for us to wash with. After getting dressed, I'd make barn nails in the shop until about 8:30, when Mrs. Mahnke would call me for breakfast. Mr. Mahnke and I would go back to the shop and work from 9:00 until lunch and from lunch until 5:00. During lunchtime, I'd read the Bible, and after work, I'd often read some other Christian book, such as Pilgrim's Progress, or I would go visit some Christian friends or play soccer with some kids from school. Washing up in the evenings was the same as it was in the mornings.

Months passed by this way, and I grew tall and strong. More than that, I was growing in the Lord. Life was exciting, and everything was an adventure. The one part of my life that was dark was that I missed my Papa. Mr. Mahnke was a powerful man, for as old as he was, but he didn't have my Papa's compassion or love for the Lord. Hans, Tante Martha's husband from Masuren, had finally been released from his Russian prison and had made his way to our new house back in April, 1946. He was so sick and weak that he'd fallen flat on his face tripping over the step into Tante Martha's room when he first walked into the house. Since then he'd recovered, and it was good to have a friendly male adult relative around, but he still wasn't my Papa.

The only news we heard from Papa was an occasional letter, in the form of a postcard. These postcards were provided to him by the Red Cross, and they were two-layered and folded, so that he could write his message and our address on the one side, and then when we answered him, we could flip the layer fold inside out and write his address and our message on the other side. He was restricted to just 25 words in his message, and he couldn't talk about certain things, like describing the conditions he was living in. He had to word his messages very carefully, conserving every last word to try to get the fullest meaning through with the fewest words, while not offending his censors.

That was extremely difficult for him, and it was strange how he tried to do it. He would say how he loved it there and how sorry he was for what the German people had done to the Russians. He praised his captors and lauded the wisdom and judiciousness of their Communist system. He said he was glad that he was able to do some work for the Russians as restitution to help make things right with them again, or as they called it, "Wieder gut Machung." Sometimes we had to laugh at his messages, because we knew that he didn't believe one word of that. He was saying the exact opposite of what he meant to say, so the censors would let it pass. We knew it, but they didn't, so it was funny.

Even with that though, the censors still sometimes blacked out up to a third of his words. We could tell what they would probably be in most cases, since we knew Papa, but it made it frustrating, and our hearts went out to him. Our own messages had to be crafted with care too, as they were limited to twenty-five words and would be censored as well. At least we knew that he was still alive, so we always looked forward to receiving them.

Time seemed to drag on between them though, and it was getting to the point where we wondered if he would ever be allowed to come home. After all, he hadn't come home by the time I got baptized, on December 4th, 1949, and the war had been over for more than four years already. An interesting thing happened during my baptism though, and it related to Papa.

My baptism was quite a big event. Elim Assembly had to rent out the city's huge indoor swimming arena for it, since all of 104 people were getting baptized, and since there were well over twice as many other people present than what could fit into the sanctuary of their new building. Elim's congregation was much bigger in reality, than the number of people that attended Sunday morning services. The reason for this was the revival that Elim had been experiencing. So many people were joining the church that they began to spin off daughter churches, which were really cell churches meeting in people's homes. Every so often all these daughter churches would meet together with the main church in someplace larger than Elim's building. That's what they were doing for our baptism.

The swimming arena was crowded, even as big as it was. There was an Olympic-sized swimming pool, and around it there were bleachers enough for over a thousand people. They had the entire pastoral staff in the water, baptizing people, and in between baptisms, the various choirs and bands would play, and everyone would sing and praise the Lord. There was a Guitar Choir with over 100 members, all of them playing guitars in harmony, and there was a brass band and a fifty-piece orchestra set up next to the pool too. On any given Sunday, these choirs and bands were much smaller, because some of the members played in each of the daughter churches too. There were also a couple rows of booths set up in front of the bleachers for people to change their clothes in before and after being baptized. Each booth was big enough for two or three people, and you would wait in there until it was your turn to get baptized.

The service had been going on for quite a while by the time it was my turn to occupy a booth and get into my white baptismal robe. The Spirit of God was moving powerfully, and everyone was excited to see so many people being baptized at once. And this wasn't the first time that year for this either.

There was an older man in the changing booth with me, though I don't remember his name. He and I were friends, and I'd already told him about Papa months earlier. He was from one of the daughter churches, so I introduced myself, and we got to talking while we waited for our turns. At one point, I told him about my Papa being a prisoner of war in Russia, and he offered to pray with me that my Papa would return home soon. So right then, we turned around and knelt down at the bench, and he prayed.

As he was praying though, I smelled smoke on his breath. Realizing that he must've been smoking a cigarette just before the service, I thought, "You smoke cigarettes, and you're getting baptized?" I know, perhaps that was being judgmental, but that's what I thought.

When he got done praying, he turned to me and said, "You know, the Lord told me, 'You're Papa will be home by Christmas.'" I very religiously replied, "Yes, yes, I know!" But inside me, I was thinking, "Ah, what do you know about this? You're smoking, and you're trying to give me a prophecy?"

Just then, our names were called, and we had to go out to the pool. I didn't think any more about what he'd said, and I quickly forgot about the whole thing.

16

Papa

Several more days passed without me thinking about what that man had said, but then about the middle of the month, we got a notice from the Red Cross in the mail. It said that Papa had returned from Russia and was in a repatriation camp near Wolfsburg. When Mom read the letter, she leapt in the air and screamed, "Otto is back in Germany!" All the rest of us started laughing and shouting and running around, hugging each other, and thanking God for His mercy. It took Mom maybe another two minutes to get ready and head out the door towards the train station to go visit him.

Mom didn't return until the next day. She was more relaxed and happier than we'd seen her in years. She practically floated through the doorway, and she began singing as she started her housework the day after that. She said that Papa was going to be coming home on December 23rd, two days before Christmas. The old man in the changing booth had been right.

253

Christmas was on a Friday that year, 1949, so I was still at work at Mr. Mahnke's blacksmith shop on the twenty-third. Papa was due to arrive on the Borstel ferry from Hamburg that evening. I had off from school on Christmas Eve, so as soon as I got done with work, I rode my bicycle home, and then we all went out to Borstel to be at the dock when the ferry arrived.

Our whole family was in a festive mood as we walked the two kilometers to Borstel. Normally, Ursula and Gerhardt would complain about being tired, but this time, they were jumping and skipping as they went, while the rest of us talked on and on about what we were going to do when Papa got here.

The Elbe was at low tide though when the ferry pulled up, so it couldn't get close enough to the dock to tie up. There were dozens of people waiting to get off the ferry and dozens more waiting to get on it to go to Hamburg, but they were just going to have to wait until the tide rose enough to let the ferry finish mooring. Meanwhile, we scanned the ranks of passengers standing on deck to see if Papa was among them. We looked back and forth and even checked up on the superstructure and wheelhouse, but we couldn't see anyone that looked remotely like him.

On the other hand, we weren't sure what he looked like anymore either. We could be looking right at him and not know it, and since it was getting dark, it was easy to miss someone too. Someone caught my eye on deck, so I hollered out, "Do you have an Otto Flemming on board?" He shouted back, "What did you say?" I returned, "Is there a man named Otto Flemming on the ferry?" He answered again, "Just a minute. I'll check."

With that, he backed up from the railing and disappeared inside the ferry.

A few minutes later when he returned, he shouted, "There is no Otto Flemming here. Sorry about that."

Discouraged, we turned around and started walking home. This time, everyone was silent. With no word from Papa, we thought perhaps something had gone wrong, and he wouldn't be coming home until the next week, or more likely, the week after New Years. It was a long, dark walk home, and when we got there, everyone was grouchy and irritable.

Nevertheless, the next day, Mom ordered us to prepare for our Weihnachtsfeier, or Christmas celebration. We didn't have a tree or decorations or presents, but we had each other, and that was enough. Mom prepared a dinner that was a little better than usual and had some meat in it, and after eating it, we lit some candles and sat around the table in our one room in Oma Moje's house. Mom had each of us tell what Christmas meant to us and say what we were thankful for, and then we took turns reading the Christmas Scriptures, starting with the Old Testament prophecies about the Christ.

About the time we got to Luke, Chapter 2, we heard a knock on the front door. We all stopped and looked at each other. A few seconds later, Oma Moje's crackling voice announced from the hallway, "There's a strange man here," hoping that someone from one of her refugee families would come out and claim him.

Mom was sitting in front of the door, so she peeked out to see who it was. All we could see from inside was the silouhette of a man against the light in the hall. When Mom saw him though, she gasped and exclaimed, "Oh, Otto!" and she nearly fell off her chair in her haste to get out the door.

We all rushed out behind her, scrambling to get over or around everyone else's chairs in the small apartment. Once in the hallway, we found a gaunt, pale man standing there, looking tired and much older than he really was. His cheeks were sunken into his face, and his skin seemed thinly stretched over his bones. He had on a long, gray overcoat, with a beat up pair of coveralls underneath it and a Russian bomber cap on his head, and he was carrying a small sack of stuff in one hand - all his worldly possessions - letting it drag limply on the floor. The door was still open behind him, revealing piles of icy slush and a mixture of snow and rain in the bleak glare of a street light. If we didn't know any better, we would've thought him a homeless tramp.

The sight of Papa standing there like that caused everyone to hesitate for a second. None of us but Mom really recognized him, and Ursula and Gerhardt stopped in their tracks and weren't sure what to do about him. My first thought upon seeing him was, "He's so small." I remembered him being big and powerful, but now he was weak and frail, and I had grown to be three inches taller than he was.

Finally, Papa broke the spell by saying, "Maria, children, it's so good to be home." At that, all of us rushed up to him and began hugging and touching him. Karl took his sack from him, while Hildegaard helped him take his coat off. Ursula and Gerhardt jumped up and down, begging for him to hold them. Mom got in a good hug and then walked arm in arm with him back to our door, while he tried to remember what all our names were.

He said, pointing at Karl, "Now is that Karl or Horst?" So Karl answered, "I'm Karl," and I said, "I'm Horst." Then he pointed at Hildegaard and said, "And you must be Hildegaard, but which ones are you all?" as he motioned to the younger girls. They all shouted their names, to which he replied with, "Oh, YOU are Waltraut!

My, how you've grown. And THIS is Mariann! YOU are
Ursula? You've grown so big! RUTH, why, you're a
young woman now." And turning to Gerhardt as we
crowded into our room again, he said, "Gerhardt, you've
become a young man while I've been gone. Everyone
has grown so much. I don't know what to make of you
all."

Just then, Papa's and Mom's eyes met, and he
asked her poignantly, "And Maria, what ever happened
to..." and his eyes dropped to her belly. Everyone
became quiet at this serious note, but Mom merely
shook her head and said, "Not now, Otto. I'll tell you
about Ulrich later."

Gerhardt asked, "What's in the bag, Papa?"

Papa took the sack from Karl, opened it, and bent
over for Gerhardt to see in it. "Oh, these are some
things that I made for myself while I was in prison.
There's a cooking pot, a cup, a spoon, some socks, and
some gloves. Not much, but I made them, and they
made life easier for me while I was there." Gerhardt
picked up the pot, which was only about two-quart size,
to look at it, and then he handed it to Karl, who handed
it to me. It was very roughly done and had seams
instead of welds, but he had fashioned a handle on it,
and it looked like it would hold water fairly well.

Papa straightened up and gestured towards the
table, with our Bibles and a couple of candles and a
hymnal on it, and he asked, "What have we here? What
have you been doing tonight?"

Mom answered, "We've been having our
Weihnachtsfeier. We were just about to begin reading
Luke, Chapter 2, when you walked in."

"Well, don't let me stop you. Let us continue with
the celebration." And with that, Papa sat down at the
table, picked up a Bible, and began reading Luke 2:1,
"And it came to pass in those days, that there went out

257

a decree from Caesar Augustus, that all the world should be taxed..."

As he read, a calm descended on our family. We all sat down around the table with him, listening with rapt attention, tears coming to our eyes. When he was done reading, we began singing Christmas carols as we'd never sung before, and when it finally came time to pray, every one of us was fervent and effusive in our thanks to God Almighty for bringing our Papa home.

Our Papa was home for Christmas after all, and there could be no greater Christmas present for any of us than that.

We stayed up until late that night, talking, telling stories, laughing, and crying. Everyone got to tell what he or she had done during the four years since we'd seen Papa last. Then it was Papa's turn to tell us what had happened to him. We'd been asking him this off and on since he'd arrived, but he always said it really wasn't all that interesting, and he put it off, asking us to tell him about our stories first. When he finally couldn't put us off any longer, he only gave us a brief overview and then explained, "Ah, children, children. It was hard, and I'm not sure if I can tell you all of it right now. I'll be able to tell you more in the morning, but you may have to wait for some of it until I'm stronger."

Christmas morning and all that weekend was largely spent telling and retelling Papa's story. First it was him telling it to us, but then it was us telling it to our friends and the people at church. It took me a couple of years of asking him questions before I felt that I really understood what he went through. He gave us the basics that Christmas, but the real details had to wait until I could ask him questions alone. Some things he only told other adults, such as our friends, the Zopkes and the Lüks, when we would go over to their houses on Sunday nights, after getting home from church. I had a youth group meeting to attend, and then I would go to whichever of their homes my parents were at and listen in on their stories.

So here is Papa's story, as if he had told it all at once...

****

There was an important-looking officer silouhetted in the light just to the right of the gate on the Lotringen as our family rushed up to the gangplank. He was there with several sailors, apparently monitoring the loading of the refugees onto the ship and turning back anyone who might be a soldier trying to get away. There was a third officer and one of the port's officers down at the entrance to the gangplank for this too. Papa was near the front of the line, just behind us kids, and he was in uniform, so he was easy to spot despite the gathering darkness.

He hadn't even set foot on the gangplank before one of them held out his hand to stop him and said, "Excuse me, Sergeant, but you realize that soldiers are not permitted to come aboard with the refugees. You'll have to stay on shore."

Papa turned to the officer to salute, and then he responded, "Yes sir, I'm aware of that. But you see my wife here is eight months pregnant, and she's having a very hard time with this. If you could help her get settled in somewhere, I'd appreciate it." As he did that, he had to let go of Mom, since he'd had his right arm holding her up around her waist and his other hand holding her left hand. He realized he may have just touched his wife for the last time.

The officer said, "I'll see what I can do, but you need to stay here, and you too, Private." He said that last part to Markus, and he motioned for both of them to get out of line.

As they complied, Papa patted each of us on the head or the back and said one last Good-bye. He watched us ascending the ramp, praying silently that God would protect us. It was hard for him to let us go like that, and his eyes became moist with emotion.

When Mom got to the top and stepped out on deck, she turned around to wave, and then she was gone, caught up in the surge of people around her. There was a bit of extra commotion right after that, and the officer who'd been standing watching everything turned quickly to see what it was, and then he too disappeared.

Papa sighed and said, "Come on, Markus, let's get back to the unit."

They managed to get to their base at about 7pm, but by this time, everyone except for the guards and the CQ (Charge of Quarters) had gone off duty. They reported in, but the CQ only told them to see the commander in the morning.

After returning to his barracks room, Papa pulled a little address book and some family photos out of his uniform blouse pocket, and he began writing letters. He stayed up all that night, writing to everyone that he'd ever met in central Germany, asking them to keep an eye out for his family and to help them if they found them. As he got done with each letter, he prayed over it and asked God to give him and his family favor with the recipients and that God would somehow direct one of them to run across his family somewhcrc and help them. When all of them were finished, he spent another hour on his knees by his bunk, weeping and praying, begging the Lord to have mercy on his family and to spare them from harm. He fell asleep that way, only to be awakened a mere thirty minutes later by the base reveille call.

Papa got himself ready for duty again quickly, oblivious to his fatigue. He was determined to deliver his stack of letters to the base mail office, despite the unit's frenetic defensive preparations. The troops manning the coastal artillery guns had finally managed to get them off their mounts, and now they were in various stages of trying to secure the guns to the backs of several wagons and trucks. Papa had to rejoin his observation section in their defensive trench at one end of the base, but he was able to take a short break mid-morning and run over to the mail room with the letters, since the expected Russian assault hadn't materialized.

By noon that day, February 3rd, 1945, word reached the base that the Russians were retreating back towards Germau in the face of several German counterattacks and the heavy bombardment from the pocket battleship Admiral Scheer. The XXVIII Corps in southwest Samland now issued an order consolidating all the disparate units in Pillau under their command and rallying them for a general counterattack up the coast and from there inland towards Königsberg. Papa's observation battery became an infantry company in a regiment that would push towards Palmnicken, on the coast north of Rothenen.

It took the regiment another day to organize itself and to collect food and extra ammunition. They found transportation largely the same way that they'd found it on their way in to Pillau during the earlier retreat - by commandeering civilian automobiles, horses, and wagons, often their own. Once they finally set out on the march, it was another day before they reached the German front lines, since it was very difficult negotiating their way around all the wrecked and abandoned military and civilian vehicles, the shell craters in the road, and the bridges that had been blown up. When they were joined to the battle, they pursued the Russians northeast to Thierenberg, which they captured after a considerable fight on February 7th. Then they set up defensive positions just east of there on a bluff overlooking the highway crossroads between Weidehn and Pojerstieten. They held those positions until mid-April.

On April 2nd, the Russian 43rd and 39th Armies in Samland, together with the 50th Army north of Königsberg and the 11th Guards Army to the south, began their

second siege of Königsberg, and by April
10th, the city fell amid a tremendous
slaughter. Then, on April 13th, the 43rd and
39th Armies again turned their attention to
Samland itself.

On the very first day of the attack, the
Russians broke through the German lines
north of Thierenberg and began a mad dash
for the coast. The German front seemed to
pivot on Thierenberg, which was also under
attack, so Papa's unit had to retreat in order
for them to stay in contact with the units to
their left. By April 15th, the entire front had
collapsed, and all the German units were
retreating in total confusion.

Since Papa's company was composed
of men from the old Marine Artillerie's
coastal observation sections, they naturally
wanted to head for the coast around
Rothenen, instead of directly for Pillau like
everyone else. They thought that perhaps
they could hide somewhere until the
Russians had passed over them, and then
maybe they could come out, change into
civilian clothes, and melt into the local
population.

With that in mind, they made haste
for the Kraig, south of Rothenen, which Papa
knew was a good hiding place, as he told
their commander. Along the way, however,
they fell into combat with Russian units on
several occasions and were also attacked
from the air. By the time they reached
Rothenen, the company had lost over half its
men, and the remainder had splintered into
several separate groups that lost touch with

each other.

Late on the night of April 16th, what was left of Papa's squad and a few men from a couple other squads slipped under the bridge from the road between Rothenen and Saltnicken and made their way into the Kraig. They moved far down into it, beyond where we had our fort, nearly to the beach. They slept among the trees on the bluff nearly all day on the 17th, and when it was dark again, they came out and began digging a tunnel into the side of the bluff. It took them all night and well into the next day, but when they were finished, they had some respectable living quarters, for soldiers in a desperate situation anyway. All day on the 17th, 18th, 19th, and 20th, various Russian units passed by on the road, on the beach, and in the fields between the road and the beach, but they never entered the Kraig itself. From the 21st on though, the only Russians that they saw were supply and reinforcement convoys moving along the road. It looked as though their plan was working.

All through the week that followed, they continued to hear the sounds of artillery and tank fire, and the sky was filled with Russian fighters and bombers on their way to attack Pillau and the Nehrung spit. Pillau fell on April 27th. Papa and his squad knew this because on that day, the sounds of firing stopped, and there weren't anymore aircraft flying overhead. They knew the war was over for them then, so now the only question was when and how to come out from hiding and whether to surrender or to try to sneak back into town and try to hide among the civilians.

They didn't have much food or water left, so the debate didn't last very long. The ones who wanted to stay hidden longer prevailed only a few more days, but there was still the question of whether to try to return as civilians or not. This was answered for them in the first week of May, when they heard some more shooting from the direction of Rothenen, and then there were some loud crashing noises. Shortly after that, a pall of smoke rose from the village and grew in intensity until it filled that whole side of the horizon. We didn't find out until our return to the area in 1999 that the Russians had completely razed the village after executing a number of residents because of the bodies of those Jews that the Gestapo had shot had been discovered on the beach near there.

The day after that, Papa and his fellow survivors took their white undershirts off to use as surrender flags, slung their rifles upside down over their shoulders, and hiked up to the top of the bluff and out onto the field. The dozen or so men walked in a loose line across the field, waving their undershirts over their heads, hoping that the Russians would see them and accept their surrender instead of shooting at them.

There wasn't any static Russian military presence in the area, so they had to walk all the way out to the road before anyone saw them. The Russian unit that they surrendered to was a supply convoy heading for Pillau. They stopped, and got out of their trucks, but there were only a couple dozen of them, and they didn't really know what to do with this suddenly appearing squad of German soldiers. They did have the presence of mind to point their rifles at the Germans and to order them to lay down their weapons, but then they talked among themselves for quite a while about what to do with them.

These Russian troops seemed to treat them with soldierly respect, and they even offered them some food. Nonetheless, Papa had an awful feeling of helplessness as he stood there with his hands on his head and a Russian rifle pointing at his back. His whole life seemed to parade before him as he contemplated how he'd come to this point. His only comfort was that he knew he was in God's hands, and He would take care of him - that, and his family was hopefully safe somewhere in central Germany.

After several minutes, the Russians motioned for Papa and his group to get into two of the trucks near the end of the convoy, and then they started up again and continued on towards Pillau.

Pillau from the back of a Russian truck was completely different for Papa when they got there. The Russians had set up a huge supply distribution camp there, and they were shipping those supplies out by boat across the Frisches Haff. More than that, Pillau was a lot flatter than it was before, that is, most of its buildings were in rubble, so he could see farther.

Once they stopped, the Russians made him get out of the truck and sit down on the ground with his hands on his head. They stayed this way until the Russians had unloaded the supplies from the trucks, and then they made them get back into the same two trucks that they'd ridden in before. This time though, the Russians only took them a short ways, over to the other side of the peninsula, where there was a large POW camp.

Thousands of German soldiers in tattered uniforms, often with bandages, splints, or crutches, lolled around in the open. Their guards made them sit in squares of several hundred, all bunched up together with nothing but some hastily stretched concertina wire and the guards themselves to prevent a mass exodus. At one end of the camp, some other Russian soldiers were setting up several large tents, and there was a convoy of trucks with more tents waiting nearby, but it would be a long time before all of the prisoners were provided with shelter. Every so often, groups of Russians would come and take several of the tents off the trucks and walk away from the camp with them, prompting Papa to wonder what they were doing with them. The smell of urine and feces filled the air. There was also a long queue of prisoners leading up to some kind of platform in one corner of the camp, where Papa thought they might be serving food, and there were several groups of prisoners digging what he thought were latrines.

Where he was near the gate of the camp, there was an administrative tent where he had to turn in his identification papers, get fingerprinted, photographed, and be given a prisoner number. It was a long process, as there were dozens of Germans in line ahead of him, and by the time he reached the desk, dozens more had arrived behind him. Once he was done there, he was made to sit in one of these squares.

Time passed slowly by. It was a nice day, and Papa enjoyed watching the clouds go by. But the day turned into night before he was allowed to visit the latrine, and it was day again before they let his square go up to get fed. This became a pattern that lasted for a week before his square received a tent for shelter. Then the tent wasn't big enough for the number of men in his square, but the Russians demanded that they all fit into it anyway. This resulted in many of them having to stand or lay on top of each other, since no one was allowed to touch the tent walls.

Another week went by like that, and then Papa's square was organized into a large work detail. They were marched over to the railroad station and were given pick axes, crow bars, and tongs and were told to begin dismantling one of the two rail lines servicing the city. Once they got a rail loose, they had to put it on a flatbed rail car on that same line, just up the way a little. As they removed all the rails up to where the flatbed car was, an engine pulled the car a little further on to allow them to continue working. Over the next few days, they pulled up the rails on that line all the way to Godnicken and Sacherau, across from Rothenen, and eventually they worked their way up to Palmnicken and Gross Dirschkeim. They were told that they were doing this to provide materials to repair railroad tracks in Russia that the Germans had destroyed.

Along the way, Papa saw other prisoner work details dismantling factories and warehouses in Pillau and even taking apart small villages in the countryside. Rumor had it that the Russians were removing everything of value and taking it to Russia. Papa wondered what had happened in Rothenen and whether they would take even a small village like that.

At one point, he got dysentery and became very sick, but the Russians refused to allow him to stop working. Eventually, the illness passed, but Papa lost a lot of weight and became much weaker during that time.

After a couple months passed like this, and there wasn't anymore dismantling work to do in East Prussia, the Russians moved Papa with the rest of the prisoners by train through Byelorussia to Smolensk, on the Dnieper River. There, in the middle of the woods, the Russians had built a large concentration camp. Unlike the first camp he was in, this one had wooden barracks houses where about thirty men could sleep in bunks. It was very similar to some of the

German concentration camps that were exposed at the end of the war, though they didn't have any gas chambers or human furnaces.

Much like any military prisoner camp of those days, they would have accountability formations in the morning and at night. There were work details around the camp during the day, and some of the prisoners had work assignments outside the camp too. The Russians didn't like the prisoners to talk to each other, but no one that Papa knew of was ever beaten or killed or anything. On the other hand, they weren't cared for very well either. They received a bowl of kasha, which was like grits or Cream of Wheat in the US, in the morning, and they received a bowl of watered down kapusta, which was cabbage soup, in the evening. Their bunk houses weren't heated, and they received only one blanket and one set of prison clothes to keep warm with. Their bunks were rather wide rough-cut wood shelves with thin, straw-filled mattresses on them that attracted bugs and vermin which would come out at night to feed on the sleeping prisoners.

Perhaps as a result of the bugs or perhaps as a result of the poor food, dirty water, and lack of sanitation, Papa got sick again shortly after arriving at this new camp. Everyone had dysentery at various times while they were there, and at first it appeared that this was what Papa had too. He had a fever, chills, and terrible diarrhea, so they put him in the camp hospital.

This hospital was really more like a morgue for people that weren't quite dead yet than it was a genuine hospital. It was cold and damp, with tile floors, painted cinder block walls, and bare bulb overhead lighting that they never turned off. While there were bathrooms, the sleeping facilities were just large bay rooms with 3m x 2m plywood tables upon which they would lay the patients not length-wise, but width-wise, in rows so tightly packed that the men had to lay on their sides just to fit in together. This way, if someone wanted to turn over, the whole table full of them had to turn over all at once and hope that the guy on the end wouldn't fall off the edge. The Russian attendants would just leave them there, not really treating or checking on any of them individually, but just hoping that they would either die or get better.

Every morning, they did receive a visit from a doctor, a snitty old woman named Dr. Aznabaev (not her real name). She performed a cursory examination of each of them that was more like checking the condition of packages of ground beef at the grocery store than it was a medical diagnosis. She kept a tally of their statistics on a clip board, but the number that she was most interested in was how many of them had died overnight. Whenever she or the orderlies would find a corpse on one of the tables, she would gleefully proclaim, "Das Gut!" But any day that there weren't any deaths among the patients, she would complain, "Nicht Gut." Then she would

271

encourage more of them to die to make more room because of the overcrowding.

Dysentery was probably the most common sickness in the camp, and you can imagine what kind of horrid mess resulted from piling a dozen or more men like that together on a table and leaving them there all day. They were already in terribly weakened conditions, and the orderlies weren't about to help them get to the bathrooms. Papa only stayed there a few days though, because he didn't have dysentery. Dr. Aznabaev eventually noticed the big red spots on his skin and diagnosed him with typhoid fever. Then she sent him into quarantine.

Quarantine there was a euphemism for solitary confinement. Papa was placed in a cell about the size of a bathroom, with a single wood bunk, a bucket, and a drain in the floor. There was a light bulb in the ceiling, but the orderlies only turned it on when they opened the slat in the door once a day to change his potty bucket and to give him another bowl of kapusta. That was the only human contact he had during the weeks that he was in quarantine, just a single hand replacing his bucket and his bowl. The rest of the time he was in near darkness, except for a small window high up on the far wall. Papa spent nearly all of his waking hours gazing out that window, watching the clouds go by, and dreaming about his wife and children that he might never see again.

There was one consolation about being quarantined like that though. Papa was finally free to spend as much time

communing with the Lord as he wanted to.
He prayed and he worshipped like never
before, and for the first time, despite all his
years as a Pentecostal lay preacher, God
finally gave him a heavenly prayer language.
With this, he could keep right on praying
and praising God, even after words failed
him. With this, he could also fully express
the grief and anguish in his heart. And with
this, he was able to forgive his captors. So
by doing that, Papa found the strength he
needed to carry on, and eventually the day
came when he was well again, and Dr.
Aznabaev let him out and sent him back to
his bunk house.

In many ways, Papa was a new man
after coming out of quarantine. He looked at
life with a new appreciation that he'd never
had before, and he developed a love of God
and a sense of contentment beyond anything
that he'd known before. The other prisoners
sensed this, and soon several of them
secretly approached him and revealed to him
that they were Christians. Of course he told
them of his own Christianity, and before
long, he was part of an underground network
of believers at the prison camp.

The Russians, being Communists and
atheists, prohibited the prisoners from
having Bibles or any other kinds of religious
materials, and they would punish people
that they caught practicing religion. But
their scrutiny wasn't so close that the men
who were believers couldn't get around it.
They developed their own little codes for
letting each other know what to pray for and

when they had something to praise the Lord about. They would whisper in the bunk houses and leave scribbled Scripture verses on toilet paper in the outhouses. Sometimes they would even hum Christian songs or sneak in a "Praise the Lord," or a "God is good" during morning formations. In these ways, they encouraged each other and drew strength from each other as the months dragged on and became years.

After a couple years had passed at the prison camp near Smolensk, Papa was transferred to a regular prison near Kiev, in the Ukraine. This was a brand new prison, and it was probably under construction while Papa was in Smolensk, which was only a temporary facility. In fact, there were parts of it that were still under construction.

One of those parts was a sawmill which was to be operated by the inmates. This was a German sawmill that Russian troops or their German prisoners had dismantled and sent by rail into Russia for use there, along with so much of the rest of the German infrastructure. The prison wardens queried the new prisoners as they came in about any skills that they had, since there were other projects that needed manning at or near this prison too. Papa used to sharpen the blades for a local sawmill in Samland, and he was a blacksmith too, so he knew about the mechanics of how a sawmill operated and was set up.

As soon as he heard that the prison wardens were looking for people to work at the sawmill, he volunteered for the position. This was interesting work for him, his first in two years, and he dove into it with as much gusto as his weak frame could muster. Once the mill was assembled and operating, he became their blacksmith and was able to make tools and fix things more or less as he had back in Rothenen. This was where he made the spoon and cooking pot that he brought to Jork with him after his release.

Oddly enough for a prison work detail, Papa's job at the sawmill was at night, which left the daytime open for him to do other things. When he learned that there was a dishwasher position open in the kitchen, he volunteered for that too, since he figured that he'd have better access to food that way, and if nothing else, he could at least scrape up what was left in the cooking pots and eat that.

The first time he did that however, he nearly got himself killed. He was all alone in the kitchen washing the huge 50 gallon kettles that the cooks made their kapusta in. He knew beforehand that there must be some sediment or something left over from the vile soup that they had to eat day after day, and he imagined that it would be more concentrated in its evaporated form than it was in the soup. He was right about that too, as each kettle had a thick line of scum around the top of it. Greatly encouraged, Papa hurriedly scraped as much of the scum off of each kettle as he could before washing it. He ate more by the time he was done washing those kettles than he'd eaten on any

275

one day in over two years, and he was feeling pretty good about himself as he dried his hands off that afternoon.

But that only lasted until he showed up for work at the sawmill that evening. Within just a few minutes after reporting for work, he felt the first pangs of stomach discomfort, and he wondered about the wisdom of his secret feast. Before an hour had passed that night, he was having severe gas pains that just wouldn't go away. Soon his stomach and intestines began to expand, filling with gas that he couldn't pass out either end, and now he began to be afraid too. He undid his belt and opened his pants, but his abdomen just kept on growing. The pain became excruciating, and his midsection looked like a balloon. He couldn't do anything but lay on his work bench, groaning, and writhing in agony. He knew from experience helping Rothenen's farmers that he was having a severe case of bloat, something the farmers cured their cows of by poking a hole in their stomachs with a special tubular knife to let out the gases. Unfortunately, no one else was around right then, and he couldn't do it himself, so he cried out to the One person Who could help him.

Papa began praying that God would spare his life once again. He prayed, "Lord, give me ten more years with my wife." Then he started rolling around on his bench, back and forth, and back and forth. All at once, he began belching and passing gas. This went on for over an hour, but the pain and

the swelling reduced, and before his shift
was over, he was well again. He never tried
eating the scum off the kettles any more
though.

This new prison had a variety of
special programs for its inmates that
Smolensk didn't have, besides the extra work
opportunities. There was a qualitative
change in the way that the guards behaved
as well, as they treated the prisoners with a
great deal more respect than what they'd
received back in Smolensk.

For one thing, they began having
classes and group discussions. The wardens
brought in a Zampolit, or political officer to
conduct these classes, and he informed them
that Russia had officially forgiven them of
their crimes against the people of Russia. He
said he knew that they were really just good
German working people who'd been deceived
by Hitler into believing in Fascism and into
fighting his war for him. As long as they
behaved well, he said that they would be
treated well and would have more
opportunities to redeem themselves, by
working to help the Russian people and to
pay them back for all the pain that the
German Army had caused them. In these
classes, Papa and his fellow prisoners were
finally allowed to talk almost freely. They
were even encouraged to give testimonies
about what Hitler and the Nazis had done to
deceive them and to confess what they
themselves had done to hurt the Russian
people. Whenever they did this, the Zampolit
would scold them, but then he would

publicly forgive them if they expressed regret for having done whatever they confessed. After going through this for several weeks, the Zampolit established something of a rapport with his class, and then he began to indoctrinate them in the tenets and superior ways of Communism. He even held open the promise that if they did well in his class, they could expect an early release date, though he added that he hoped when they were released and went home, they would remember his words and speak up in German society to prevent any recurrence of Nazism and to tell all their friends what they'd learned in these classes.

Papa was an especially quick learner, and he realized right away what the Zampolit was trying to do. Beating him at his own game, Papa went along with the Zampolit and became his best student. Soon Papa was being allowed to write home with postcards provided by the Red Cross. Playing with the Zampolit's mind became a sport for him, and he led him on to the brink of the absurd without ever letting him realize that he was being completely duped. Then Papa would go back to his cell and fall on his knees before God and pray that he would never really believe any of those terrible things he was learning in class.

Along with the class, Papa and his fellow prisoners each received a new set of work clothes and a good pair of work boots, something he hadn't had in years. And although their rations in the prison remained unchanged, they were allowed an

unthinkable privilege, the opportunity to go
into a nearby town, unsupervised, to beg for
food from the local populace.

Every week, each cell block conducted
a commune meeting to manage their affairs,
and one of the things they voted on was who
should go out to beg for food that week.
Papa was chosen for this privilege nearly
once a month, since he had a way with
people that the rest of them didn't have,
which meant that he would always come
back with more food than any of the rest of
them. This was significant, because the
local residents really didn't have much more
food than the prisoners did. Even on a good
day, the most they could expect from a
Russian family was one or two small
potatoes. Papa collected these, and then
they were divided among the cell block when
he got back to the prison. From the Russian
wardens' point of view, this became quite a
successful program, as their spirits were
raised and they gained a little weight, while
they still remained quite weak and
dependant upon the guards for many of their
needs. Papa said that he hated begging like
that, not just because it was humiliating, but
because he was taking already scarce food
away from the Russians. He said it was
pitiful seeing these dirt poor people giving
him their hard won rations and knowing that
they were only doing it because they knew
who he was, and they were afraid of what the
police might do to them if they didn't
cooperate with the government's plan to use
them to subvert Germany after they were

released. He continued to do it though,
because he wanted more than anything to go
home as soon as possible, and he knew
cooperation was his ticket.

****

Now, months later and back home with us, I
found that my Papa was indeed a changed man. He was
still stern, but people loved him more than ever. People
would flock to hear him preach or just to hear him talk.
You could see the love in his eyes now; whereas,
sometimes it was difficult before. He was more
easygoing with us kids too. He wasn't the disciplinarian
that he'd been earlier. He respected us more, and he'd
sit there and really listen to what we had to say. He
even took the time to answer our questions, which he
hardly ever had the time for before we became refugees.
He even had a different look in his eyes, as though he
understood things better now. We were all just glad to
have him back, but as time went on, our appreciation of
him deepened, and he became our friend, rather than
just our Papa.

17

Emigration

Having Papa back home again was a great boost
for our family in so many ways. Even though we were
more crowded, everyone was a lot happier. It was so
encouraging just to be a complete family again. Mom
was happier and more relaxed than she'd been in years,
especially since Papa was able to help her with keeping
us kids in line. Waltraut, Mariann, Ursula, and
Gerhardt were pleased as anything to be around Papa
again, and they quickly did whatever he asked them to.
Hildcgaard, Karl, Ruth, and I were relieved because
Papa brought some real order and such a strong,
positive example back into our lives just when we
needed it the most. All of us started working harder at
school and at our jobs, and this brought us added
success and increased confidence. But most of all,
since Papa was able to get a job at the Jork blacksmith
shop a couple of weeks after returning home, he
dramatically increased the amount of money the family
was bringing in, which helped us with the food budget

and which also took a lot of pressure off the rest of us, allowing us to think about the future again.

Right about that time, or beginning a few weeks before Papa came home, a certain Swiss Army general began coming to Mr. Mahnke's blacksmith shop to pick up horses that he was buying for the Swiss Army. He was working through a dealer who would take horses on consignment from many of the local farms. The dealer would bring the horses to us for shoeing, care, and sprucing up, and then the general would come by to select the ones he wanted to buy. Since he was such a regular customer of ours, he and I became friends and were able to talk on many different subjects. He told me what Switzerland was like, how free it was, and how so many people from all the surrounding countries were emigrating there to escape one thing or another as a result of the war. Since I was such a young lad at the time, it was only natural for him also to ask me what I wanted to do with my life. I told him that I didn't know, but that I did know that I didn't want to spend it in Germany. Upon hearing that, he offered to help me escape into Switzerland after I got my journeyman's papers. The Swiss authorities were very strict with émigrés, and they frequently had to turn back large numbers of refugees trying to cross the mountainous border on foot. This general, however, could arrange for me to get the appropriate paperwork, and then I could return with him as one of his helpers in his periodic convoy of horse trailers. The border guards all knew him and trusted him, so there shouldn't be any problems with that. So together, we hatched a plot for me to move to Switzerland in a couple of years, and from there, I could go practically anywhere I wanted.

I had this in the back of my mind when Papa came home, and I was wondering how or whether his presence would affect this plan. I had a lot of big dreams and places that I wanted to go, and getting out of Germany was at the top of my list. I probably never would have felt this way if it hadn't been for us leaving Rothenen and going through the hardships of being refugees, but as it was, life was very hard where we were, and I felt that getting my journeyman would be my ticket to a better life, out of the country. Oddly enough, or perhaps because I was just a teenager and didn't have experience planning this sort of thing, that desire and planning didn't extend to my schoolwork, where I nearly flunked my English classes because I couldn't imagine ever needing to speak any other language besides German. I enjoyed smithing though, and I worked and studied very hard to do well at that. Ultimately however, it wasn't the Swiss general or my Papa, but rather Papa's sister, that came up with the idea that would provide vision and a direction for our family to go in.

One of the first things that any family would do when their long lost Papa came home, of course, would be to write letters to all the other members of the family announcing the good news, and that's exactly what Mom did for nearly the whole first week after Papa came home. Everyone sent letters of congratulations back after they got her letter, but Tante Lisa's took the longest to arrive, since she lived in upper New York state, in the United States.

Tante Lisa had been sending us care packages, as I mentioned earlier, and she continued to do this every couple of months throughout the entire time that we were living in Jork. We always looked forward to her packages, since they were invariably large and had goodies for everyone. The most interesting and exciting part of the package she sent us in early February, 1950, though, was her letter. This time, after hearing that Papa was home, she had an idea that sparked wonderment, a sense of electric anticipation, and not a little controversy among us.

She suggested that we emigrate to the United States and come live with her on her farm.

The US economy was booming, and she said that Papa could easily find a good job there. Hildegaard, Karl, Ruth, and I could probably also find jobs without much trouble too, and so could Mom if she needed to. We could live with Lisa and her family as long as we needed to, and they would be our sponsors for US Customs. If nothing else, we should at least send Karl and me over since we could best take advantage of all the opportunities there in the US.

Karl thought this was a great idea, and he was ready to jump at the chance. I supported it, but I was a little hesitant, because I already had plans of my own that I hadn't told anyone about, to go to Switzerland, and I wanted to finish my apprenticeship before going anywhere too. Hildegaard was ambivalent towards it, since she had a lot of friends in Jork now, and she didn't want to leave them, though the thought of going to America was exciting to her. Mom was against it, because of the younger children, who didn't really have a say in the matter, and because all the rest of our family was here in Germany, and she didn't want to leave them. Papa, who had the final say, wasn't sure what to do, except that it was too early to make any decision about it. He said that we would have to pray about it long and hard, and we would have to wait for God to give us an answer.

From then on, every time Tante Lisa sent a package to us, she talked about us coming to the US in her letter. She went on at length about all the benefits of it and about all the exciting things that we could see and do. She said that anyone could make it there, no matter who you were or how poor you were when you got there. She said that practically everyone in the US was an immigrant or had ancestors that were immigrants, so the people loved immigrants and would help them in any way they could. She said that there was total religious freedom too and that the government completely kept their hands out of the church and its business. And she made a point of saying that Americans didn't hold any grudges against the Germans for what they did during the war, so it would be quite safe for us to be there.

Time flew by that year, and we measured its passage by marking the arrival of Tante Lisa's care packages. All of us were excited and upbeat about our prospects, and we were all working hard to prepare for whatever it was that we would decide to do. Mom managed things at home, while Papa worked at his blacksmithing job, which he enjoyed, but which frustrated him, since he'd had his own business in Rothenen, but in Jork, he was working for someone else. Over time, I think he began to see that as a dead end, while going to America held the prospect of being able to open his own shop again, which he very dearly wanted to do.

For most of us kids, working hard just meant doing well at school, but for the older of us, it also meant working at our trades. Karl passed his journeyman's test that April, but he continued working at the blacksmith shop in Jork. Hildegaard, who was already done with school by this time, first worked as a housemaid for a farmer in Lühe, and then she got a job in a convalescent home in Hamburg. Of course, I spent most of my time with Mr. Mahnke, in his blacksmith shop in Hedendorf.

As a blacksmith apprentice, I wasn't just learning how to shoe horses, either. It was exciting work. I learned how to build wagons, make hand tools and harnesses, sharpen knives and saws, repair or modify truck and car bodies, do household plumbing, and build things with sheet metal. We were an all-around metal working shop, and I learned a lot about all these different facets of metal working.

There were even a lot of little tricks of the trade that I sometimes liked to show off with. One time, several teenage boys from the neighborhood came over to the shop while I was working. They wanted me to come hang out with them, but I turned them down because I wasn't finished working yet. They started teasing me about that, and that kind of upset me, because I enjoyed what I was doing, and I felt that it was honorable work. So on their way out, when they had their backs turned towards me, I took a nearly spent piece of coal from the fire, spit on the anvil, put the coal on my spittle, and then hit it with my hammer. It made a thunderous BANG, like a cannon shot, and they all nearly jumped out of their skin. After that, they left me alone. Little things like that were fun and gave me a sense of power and of control over my environment that made blacksmithing a really enjoyable trade.

Things went on like that through the end of 1950 and into 1951, until it was finally time for me to take my Journeyman's Test, that April. The test was being administered in Buxtehude, at the Innung (Guild) Office, and it would take two whole days. I studied a long time for it, but I was still nervous. Mr. Mahnke was nervous too, because even though he knew he was a good teacher, he also knew that the eyes of the entire guild were on him, to see what he'd done with this refugee boy that had requested to be his student despite his reputation.

The first day consisted of writing a business letter, making up an itemized invoice, solving a lot of math problems, especially word problems and geometry, and making several mechanical drawings and blueprints. Then the second day was a practical test, where we had to take pieces of iron and mold and weld them into things, both with the forge method and with either an acetylene torch or an electric welder. I chose the electric welder. After we were done with each piece, the judges would test them by trying to bend or break them. The last part of the exam was the Gesellen Stück, or Journeyman's Piece. This was where I got to show off my creativity and imagination by designing something of my own choosing and then making it from scratch. I decided to make a horse tree, which is the cross piece that goes on the bar that sticks out from the front of a wagon, the piece that the horses are tied to. Mine was about thirty inches long, made of oak, with three forged iron loops, one at either end, for the horses, and one in the middle, to attach to the bar. I only scored Average on the written test, but I scored Good on the practical. Oh, it was such a relief to be finished with that test.

Mr. Mahnke was relieved too that I had passed the test and didn't have any complaints about him, but he didn't show it the next day when I came by to collect my stuff. I had already asked him if I could continue with him as a salaried journeyman, but he turned me down. He liked me, and he needed my help, but he wasn't willing to pay me what a journeyman should make.

We weren't in a place where I could take much time off, so I immediately started looking for a job in Hamburg. It only took me a couple weeks before the Kranz Shipyard hired me to shrink bubbles off the hulls of freighters. The bubbles would form in the iron as a result of the heating and bending process of fashioning steel plates into the hull, so I had to reheat them with a torch and then pound them out with a hammer. It wasn't really hard work, but it was new and exciting anyway. I was utterly in awe at the shipyard, as I had always loved getting close to big ships, so being up in the scaffolding on the side of a ship was a dream come true.

I worked hard to make a good impression there, since I was still only seventeen when they hired me. That hard work paid off too, because less than a month after I turned eighteen in May, they reassigned me as a tack welder, straightening out deck plates. This was more complicated than the first job. Here I had to heat adjoining steel plates and put some flux between them so that they would slide together and straighten out. One time, some of the hot flux dripped onto my bare elbow, and I still have a scar there today.

Apparently though, I did such a good job as a tack welder that within just two more months, they gave me my third job. This time I was put in charge of a team of three, as a Spantenbieger, or span bender. We worked up in the design shed, an elevated room where you could see the entire layout of the ship and where they had a complete set of the ship's blueprints laid out on the floor. We took measurements off the blueprints, and then we went down to the wood shop and made wooden patterns that we used to calculate the proper angle for bending the steel beams that would become the ribs of the hull. Next we would heat those beams in a coke fire until they were red hot and could be bent. We didn't actually join the beams to the frame though, as that was another team's responsibility.

Now all during this last year, things had been getting somewhat better for us as a family. We were still living at Oma Moje's house, so we didn't have any real need for furniture. We were able to eat a little better, and we could buy a few clothes now; whereas, for the entire time before Papa came home, our clothes were donated to us. Our one big purchase was when Papa bought a bicycle. I started saving for one as well after I got the job at Kranz. Also, about that time Papa decided it was time for us to move out and get an place of our own. We rented a four-bedroom house in Jork, which was more room than we'd ever had to live in, even back in Rothenen, but then we didn't have any furniture to put in it.

Papa didn't say anything about this, but we could tell that he had something on his mind. We made do with what little we had, plus a few donated things, but we were eventually going to have to buy some furniture, beginning with beds for us kids. I think Papa knew that if we started buying stuff and establishing ourselves in Jork, then we would have a harder time later on making a decision to go somewhere else. So he was going to have to make a decision, and soon.

At first, he just put off buying the furniture. He made excuses about this or that reason why we shouldn't buy additional beds yet. By September though, the family was starting to get antsy and irritated. Either a decision was going to have to be made to go somewhere else, or we were going to need to start buying some furniture. The lease on the house was up for renewal at the end of October too, so about the end of September, Papa gathered the four oldest of us kids together and sat us down for a talk.

He said, "You know I could live here in Germany, and I could make a good living for myself. Eventually I would get a pension, but you are young people. You have dreams and desires, and you want to go places. You don't have to live here if you don't want to." He nodded at Karl and me and continued, "You two boys, you could go to America together if you wanted to, and you could make it. Or the four of you could go. But honestly, I'd rather that we find a way that our family could stay together."

Karl piped up, "Well, Papa, why don't we all go to America, our whole family?" Hildegaard and Ruth both added, "Yeah, Papa, let's all go."

Papa returned, "Well, it's true, that's why I haven't wanted to buy anything significant here yet. I don't have my own blacksmith shop anymore, so I personally am not tied to Germany anymore. I could go, or I could stay, and I would be okay either way. Right now we have a little money to buy some furniture with, but if we do, we'll have to stay in Jork. Or, if we go, we'll be starting all over again."

All four of us chimed in, "Okay, let's all go then."

By this time, Mom had heard us, and she came and stood quietly in the doorway. Hildegaard saw her and asked, "Mom, what do you think?"

Mom smiled wistfully and dropped her gaze to the floor, shaking her head ever so slightly. "You know that my place is where my family is. If you all want to go, then yes, I'll go with you."

The four of us let out a whoop of joy and started laughing and shouting and talking about what we would do when we got to America. All of us had come to the point where we desperately wanted to get away from Germany, and we secretly wanted to go to America. We just didn't feel like we could express that longing until Papa said it was okay.

Now however, Papa got up and held out his hands and shouted above the rest of us, "Hey, quiet down! There's one more thing." He waited until we'd sat back down and were all looking at him. "If we go to America, then I want you to promise me that we will stay together and work together until we have our own roof over our own heads. Do you promise?"

We looked at each other and then back and him, and we all nodded our heads and chorused, "Yeah, we promise."

Papa smiled and said matter-of-factly, "Okay then. It is decided. We shall go to America." The four of us jumped back up and ran out of the room, screaming and hollering, trying to find the younger half of us to tell them the good news. Papa looked silently at Mom, who had tears in her eyes. She just turned and walked back into the kitchen.

What Papa hadn't said during our conversation was that he had received an invitation from the World Council of Churches to come to their office in Hamburg to apply for refugee status in the United States under the recently passed Displaced Persons Act. We were eligible on the one hand because we were refugees, especially coming from East Prussia, and on the other hand because he was a member of the lay clergy, which was why the WCC was interested in helping him. Just two days before our conversation, he had done that, but in a fit of indecision, he'd left the completed paperwork in their lobby and had walked out. The morning of our conversation, they had called him, wanting to know whether he wanted to apply for refugee status in the US or not. He told them that he'd call them back later on. So now, he called them back and said that we'd decided to accept their offer and go to the United States.

Now we immediately started getting ready to go. Papa called our landlord and told him that we wouldn't be renewing our lease. Then he called the Salvation Army, another of many Anglo-American aid agencies along with the WCC that had entered Germany since the end of the war, and he arranged to donate what little furniture we did have to them. He also sent off a letter to Tante Lisa, explaining what we were doing and giving a rough timeframe of when she could expect us. We all quit our jobs the week after that, and by the third week of October, 1951, we were admitted to an emigration camp just outside Hamburg.

We stayed at this American-run camp for three weeks, while we all underwent physical examinations and tests for small pox, typhoid, tuberculosis, and so on. Thank God, Papa had been healed of typhoid for a couple years already. After the physical tests, we had to go through political screenings where an American intelligence officer ran our names and identification numbers through lists of both Nazi and Communist Party affiliations and then asked us all sorts of questions about our beliefs and political leanings. Papa and I both got an extra grilling because of his political indoctrination classes while he was in prison and because of my involvement with the Hitler Youth during the war. Also, I'd turned 18 back in May, so now I was required to sign a statement saying that I would not refuse military duty in the United States if I was called upon. I didn't have any particular nationalistic feelings towards Germany, and it was a requirement for going, so I signed it. I had no idea that this would one day require me to return to Germany as part of my own country's occupying forces.

The camp itself was an old Wehrmacht base, currently occupied by the US Army, so we lived in military barracks. The Army had sectioned off this one corner of the base for use by the refugees, but they allowed us to visit their Commissary, Post Exchange (PX), Recreation Center, and so forth. It was a good thing that they did too, because our corner of the base was overflowing with kids.

There were hundreds, if not thousands of refugees at this base, six years after the war was over. The advent of Communism in Eastern Europe had made a bad situation far worse, since none of the original refugees of the Russian onslaught wanted to return, and since many thousands more were now fleeing who hadn't fled before.

Each barracks building was three stories high and had about thirty rooms per floor, which translated into somewhere between thirty and sixty families per floor, not to mention a fair number of singles scattered throughout. Thus, each building had hundreds of children of all ages running up and down the halls and in between the buildings. And there were at least a dozen of these barracks in this complex. None of us had anything to do most of the time, and we were going to be there for several weeks, though some of the singles apparently enjoyed this lifestyle and managed to stay there for several months, probably living off of crime and prostitution.

Very quickly, I fell in with a group of boys that wanted to explore and do things that we weren't quite supposed to be doing. We discovered, for instance, that our barracks had an attic, and there was a ladder going up to it at one end of the building. The trap door was supposed to be padlocked, but somehow it had been left open, so of course, we found our way up there. The whole attic was an open bay, and there wasn't anything up there except some old bedsprings and mattresses that were stacked up, but a couple of us had an idea about what to do with the place.

The Army's Recreation Center had sporting equipment for rent. We'd been issued ID cards, and you could turn in your ID card at the Rec Center and check out their sporting equipment for a few hours. They had baseball stuff, footballs, soccer balls, roller skates, and boxing gloves. One of my newfound friends and I went there after discovering the attic, and we checked out some boxing gloves. Then we headed back up to the attic.

Once we were in the attic again, we set up the bedsprings, which were just metal frames with springs arrayed in a layer through the middle, with four legs

293

attached at the corners, and we arranged them in a circle, setting them lengthwise around the center of the room. This was our boxing ring. Then we took off our shirts, put on the gloves, and started a little friendly sparring.

One of the other kids saw us though and started spreading the word that there was a boxing match going on in our attic. Pretty soon first one, then another, and then whole groups of kids of all ages were climbing up the ladder to watch us fight. Before long the whole attic was filled with them, and they were cheering us on. The extra attention emboldened my friend and I, and soon our little sparring match had turned into a genuine, first rate fight.

Both of us hurt each other, but we agreed to quit before either of us got knocked down. That was just the first day though. The next day, several other guys got boxing gloves, in addition to us, and we had a tournament going before lunch time. Kids from all over the base showed up to watch us and cheer for us, and some of them even started taking bets on who was going to win.

I wasn't the best fighter there, but because of my blacksmithing and my size, I could hold my own against nearly any of them. This went on for most of the time we were in the camp, and as a result of it, I made something of a name for myself among the kids there. I discovered this one evening while some of us were walking back from the PX. There was a group of twelve or thirteen-year olds standing outside the movie theater, and when they saw us walk by, I heard them whisper excitedly to each other, "There's a fighter!" and "Hey, those guys are fighters!" Then they started following us, but they were awkward and nervous, pushing and punching each other, and trying to look nonchalant, as though they were going our way anyway. Some girls their age joined them too, giggling and looking anxiously in our direction. It was funny to hear them say that, but it made us feel pretty good, as though we were somebody, and as though we had a following.

When all of our tests and so forth were done, the Americans let us out from the camp for a couple weeks so that we could finalize our affairs and pack up our belongings. Then by late November, we had to report back to the camp where we went through some follow-up medical tests. After that, they put us on a train for Bremerhaven, where we processed into yet another camp, this time to wait for a ship to arrive to take us to America.

This camp, like the other one, was a US Army base, so every morning, they played reveille over the loudspeakers at about 6am, and they followed it up with the Star Spangled Banner. All the soldiers on base were out on their parade grounds having their formation and getting ready to do PT (physical training), so they came to attention and saluted when reveille was played and the American flag was raised. Being a kid, I slept in every day at the camp near Hamburg, but we only stayed at the Bremerhaven camp for a day or two, and on the morning when we were to leave, I was up, so I got to witness this ceremony.

I was standing in our room, slowly getting dressed, at just before six, absentmindedly staring out the long, fold-out windows into the pre-dawn darkness and early morning fog. All at once, there was this loud crackling noise coming from the center of the base, and it was followed by the clear, crisp notes of reveille. The sound of it made my veins surge with energy, and my arms got goose bumps all over. I looked more intently out the window now, and I could just see the top of the big flag pole in the center of the base as the American flag was hoisted to a stop just below its truck. In a few moments, when reveille finished up, the crackling noise resumed for a few more seconds, only to be replaced by the strong, bellowing peals of the Star Spangled Banner, which as I remembered, was the American National Anthem. I didn't really know any of the words to the song, but even the knowledge of what it was seemed to clarify in my mind what I was about to do that morning. My jaw slowly dropped, and my heart raced, as it dawned on me that I was going to AMERICA! That very day, I was going to America.

I hurriedly finished getting dressed, and I packed faster than I had since the night Papa rescued us from Rothenen before the Russians came. Everyone seemed to have a sense of excitement and anticipation. People all over the camp were moving about early that morning, getting ready to leave. We showed up outside the administration building at 8:30, and there was already a long line waiting for our 9:00 outprocessing. Somehow the line didn't seem to matter that day though. Everything was going to be okay in a few hours, and we were going to be on our way to our new home in the United States.

Outprocessing from the camp was simple, once we got inside the administration building. Right by the door, they had a huge pile of dirty linens for us to drop our sheets and towels in. Next, they had someone that checked our names against a list of people that hadn't paid for stuff at the Rec Center and PX. Then they had someone else that checked our names against the boarding roster for the ship. And that was it, except for one little snag, which we didn't feel was little at all.

Hildegaard was on the roster for a ship that was going to leave the week after ours. It had something to do with the fact that she was already a legal adult, being over age eighteen. I don't remember exactly what the issue was. In any event, they wouldn't let her come with us, so she had to wait there for a week until her ship arrived. That was an emotional parting, since it was the first time any of us children except for me had been away from the family for any length of time. She said she'd be okay though, and the clerk there promised to look after her, so we continued on our way.

Once we were cleared out of the administration building, we were loaded into one of many buses or trucks that was waiting, and then we were immediately taken down to the Bremerhaven Naval Base. The gate guards stopped us and made everyone hold up their ID cards, but that was the only processing we did there. The bus driver took us right up to the side of our ship, the USS General Taylor, a Liberty transport ship from the war. There were a few people in line at the gangplank, but the line moved quickly, and soon we were being shown to our quarters for the trans-Atlantic voyage.

Our quarters for this trip were a lot different than they were on the Lotringen though. Seeing them made me realize what we'd missed by being rescued by Captain Sehlbach. We were being put up in a large bay in the center of the ship, on the quarter deck. The room was nearly as wide as the ship was, and you could see out both sides of it from anywhere in the room. Every couple meters, there were a pair of poles that went from the deck to the ceiling, and arranged between these poles were five bunks on one side of the poles and five bunks on their other side. Our whole family fit inside one set of poles. There were hundreds of bunks like this in this one room, and we had to store all of our luggage, which wasn't much, on the floor under the bottom bunk. Thankfully though, everything was planned out beforehand, and they only let as many people on board as the ship had bunks.

We boarded the General Taylor about noon that

day, and the crew cast off their lines and picked up a tug out of the harbor beginning about two that afternoon. I was half expecting to have the run of the ship, as I did on the Lotringen, and I was looking forward to doing some exploring and to hooking back up with several of my friends from the camp. This ship was a regularly scheduled service of the United States Navy, however, and the crew had no intentions of letting anyone get out of line on this voyage.

As soon as the lines were cast off, there was an announcement over the loudspeaker, in German and in English, that a meeting would be held immediately in each berthing room, and all passengers residing in each room were required to attend. The meeting began within a couple minutes of the announcement. An officer in his dress uniform, speaking with a translator, went over a list of rules, and then a petty officer standing next to him went over the room roster and divvied out jobs for everyone to do. This was not going to be a free ride after all. I got assigned to the kitchen in the crew's mess, and I was told to report there within one hour to get ready for supper.

The kitchen, or galley as the Navy called it, was on the same level as our berthing area, but it was quite a ways forward of us. The General Taylor was much larger than the Lotringen was, well over twice its size. It was a troop transport from the war, so it was something of a mix between a freighter and a passenger liner in its design. It had large holds in the forward and after sections of its hull, but it also sought to maximize the number of passengers it could carry, though without any regard to their personal comfort or privacy.

The mess hall was a large bay, similar in size to our berthing area, but instead of bunks, it had foldable lockdown tables. At one end of the bay, there was a drink island with large coffee pots and juice and soda spigots arranged along a counter. Behind the drink island, there was a cafeteria-style serving area, and behind this was the galley. A sailor in a cook's uniform met us at the door and directed us back to where a chief petty officer (CPO) was getting ready to receive us. There were about twenty refugees reporting for KP duty, and there were about ten regular crew on duty there, including the CPO, all in white cooks' uniforms.

One of the crew passed out aprons to each of us, and then the CPO dove into his class. He had some help from a refugee interpreter, but it was hard going most of the time, because he didn't want to wait for the interpreter to figure out what he'd just said. Most of us that didn't know English were left rather confused, except that he'd made it perfectly clear that we were to show up at 5 O'clock in the morning for breakfast prep every day that we would be at sea. Our schedule was rather strange after that, dictated as it was by the meal schedule. We'd work from about five to eight for breakfast, from ten to one for lunch, and from three to six for dinner, nine hours per day, but in shifts of three hours each, with two hour breaks in between.

The only other thing that I really understood from the CPO was that I was supposed to help the salad prep guy. There seemed to be little rooms positioned throughout the galley, and each room was designed to facilitate the preparation of a particular type of food. There was a large grilling area, with four two-meter long flat-top grills in two's, back to back, with a long prep table between them. Then there was a cooking room with about a dozen double-high convection ovens arranged around another large prep table. There were two huge walk-in refrigerator rooms, one much colder than the other. There was a dessert room with a dozen wardrobe-sized carts with long pastry trays stacked twenty high inside them, and there were several large mixing machines with meter-wide kettles or bowls set up beneath them in this room too. There was a wash room with four large sinks or washtubs, each with its own overhead sprayer hose, and several meters of counter space in between them, though there weren't any dishes to be seen laying around at the moment. There was a general prep room, which was where the CPO met us, and which had a large prep table and dozens of cabinets full of supplies and clean aluminum pots and pans. There was a walk-in pantry where all the dry goods were stored. And there was the salad prep room, where I was going.

The salad room had another large prep table, but half of it was a wooden cutting board. It also had several meters of counter space, two closets, and a large, double-wide sink, again with its own overhead sprayer hose. It had several of its own wardrobe-sized stacked tray carts, a couple of mixing machines, and four meter-wide bowls set up on frames with wheels on them. All of these wheeled carts also had locking devices on their sides so the crew could lock them into matching devices affixed on the edges of the tables and counters, to keep them from rolling around during high seas.

The crew member who led me into the salad room was a stately, tall Black sailor, though I don't remember his name. He didn't know German, but I knew enough about food, kitchens, and cooking that if he pointed to something, I was able to figure out what he wanted. He told me to chop up several dozen heads of cabbage and put the shavings in one of the big vats on the wheeled frames, while he was going to make sauce for cole slaw. So I got a big knife out of one of the under counter drawers that they had and started quartering and coring the cabbage. When I was done with that, I moved the vat under a grinder machine that they had attached to the edge of one of the counters, and I began putting the cabbage quarters through the grinder and dumping the mash out into the vat below it. Meanwhile, the cook poured pots of vinegar, cream of tarter, spices, and so on into a couple of large pitchers and mixed up the sauce in them. When both of us were finished, he poured the sauce from the two pitchers into the big vat with my cabbage shavings in it, and then the plunged his hands deep into the slaw to mix it up.

I was shocked when I saw him do that, and I thought, "Boy, he should wash his hands first." Of course, he had already washed his hands. What so startled me was the contrast between his jet black skin and the milky white of the cole slaw. Then I realized, "Oh no, he's Black. He can't help it. That's him." You see, although I'd seen pictures of Blacks in magazines before this, and I'd noticed a few Blacks among the rest of the American crew since boarding the ship, this man was the very first Black man that I'd ever met. Frankly, I didn't know what do make of him, but my reaction to his dark skin in the cole slaw made me embarrassed after that, because I knew I shouldn't be thinking things like that about people. On the other hand, I wasn't sure whether it really mattered or not, because I didn't know English, and he didn't know German, so we weren't exactly holding a conversation either.

After I got done mixing the cole slaw, I was sent to the grilling room to set out hotdogs and hamburgers from the freezer, so they would thaw out for cooking on the short order line. As it turned out, I was very fortunate to get this job in the galley, because it meant that I could eat practically whenever and whatever I wanted to, as long as it didn't interfere with my duties. I soon got in the habit of taking several frozen hotdogs and thawing them out against my stomach while I was sitting around waiting for something to do in between

301

meal times. Then I'd eat them raw, or I might turn on one of the grills and fry them up real quick, or I might boil them in a small pot on a stove. I enjoyed eating, and I knew I was going to enjoy this job all the way to the US.

My Papa and Karl, on the other hand, weren't so fortunate. Once I was done cleaning up after dinner that first night, I was able to catch up with them and find out what their jobs had been like. Papa was assigned to take a bucket, rag, and mop and patrol several stairways in this one section of the ship, basically cleaning up after refugees that had gotten sea sick and vomited while moving around on board. This was not a small task either, since there were hundreds of refugees on board, and few, if any, of them had ever been on a ship at sea. Just by the end of his first shift, he'd already had to clean up after more than twenty such accidents. Karl was doing the same thing as Papa was, except his patrol area was the main latrine, or head, as the Navy called it. This was a smaller area, but it was more notorious for accidents of that nature. Karl had cleaned up over thirty messes by the end of his shift.

That night, as I crawled into my bunk above Karl's and as the ship gradually quieted down, I could feel the slow throb of the engines, I could hear the sloshing of the waves against the hull, and I could smell the salty savor of the sea. The noises and the smells all brought back to me those wonderful days on board the Lotringen, with all their excitement and danger. On this my second sea voyage, I was excited for a different reason. This time, instead of towards safety, we were heading towards freedom and opportunity. My entire future, grand and unknown, seemed to lay before me as wide as the sea, and as the ship's gentle swaying lulled me to sleep, I dreamed great dreams of doing wonderful things in a new land.

Morning broke early, with the hard reality of having to get up at 0430 and be in the galley by five. I quickly got used to it though, when I found out that breakfast was scrambled eggs, pancakes, sausages, and a half dozen other delectable things that I'd never had for breakfast before. "Wow, these Americans sure know how to eat well," I thought. And I could eat as much of it as I wanted to.

Later on that second day, in between my lunch and dinner shifts, I was standing out on deck, watching the waves go by, when someone shouted that they saw land. Upon inquiring which land, I found out that it was England, somewhere around Dover. They said that pretty soon, we should be able to see the famed "White Cliffs" of Dover. I had over an hour left before my next shift started, so I decided that I would watch and see what they really looked like.

Sure enough, in about twenty minutes, I could see a distinct white line spreading out across the horizon to our north. In another twenty minutes, it had grown to half a centimeter high and was beginning to fall astern of us at its eastern-most edge. It was beautiful, almost as if someone had taken a piece of chalk and drawn a line across the earth with it. I wondered what was in the rocks that made them so white.

All at once, there was a commotion on the deck below me. Several refugee men were running forward as if their life depended on it, but no one was chasing them. A minute later, they came running back the other way, with a several tan-uniformed officers and dungaree-clad sailors running right behind them. Five minutes after that, one of the officers went running back towards the stem, and another five minutes later, the ship suddenly slowed and heaved over, beginning a

ponderous turn to the right, or starboard, as the sailors
say.

Curious, I asked the refugee translator in the
galley if he knew what was going on, why we had turned
towards land like that, and he in turn asked the CPO.
The CPO answered that a pregnant woman in the bay
below ours had gone into labor, and the ship's medic
wasn't prepared to handle giving birth, so they were
turning about and heading towards Dover to take her to
the hospital there.

Dinner was cut short that day, needless to say,
since the crew needed to be up on deck to help us come
into port. I managed to get released early from the
galley, so I went outside with everyone else to see the
sights. It took us about a half an hour before we got
there. Dover was right on the coast, in a low place
among the cliffs. Part of the city was down below the
cliffs, and part of it was up above the cliffs. There are
roads and a railroad track that cut through the cliffs
and dropped down to the lower half of the city, where
there were two sets of piers, one at the east end of the
city and one at the west end of the city. Each set was a
pair of one long pier on the outside and a shorter one on
the inside, and there were wharves between them where
ships could actually dock. Both sets had a place for a
ferry to land, but the eastern one also had a marina,
while the western one had slips for larger ships.
Together, the larger outside piers curved back over in
front of the city's beach to protect it from the waves in
the English Channel. The cliffs themselves ran right
through the city, but they were more of a series of steep,
tall bluffs than they were vertical cliffs. They were a
dull white, almost like chalk, and they gave the city a
very unique feel, as if it came right out of a storybook.

The Dover Port Authority sent a tug out to meet

us, and they transferred a pilot to our ship to help us navigate into the western set of piers, since the space between the docks was very narrow. A speed boat from the local police came out and transferred a doctor to us as well, to help the ship's doctor with the pregnant lady. Apparently, she was having complications with her pregnancy. A number of other small boats came out too, because they'd seen the police boat go out, and they wanted to watch what was going on. When we docked, our doctor, the city's doctor, and several of the crew moved the pregnant woman to the wharf on a stretcher, and then they loaded her into an ambulance and took her to the hospital. No one else was allowed to get off the ship.

We stayed in Dover harbor for about four hours, long enough for the hospital to send back a report that the woman wasn't going to be able to come with us. Whatever her complications were, she was going to need time to recover. I never did find out how her baby was doing.

The tugboat's pilot boarded the General Taylor again for the trip back out of the harbor. None of the pleasure boats came with us this time, since it was after dark. We could see Dover's street lights getting smaller in the distance for a long time afterwards, and it left me with an enormous sense of leaving everything that was familiar and of launching out into a great unknown.

The next morning someone in the galley started passing around the ship's newspaper. I didn't know that ships could have newspapers, but the General Taylor did. It was in English, so I couldn't read it. But it did have a map of the Atlantic Ocean on the front page, with a big X marking our location at 6am that morning. It also had some dotted lines tracing where we'd already been. I could understand that without having to be able to read it, so I looked forward to looking at it each morning that we were out. According to the map, we were traveling along the coast of France, a couple hundred nautical miles south of Dover.

That afternoon, right after I got off my lunch shift, a couple refugee men and a sailor approached me and asked if I was a fighter. I wasn't sure where they'd gotten this idea, but several of my friends from the American Army camp outside Bremerhaven were on board, so it was possible that they'd bragged on me somewhere. I was feeling cocky and wanted to impress them, so I said, "Yeah."

The leader of the group responded, "Good. We've got a fight lined up for you. Come on over here with us. We've got some gloves for you." I wasn't sure if I wanted to be a part of this or not, since these were grown men, but I followed them to see what they had.

They took me up to the fifth deck, on a stairway landing which was about three meters in diameter. A crowd of men, some refugees, some sailors, had gathered. They were talking boisterously, slapping each other on the back and looking around. When I showed up, I created quite a stir. They were keenly interested in me and started comparing me to this other guy, a sailor, who was standing nearby. One guy seemed to be the ringleader, and he started taking bets from everyone. The guys that had contacted me helped me take my shirt off and gave me some gloves. The sailor that I was supposed to fight stood opposite me with several of his own supporters as they helped him put his gloves on too. Most of the refugees were betting on me because of my size, but the sailors were betting on their man. He was a little smaller than I was, but I took it that he had more experience than I did. I figured that it would be okay though, because I was in pretty good shape and because of how big I was. I hoped he didn't have too much experience though.

Then I noticed that several guys on the edge of
the circle didn't seem to be paying any attention to the
betting at all. Instead, they were looking away from us,
up this gangway, back down the stairway, or into the
rooms on this deck through a port hole. They seemed
nervous, and it dawned on me that we weren't supposed
to be doing this. Now I was more edgy about getting
caught than I was about getting hit. What would
happen if I got knocked down just as someone came
around the corner?

The ringleader, who had two hands full of dollars
and Deutschmarks by this time, raised one hand and
announced, "Okay, let's do it!" The leader of the trio
that was "managing" me brought me into the middle of
the circle and had me shake hands with the sailor that I
was to fight. Well, it was more like politely knocking
each other's fists, because of the gloves on our hands.
Then another guy that probably was going to be the
referee told us to go back into our corners and wait for
him to ring the bell, which was a spoon and a coffee
mug. Or I imagined that was what he said, since it was
in English, so I didn't understand him.

The referee held up his mug, waited for the crowd
to quiet down some, and then struck the mug with the
spoon. The sailor and I both advanced a couple steps
towards the middle of the ring, and then we started
circling each other.

Suddenly one of the guards yelled, "Hey!
Someone's coming!" Pandemonium erupted.

Men were running all over the place, some inside
the cabin, some down the stairs, and some around back
of the cabin. I felt rough hands picking me up bodily,
and within seconds I was down the stairs onto the lower
deck, without ever walking an inch. My manager was in
my face, grabbing the gloves off my hands and telling
me to get lost. One of the other guys in my trio gave me

back my shirt. The other fighter ran past us. The ringleader had simply disappeared. Everyone else that was still around just started walking away as if nothing had ever happened.

That was the end of my boxing career. I saw some of those guys around later on, but none of them acknowledged me, and no one ever asked me to box again. I guess the officers were too strict for them to risk it, or something like that.

On our fourth day out, I noticed in the morning's newspaper that we were still heading south. We were now off the coast of Portugal. I thought this was odd, so I asked the galley translator why we were heading south instead of west. He dutifully asked the CPO, and he answered that there was a big storm in the middle of the Atlantic. We were going south to try to get around it. He pointed at a little squiggly mark in the center of the map and said, "That's the storm."

It didn't seem like there was any storm near where we were. The weather had been getting progressively warmer, and it now seemed more like summer than late November. Everyone had shed their coats and jackets, and most of the men were going around without any shirt on at all. No one was prepared for this, since it was cold and wet in northern Germany this time of year, and we just figured that it would be the same in the US.

The morning paper on our fifth day out had us positioned across from the Straits of Gibraltar, and about mid-morning, I felt the ship come about and begin heading west. I thought that we would be clear of the storm, which looked as if it had moved north and east from its position the day before.

On the sixth day, the storm and our position still seemed like they were far apart on the map, but when I came out of the mess hall after my breakfast shift, I found that the crew had strung a rope along the center of the outer gangways that ran around the edge of the ship. There were signs hanging off this rope in both English and German that read, "DANGER! Do not cross." I also noticed that crewmembers were tying things down and picking things up all over the ship. Several of them cruised through the refugee berthing areas with translators, warning people to secure their belongings and passing out "Barf Bags." I couldn't figure out why they were doing this, because the sea was still calm, and there weren't any serious clouds anywhere to be seen.

Halfway through my lunch shift though, the CPO strode into the grill room where I was working and ordered everyone to secure all the carts. He said we needed to hurry, because we were going to have a short lunch.

The serving lines got crowded as soon as they opened. It was as if the whole crew showed up all at the same time. They even called me over to help dish out food. The tension in the air was palpable, and the men ate quickly and in silence. The servers were issuing paper plates and styrofoam cups too, instead of their usual aluminum trays and ceramic mugs or soda glasses. Extra garbage cans were stationed and locked down at all the entrances.

The CPO and some of the other kitchen staff filtered among the eating sailors about halfway through lunch and began urging them to hurry and finish up. Many of them quit without actually finishing their meal. I had to empty several of the garbage cans twice, because they filled up so fast.

Just before I was released from lunch shift, the CPO rounded up the mess crew and announced that we were all going to have to help the deck crew clean up after people during the storm. Supper, if we had it, was only going to be sandwiches.

As I went out on the deck to return to our berthing area, I finally saw the edge of the storm. We had already passed under it by this time. There was a line of high clouds behind us, and they grew darker and more ominous over and in front of us. The sea was choppy now, and the wind was picking up, sending streams of spray and foam flying through the air. One of them hit me in the face and took my breath away.

Back in our berthing area, people were lounging around taking it easy. Children were running and playing in between the bunks. Men and women were chatting back and forth, comparing this to previous storms that they'd been in and commenting on the clouds and the waves. A few were looking out the porthole in the door, watching the storm come up. They were excited about seeing a real ocean storm. Some were nervous too, but they didn't seem to have quite the same appreciation for it as the crew did.

An hour later, all that had changed. The wind roared and howled, and the sky was nearly black, even though it was only two in the afternoon. Rain fell in sheets, and low clouds scudded across the horizon. The waves had grown into mountains, and the ship drove down the side of them, plunging into the sea at the trough. The sides of the ship would resonate with earsplitting BOOMs as the steel ribs and plating of the deck and hull bent and contorted in agony at being wrenched so by the sea. Sometimes the whole front quarter of the ship disappeared under the waves. Then we would pop up and go soaring towards the crest of the next wave, silouhetting the forecastle and bridge against the glowering sky as the bow shot out of the water at the top before diving towards the sea again on the other side.

310

Now I understood why the CPO wanted us to help the deck crew with their clean-up duties. It seemed as if every other person in our berthing area was getting seasick and vomiting all over the place. Some of them used the bags they'd been given, but many didn't or didn't have time to, and even those that did often missed and spewed vomit across the deck. Nearly everyone moved back up onto their bunks, partly out of seasickness and partly out of fear. Children cried and whimpered. Their mothers tried to comfort them, but they were just as scared and cowered or cried right along with them. Some women became hysterical and screamed and cried when we would go under the waves and the hull made all those crashing sounds, thinking the ship was splitting apart.

Thankfully, we had the doors closed to keep the water out, but every now and then someone would come or go and would open the door, allowing a blast of cold air and many liters of water to come surging in. Some of the men were still standing up against the porthole, watching the storm, but most of them were sticking to their bunks too. I had to be out by the door, because of my duties, which was how I got to see all of this. It seemed as if I was mopping up someone's lunch every couple of minutes. Sometimes they let go in groups too. One person would lose it, and then half a dozen others would see or smell it, and then they'd vomit too, all at the same time. I myself didn't really get sick, except once when I was dumping a bucket full of garbage and vomit down the refuse chute in the bulkhead, and a sudden pitching of the ship blew some of it back into my face.

Some of the garbage cans that the crew had stationed around our bay came loose from their stanchions too. The violent twisting and wrenching of the hull probably bent their snaps and caused them to break away and tip over, emptying their smelly contents across the floor. Then the pitch and roll of the ship sent them careening across the room until they'd crash into the bulkhead and bounce off in another direction. The ship wasn't just rolling up and down the waves two-dimensionally; rather, it often slid sideways down a wave or would sometimes get caught in a vortex and might spin around some. The affect was violent and unpredictable, and people often had to scurry to get out of the way of one of the errant cans.

When dinner time came, I had to report back to the crew's mess to make sandwiches. Now, the General Taylor was a naval ship, so it had elliptical doors with watertight seals, and the lower edge of the door was raised about ten inches above the deck to help keep water out. As I opened the door and was stepping out over this raised door jam, the ship chose that moment to dive down the side of another wave. It changed course so suddenly that the deck simply disappeared out from under my feet, and I was left standing in mid air, wondering where the ship had gone to. That only lasted for a second before I went flying down to meet it, landing with a thud on my back in the middle of the gangway. The way the ship was moving, it was a miracle I wasn't swept overboard.

I looked up from where I was laying, sore and wet all over, and I saw that safety rope suspended directly over me, a line of white cutting the violent gray sky. In that moment, I sensed the enormity and power of the storm in all its vastness, and I realized with stark clarity how tiny and vulnerable we were in this ship. With that fresh understanding, I reached up and grabbed the rope and pulled myself upright, and then I ran back into our berthing area to catch my breath.

It was several more minutes before I found the courage to venture out again, but when I did, I had a lot more appreciation for what the crew had to deal with. They had to continue moving about the ship, performing their duties, no matter what the weather was doing. If you were aware of the danger though, and you knew what to do about it, you could manage it and get through it.

After that, I was more careful with my footing, and I made sure that I was always holding onto something wherever I was, inside or out, and especially when I was going up or down stairs. Most of the stairs were outside, and those were slippery. But even the ones inside were treacherous in this storm because of the effect of the waves. Just as happened with me as I was stepping out through that door, if you were going up some stairs with the ship going down a wave, it was as if the stairs were falling out from underneath you, so you had to run up them. On the other hand, if the ship started going up a wave while you were climbing some stairs, the force was so great that it pinned you to them, and you couldn't moved until the ship had crested the wave. Going downstairs, it was the opposite. If the ship was going up, you ran down the stairs, at least if your feet could move that fast. Or if the ship was going down, you grabbed onto the railings for dear life and got ready to slide down them and slam into the deck as soon as the ship entered the trough. It was almost like a game once you got used to it though.

The storm lasted for three days. By the morning of our ninth day at sea, it was calm again, and the map on the cover of the ship's newspaper put us just under 800 nautical miles southeast of New York City. During our ordeal in the storm, we had trekked a ways north again, so the weather was quite cold that morning, despite the sunshine and a few high clouds. On the other hand, that morning the map also featured a river-like swath of shaded gray between our location and the

North American coast. The refugee translator in the galley told me this was the Gulf Stream, and our weather should change for the warmer as soon as we crossed into it.

Sure enough, later that afternoon when my lunch shift was over, I stepped out of the crew's mess onto the gangway and into a totally different world than what I'd seen that morning. The air was warm and strangely fragrant. The clouds were fluffy white cumulus. The sea was bluer than I'd ever seen it before, and it was alive. Fish were jumping out of the water everywhere. There were porpoises and dolphins, flying fish, sail fish, and others leaping into the air, while unimaginably large schools of smaller fish zigged this way and that just under the surface. Transfixed by this unexpected beauty, I joined a hundred or so other refugees standing along the gunwales and whiled away the rest of the afternoon watching this landless paradise flow by.

All through the tenth day and into the morning of the eleventh, we were still in the Gulf Stream. On that morning though, just after breakfast, I was again standing against the gunwales, this time near the bow, when I noticed the sea turning a lighter color ahead of us. There was a definite line that stretched from south to north where the color of the sea changed from the dark blue where we were to a lighter grayish blue beyond, and we were fast approaching it. This line was also marked by an odd choppiness among the waves, as if they were fighting each other. The waves on our side of the line seemed to be rushing north, while the waves beyond it didn't seem to be going anywhere.

There was a sense of excitement and wonder among the lines of refugees watching from the gunwales and railings on various decks as we approached that line. You could see the line as it passed, and the ship seemed to shudder ever so slightly as we crossed it.

Then, as if on command, the air became colder. Just by crossing that line, we had traveled from the subtropics to the mid-Atlantic, or from July back into late November. Within minutes, every person that had been watching this happen from the decks of the General Taylor had disappeared into their cabins or berths to change their clothes and to don their jackets.

Our excitement, however, continued to grow, because we knew from the morning's newspaper that once we crossed the western edge of the Gulf Stream, we were only about 70 more nautical miles from New York City.

18

America!

About an hour after crossing out of the Gulf
Stream, we came under another weather system. It
wasn't really a storm, but it was overcast and dreary
and cold. The wind picked up a little, and a soaking
drizzle fell. It felt very much like being back in
Germany, but it didn't dampen our spirits at all.

When I'd been released from breakfast duty by
the Chief Petty Officer (CPO) in the crew's mess that
morning, he'd announced that we were finished with
our duty on board the General Taylor. We'd be docking
in New York Harbor in a few hours, so there wasn't any
need to get lunch ready. He thanked us for our help
and wished us a good life in America.

I'd gone out on deck to watch our passage out of
the Gulf Stream, but when it got colder, I returned to
our bunks in our berthing area. Mom and Papa were
already helping the rest of us kids pack things back up
and get ready to disembark. All the refugees were
packing or running about, doing things, and there was

an excited buzz among them as they whispered or chatted or giggled about what they might see or do once they landed. Some crew members circulated among the refugees, passing out Customs forms for everyone to fill out, for declaring what we had in our bags and so forth. Once we'd changed our clothes and packed everything away, we joined the throng of other refugees out on deck to watch our entry into New York Harbor.

Visibility wasn't very good, because of the drizzle and the clouds. The sea was gray, and the clouds were gray, and the sky was gray. When someone up in the port flying bridge shouted, "I see it! I see land!" all of us peered into the grayness. Soon there was a smudge of darker gray on the horizon at the port bow. Then another smudge of darker gray appeared on the starboard bow. These smudges gradually broadened and thickened until the entire horizon, except for the part immediately in front of us, was filled with this dark gray smudge that was land.

A sense of excitement and wonder rippled through the crowds of refugees standing on the decks of the General Taylor. Men and women pressed towards the front against the railings, while children wriggled their way between bigger legs to get a glimpse of whatever was so entrancing the adults. Muted conversations and exclamations of joy in German, Polish, Russian, and half a dozen other languages passed from side to side among us like the very waves we were riding over. Along with probably all the other passengers, I suddenly realized, "This is the land that's going to be my home!" My heart raced with expectation and even a little anxiety. This was it. This was what we'd come for. We were going to be home soon.

In another few minutes, the smudges began to resolve themselves into bays and headlands, and then beaches and lights appeared. Other ships, freighters and a passenger liner, appeared in various places around us, some going out of the harbor, some going into it, and they began blowing their horns to acknowledge each other's presence. Our own horn blew, great and bellowing in the mist. A shiver of excitement ran through the ranks of refugees, as if it announced, "Welcome to America!"

Before long, the land was beginning to close in around us. Coney Island passed us to starboard, and the Gateway National Recreation Area approached us to port, along with a couple small islands. As we entered the Narrows, several of us noticed movement on the starboard shore. Office buildings, trees, and what looked like military barracks could be seen higher up on shore, but there were moving things right along the beach. Someone finally pointed out, "Oh, those are cars!" And they were. Big cars too, on a vast highway. People remarked about how big they were and about how many of them there were. Hundreds of them flocked in both directions along what I guess was the Shore Parkway. We gawked at them with their rakish, flamboyant tail fins and gaudy styles. We'd never seen anything like this in Europe before, not even in Hamburg, which was also a big city. We started calling them "Strassen Kroetzer," or Street Cruisers, because they reminded us more of navy ships than of the cars that we knew of.

Even while most of us were still staring at the cars on the Shore Parkway, someone up front screamed, "Das ist die Freiheits Statue!" (There's the Statue of Liberty!) People repeated that call in all their different languages from the front of the ship to the back. Some ran back inside the berthing areas to tell others who hadn't or couldn't come out yet, and a small surge of others came back out to see a sight that literally everyone had heard about and wanted to see. Everyone pressed closer to the railings. The sight of it thrilled our hearts and brought tears to the eyes of some. One or two of us even broke down, weeping for joy.

Slowly we approached it, and as it passed a mere half a kilometer off our port beam the weight of the ship shifted to that side, for perhaps a thousand people on the starboard side ran to the port side to get a better glimpse of the Noble Lady. She was beautiful. Tall, strong, and calm, she spoke volumes of acceptance and freedom to all of us disparate, displaced persons. I felt as if we'd been following the light of her torch for years without even knowing it, and now we were finally here. All eyes stayed riveted on her as she passed astern until a chorus of Ooooh's and Ahhh's broke out among the people in the bow.

What lay ahead of us that people were exclaiming about was Manhattan, particularly the southern tip of it, with Wall St and the Financial District. The towering skyscrapers were simply beyond our imaginations. Their gleaming glass walls seemed to rise straight out of the water. Building after building, as far as the eye could see, stretched tall and mighty, dwarfing everything else around them, including our own little ship. It made my head spin looking up at them, as we came abreast of them on our starboard side and entered the Hudson River.

Now a small gray tug boat approached us and pulled alongside. They lashed themselves to us, and some of our crew let down a rope ladder for someone, probably a pilot, to come aboard. As he mounted the deck, all the crew saluted him, so I imagine that he was a Navy officer. Some of them escorted him up to the bridge, which was the last that I saw of him, and then the tug cast off again.

As we went up the Hudson River, we passed row after row of ships moored in wharves. The entire coast on both sides of the river was one continuous mass of docks, from the end of the Narrows all the way up as far as we could see ahead of us. There were freighters and steamers and tankers and fishing boats and naval vessels and passenger liners and tug boats and smaller craft of every description. Most of them were docked, but many were also moving up or down the channel and blew their horns as they passed us. Our own captain returned the favor, as if this was their way of greeting each other. The effect was deafening, but I enjoyed it because of all the different kinds of ships I got to see.

We went on up the river quite a ways, past a long elevated railroad, several rail yards, warehouses, factories, and office buildings, until the pilot and a couple tugs backed us into Pier 86 just past the Lincoln Tunnel, with barely enough room for one other ship between us and Pier 84. Cargo trucks were parked by the dozens in a large lot off to the south, in front of where the Tunnel probably came out, and right along the waterfront ran a double-lane elevated highway, with ramps going up and coming down every block or so. There was a long stone office building at the base of the pier, running across its width, and a large warehouse made of corrugated metal sides was connected to it, right on the pier, only a few meters from our starboard aft. A crowd of people stood around in front of it, watching us. Many of them were waving at us, and nearly everyone on board waved back. Every now and then someone on board would recognize someone on the pier, and they would begin jumping up and down, waving frantically, shouting for joy, and trying to communicate with their relatives on the pier. A number of sailors on the pier helped tie us up to the bitts, while longshoremen with hand trucks and fork lifts waited nearby to begin unloading the baggage. Once we let down the gangplank, several men in business suits came aboard, and the ship's loudspeakers announced that everyone had to go past the Customs desk by the gate before we could leave the ship.

It was going to be a long time before everyone could get off anyway, since there were so many of us. I wanted to stay out on deck and watch what was going on, but Papa made all of us go back to our berth to pick up our baggage and get in line. Mom and he had to fish out the sheaf of forms that they'd filled in back at the emigration camp in Germany, so they could turn them in at Customs. The line was already snaking around from the Customs desk by the gangplank over to the port gunwale and from there aft to the fantail by the time we reached it. Papa didn't see any reason for us older kids to stand in line with them, so he allowed us to go back over to the gangplank gate to wait for them there.

While we were waiting, we had a ringside seat to watch the spectacle that was New York City. For over an hour we marveled at the giant American fishtail cars zooming back and forth on the West Side Expressway. We wondered who they were and where they were going. Freighters and tug boats and a local tour boat plied up and down the river, and the passenger liner that we'd seen earlier out in the bay came and docked two piers further up from us. A freight train loaded down with coal moved slowly through a massive rail terminal on the New Jersey side of the river. And over a hundred cars and buses queued up under the expressway overpass to wait for the refugees to begin coming out of the office building on the pier.

I knew that's what the cars were doing because we saw the refugees that got off the ship go into the building and after an hour or so, they started coming back out and wandered in the general direction of the parked cars. Eventually some of them were met by various people, but it looked like they spent quite a while searching for them in the parking lot and under the bridge. We knew that Tante Lisa and her family would send someone for us, because Papa had telegraphed them the day that we left Bremerhaven and again from the ship after we got out of the storm, but we didn't know who would actually come or when or in which vehicle. We tried to see if we recognized anyone in the crowd in front of the building or among the cars under the bridge, but it wasn't any good, because Tante Lisa had emigrated to the US before any of us were even born, so of course, we wouldn't know what she looked like.

When Mom and Papa finally showed up at the Customs desk behind us, the men in the suits took their baggage forms, stamped them, and then gave them some more forms to fill out, telling them to go to the office building on the pier to inprocess with Customs. After that, they joined up with us, and we all walked down the gangplank and set foot for the first time in America.

It was as if the sun had come out, even though the sky was still gray and drizzly. We all stretched and looked around, not wondering where to go, but sizing up our new home, eager to explore our new opportunities. Everyone was in a positive, upbeat, cheerful mood. Papa asked if we'd seen Tante Lisa at all, but we said we hadn't. The younger kids wanted to play and run around, but there were so many people milling around that Mom didn't want them to. Amazingly, they didn't even complain.

We started ambling on over to the Customs building on the pier. There were piles and piles of luggage stacked up in a line from there all the way out towards the end of the pier. The longshoremen had left them there after retrieving them from the hold of the

General Taylor. They had another ramp going into a garage-like opening in the hull, and even now a series of fork lifts was still shuttling back and forth with people's belongings. Dozens of people were trying to get over there to retrieve their baggage, but some Customs officials had put up a rope fence separating where the fork lifts were running from where people could walk. Consequently, everyone had to go around by the building where there was a way they could get through to the other side of the luggage piles. We didn't bother with that since we'd brought so little with us that we could carry everything in our hands, all our worldly possessions.

Once we'd entered the warehouse, we were greeted by a vast room with high unfinished ceilings and a bare concrete floor. The room was mostly empty except for a broken down fork lift and a pile of abandoned luggage in a dark corner to our left and a line of gates - what looked like railroad station ticket counters - under some flood lights to our right, in front of the back of the stone office building. There were perhaps a half dozen of these gates, with a uniformed Customs agent sitting behind each ticket counter next to each gate. A line of refugees twenty deep had developed in front of each of these gates too, so we picked one and settled down for another long wait.

Probably an hour passed while we were waiting, or at least it felt that way. There was a constant low buzz of people talking, punctuated by an occasional shriek of joy or gasp of fear, depending on the individual's situation. The cavernous warehouse magnified people's voices so that everyone sounded louder than they really were, but you couldn't understand what anyone was saying because all the voices seemed to blend in together. The air was stale and dank, with a hint of diesel fumes and cigarette smoke, and this irritated the noses of the smaller children, making them sneeze and cry. A sense of boredom prevailed among the older children, but everyone was trying to be patient, knowing that our entire futures lay just to the other side of that row of gates.

When we finally reached our gate, Papa turned over a stack of all of our residency papers, Displaced Persons Act eligibility forms, immunization records, Customs declarations, and several other forms to the clerk behind the counter. The clerk looked at each of them briefly, gave each of us a quick look-over too, and then said something to Papa in English, which none of us understood. She shuffled the papers back into a more coherent pile, and then she picked them up and walked off towards the stone façade of the office building adjoining the warehouse. Wondering what was going on, we watched her mount a set of iron stairs and disappear into a door on the second floor of the building.

Ten minutes later, she reappeared from the same door, came down the stairs, and rejoined us behind her counter. She still carried Papa's stack of papers, but it had shrunk in size by half, with only the carbon third copies remaining. Once again, she went through each form, stamping it and telling Papa something about it in English. When she was done with all of them, she gave them back to Papa, pointed at a truck-sized passageway that went through the stone office building out to the street, welcomed us to America, and then called for the next person in line.

We breathed a collective sigh of relief, picked up our stuff, and headed through the gate, past the clerk, and out through the passageway under the building.

Outside, the drizzle had turned into a light rain. We didn't see anyone that we knew right there waiting for us, so we hurried across the parking lot at the foot of the pier and took cover under the expressway overpass. Cars were parked all over the place, without any semblance of order. There was one narrow lane for them to get in and out, but that was frequently blocked by someone having trouble backing out from where other cars had wedged them in. Refugees milled about in droves looking for their sponsors. Some seemed as if they were despairing of finding anyone. Groups of well-dressed Americans looking for refugee families were there too, often with signs proclaiming someone's last name. A row of taxi cabs was parked along the inland side of the overpass, their drivers hoping to attract someone's attention. And there were even a few individual American men in suits standing around and occasionally talking to some of the more lonely-looking refugees. One of them walked off with a family as if he was their best friend.

After looking around for a while to get our bearings, Papa saw three men standing against a bridge pylon, and one of them was holding a large sign that said, "FLEMMING." Papa waved and shouted to get their attention, and we started off towards where they were, negotiating our way around several parked cars and barely squeezing by a couple of them.

When we reached the men, none of us recognized each other, but the American holding the FLEMMING sign did speak German. After some lengthy introductions and explanations, we discovered that they were indeed our relatives. The oldest of them was our Uncle Otto, Tante Lisa's husband. He looked like he was in his late forties. One of the other two was his son Herman, and the third man was Herman's friend, Michael Hipich, both of them in their early twenties.

They'd come for us in three cars, and although they were parked up the street, it only took a couple minutes for them to go back and get them. Karl and I were immediately interested in looking all over the cars. Uncle Otto had a large Ford with fins on it. Herman and Michael had big cars too, and we took the time to look at each of them up close before we divided up our luggage and stowed it in their trunks.

The nine of us Flemmings then split up between the three cars too. Mom, Papa, and I got into Uncle Otto's Ford, with me in the front. Karl, Ursula, and Gerhardt rode with Herman; and Mariann, Ruth, and Waltraut got in Michael's car. Uncle Otto led the convoy up the West Side Expressway and then cut across the island on US 19 to the Bronx, where we took the Major Deegan Expressway north. Once we got out of New York City, we took the New York State Thruway until we got to Newburgh, where we crossed the Hudson River again and continued north on US 9.

Shortly after this, the light rain turned to snow. We didn't have any problems driving in the snow for the time being though, as the cars were all very heavily laden with passengers and gear. We drove for over three hours that way, through some of the most beautiful country I'd ever seen. We were in awe at the beauty of the land, even though there were no leaves on the trees, and much of it was hidden by the snow. One of the most striking things for us was to see how few houses there were outside of New York City, or rather I should say, how far apart the houses were from each other, compared to how packed together they were back in Germany. I was amazed at how long it was taking us to get to Tante Lisa's house. I had no idea that New York State was so big, let alone the entire United States. Another thing that surprised us was that there was not a single shell crater or bombed out building from the war anywhere to be found. Compared to Europe, it was as if the war had never happened.

Eventually, we came to US 20, where we turned right and came into the town of Nassau. From there, Uncle Otto took some back roads out into the countryside, explaining that this was a short cut to his farm outside of East Nassau.

At one point, where there was a 90-degree turn to the right, we passed a beautiful farm with many well-kept large outbuildings and a sign on the road that said, "Smith's Farm." Uncle Otto said that this was a resort where rich people came for the summer. As he went on about the place and the people that visited it, we drove over first one large hill, and then another, and then there was an even steeper third hill.

It was half-way up this third hill that the car spun out in the snow. Herman and Michael were behind us, and they had to stop to keep from hitting us. Uncle Otto spun the tires for all he was worth, but we got no where, except closer to the ditch on the side of the road. Finally, he put the car in reverse, and signaling to Herman and Michael to back out of our way, we all backed down the hill. Unfortunately, none of the three cars was able to back up the previous hill. Herman and Michael got stuck just as the road began going up the second hill, so Uncle Otto was left at the bottom without any room to gather up speed for getting over the top of the third hill. Nonetheless, he gave it first one try and then another, but each additional try left him spinning out a little short of where he'd gotten to on the previous try.

Frustrated but undaunted, he stopped the car at the bottom of the hill and said, "Okay, Horst, let's you and me get out and put the chains on the tires so we can make it home."

"Huh?" I thought, "What chains? And how do they get attached to tires?" He was already out the door and moving around to the back of the car though.

In the car behind us, Ursula and Gerhardt waved and smiled at me as I got out of the car. Karl had an expression on his face that said, "What's the matter with you?" I just shrugged and pointed to Uncle Otto. Neither Karl nor Herman volunteered to get out to help us, and Papa and Mom stayed put too.

Uncle Otto sorted through the stuff in his car trunk, pulling out several suit cases, until he found his tire chains, at which point he put the suit cases back in the trunk and closed it. He told me how to lay out the chains in front of the back tires, and then he got back in the car and drove forward a little to put the tires on top of the chains while I guided him. Next he got back out and showed me how to connect the ends of the chains around the tires. He did one set, while I did the other set. Neither one of us had it easy though.

The problem was the cold numbing our fingers. Uncle Otto had gloves and boots on, but he took off his gloves so that he could work better, since the gloves made him clumsy with things as fine as these chains. I didn't have either gloves or boots. We didn't think we'd need heavy winter clothes in New York. After all, New York is over a thousand miles south of Germany, and it wasn't anywhere near as cold in Germany as it now was in New York State.

And it was cold. The cold went right through my jacket and made me shiver and shake. The snow was deep too, and wet, and my feet quickly became soaked from it without boots to protect them. By the time we started trying to connect the ends of the chains, my fingers and toes were already hurting from the cold. My inexperience with the chains made me have to start over a couple of times, and by then my fingers had become so numb that I couldn't even feel the metal of the chains. To make matters worse, I had to kneel down in the snow to do all this, so my knees and calves became wet and cold too. Uncle Otto finished his side before I did, and he came over to offer to help, but here my pride got in the way. I knew Karl was watching me from the other car, so under no circumstances could I accept Uncle Otto's assistance. Instead, I just got angry and blamed Papa and Karl for my numb hands and feet, because they didn't come out to help me.

Uncle Otto patted me on the back and thanked me for my help when I got done though. Then with the chains on the tires, it was a cinch getting over the hill. His farm was only another hill beyond that, and I quickly got over my anger as we pulled into his circular driveway.

Tante (Aunt) Lisa and Uncle Otto lived in a typical American farm house on a rolling 200-acre farm in the foothills of the Berkshire Mountains. Their snow-covered yard and fields extended beyond their house for quite a distance and also across the country road and up the hill to where there was an old foundation, all that remained of someone else's house from long ago. Their house itself was two stories, had white clapboards and a steeply sloped metal roof with a dormer in the middle, and featured a covered porch that spanned the entire front and one side of the house. There was also a barn and two small sheds near the end of the driveway, and their yard rose into a steep hill immediately in back of the house, which was situated off to the left of the driveway, rather than at its end.

Uncle Otto turned his car around in the driveway, and then he parked in front of the house. We all got out and retrieved our luggage from the car trunks, and then we trudged up a short flight of stairs to a sidewalk and another short flight of stairs to the porch.

Tante Lisa, who'd been cooking supper and so had her apron on, met us at the door. She practically pounced on Papa when she saw him, squealing with delight and hugging him wildly. Papa dropped his things and returned the hug, since it had been more years than I was old since they'd seen each other. They started laughing and talking, while the rest of us were still waiting outside on the porch. Uncle Otto finally broke it up by suggesting to her that she let everyone in so we could take our coats off and settle down before she tried to catch up on all the stories.

At that, everyone moved on into the house. Uncle Otto directed us where to set our stuff, while Tante Lisa took our coats and laid them in their bedroom. A line quickly developed at their sole bathroom, but after we got done with that, Tante Lisa began serving us some steaming hot chocolate with whipped cream on it. Everyone gathered in the kitchen, where Tante Lisa was still cooking, and a round of introductions followed.

Tante Lisa had to come and hug each one of us, and she even picked up Gerhardt and twirled him around. She made much of us, and we instantly fell in love with her. It was as if we had known her all our lives. She put us at ease and made us feel welcome, and we knew we had come home. Of course, a plate of freshly baked cookies helped, and soon Gerhardt and Ursula were chasing each other through the house like they'd grown up there.

When dinner was ready and everyone had already started eating, Tante Lisa finally allowed herself to indulge her curiosity again. She started asking Papa questions about everything. How was the war? What happened to Rothenen? How were all the other relatives? Did he see any action? How did he get captured? Were the Russians terrible? How was prison in Russia? What was Jork like? How did he get out of Russia? Did he get seasick on the trip over here?

She went on and on with these questions. The funny thing was that she'd let Papa get about one sentence into his answer, and then she'd cut him off, answer his question for him with what she thought, and then also tell him about something that had happened at the same time in her life. She was a great storyteller though, so no one minded or complained. We just sat there and ate and listened, fascinated by how fast she talked and how beautiful her laugh was.

Somewhere along about when she was telling us how awful it must've been for Papa to have spent so long in the Russian prison, she suddenly switched to speaking English. The change was so smooth that she didn't even break the rhythm of her speech. It took most of us several seconds before we even noticed what had happened, and Tante Lisa never did notice. Uncle Otto shook his head and rolled his eyes, letting us know that this wasn't the first time that she'd done this. Mom got a scowl on her face briefly until she caught Uncle Otto's expression, and then she shook her head too. Several of us kids nearly spit up our food as we smirked and giggled. Papa's eyes just glazed over, and he let her continue talking like that for over a minute.

Finally, Papa interrupted her and said, "You know, Lisa, I'm sure that's really great, but it would help if you spoke German so that we could understand what you were saying."

She stopped in mid-sentence with a surprised look on her face and asked, "Have I been speaking English?"

Papa answered, "Jah, but it was very nice English." And the rest of us broke down with howls of laughter, some of us nearly falling out of our chairs.

Tante Lisa loved laughing, even if it was at herself, so she joined right in and told us about several other times when she'd done the same thing for other people. We laughed at each of her misadventures, and then we encouraged her to go on and tell the rest of her story, where she'd left off when she broke into English.

Tante Lisa loved talking and being the center of attention too, so she dove right back into her story. Every so often, she'd stop and ask Papa more questions, but neither he nor any of the rest of us did much more talking that evening. We just sat there and ate and listened to Tante Lisa.

When dinner was finished, Tante Lisa took everyone's plates and replaced them with hot apple pie and ice cream for dessert. When dessert was done, she cleaned up from that too and began washing the dishes in the sink. The whole time though, the rest of us sat around the table and listened to her talk. She lost track of herself and broke into English twice more before we went to bed that night, to the great amusement of us kids. It was fun listening to her.

Towards the end of the evening, Uncle Otto managed to get a few questions in too, and he let Papa or Mom answer at length, however they wanted to. We talked late into the night, and even though everyone felt exhausted, no one wanted to go to bed. We were excited about being in America, and we finally felt as though we had a home, for the first time since leaving Rothenen.

The next morning, Papa, Karl, Gerhardt, Uncle Otto, and I got up early, and Uncle Otto began showing us around the farm. Tante Lisa had split us kids up between the two bedrooms upstairs, while Mom and Papa slept in the spare bedroom downstairs. The girls all wanted to sleep in, but us guys wanted to go exploring.

Uncle Otto's farm was wonderfully huge, and it took us several hours to see the whole thing. As we were coming back to the house, Papa asked him what he was going to plant the next spring, and Uncle Otto replied that he was thinking of selling the farm, or at least most of the land, since it was getting to be too much work for him. Then he asked what Papa was planning on doing here in the New World.

Papa started by reminding his brother-in-law that there were three blacksmiths in the family, and we were sure that we could find work. But then he explained about our pact, where we had all agreed to stay together until we had a house of our own. Staying with Uncle Otto was great, and Papa thanked him for his hospitality, but it wasn't the same as owning your own home. No, the German government had given him a fair sum of money as compensation for having lost their home and also for the last few months that he was in the Russian prison, so he was going to look for some land that he could buy, and then he was going to build a house on it.

At that, Uncle Otto brightened as if he had an idea. He said, "Well, why don't I sell the farm to you? That way we could still be close to each other, and I wouldn't have to worry about who was going to be living next to me. You could build your house right over there, on the old foundation." He pointed across the street towards a small pile of rubble in the snow.

Papa responded, "Hmm. Jah, that might just be a good idea. Let me talk to Maria about that."

That evening, the adults talked late into the night again, while us kids played games for a while and then went to bed. In the morning, Papa announced that he had bought 136 of Uncle Otto's 200 acres and that we were going to build a house where the old foundation was. Karl and I had an idea that this would happen, since we'd heard them talking before, but the girls were completely surprised. We all cheered and hollered, and then we put on our coats and paraded across the street to look at where our new home was going to be.

Uncle Otto had already shown the foundation to the male side of the family, but it was new to the girls. He and Papa walked around it several times, pointing here and there and sharing ideas about how the house would look and where this or that would go. Mom or one of us kids sometimes added one of our own thoughts, but Papa was the one coming up with most of the ideas. His creative juices were really flowing, and he was getting pretty excited. A dream had ignited inside Papa's heart, and with it, Papa had become a young man again.

The two of them spent the rest of the day planning things out, from drawing architectural sketches to writing down lists of materials. We would be doing nearly all the work, and Papa warned us that it would probably take at least a year before it was finished. Karl and I didn't really know much about building houses, but Papa and Uncle Otto had both built their own houses before, so they inspired us with their confidence.

The one problem that could slow us down, Papa noted, was finances. He had paid Uncle Otto for the land, so it was ours, but he'd used up all the money that the German government had given him in the process. Now we had to figure out how to buy the materials to build the house with. Papa thought perhaps we could set up a blacksmithing business, but Uncle Otto warned that the economy here was different than it was back in Germany. Everything was mechanized here, and although some of the local farmers had a few horses, they all used tractors for their plowing, etc. There was one blacksmith in town, but he barely had enough customers to stay in business. Instead, he said that we would do better with our skills to go into metalworking or manufacturing of some kind.

335

So upon hearing that, Papa informed Karl and me that the three of us were going to have to start looking for jobs the very next day.

Tante Lisa gave us a newspaper and showed us where the Help Wanted ads were, but that brought up another problem. None of us knew how to speak English. Not only could we not read the newspaper, but there was no chance at all that we could explain ourselves to an employer or understand what he was saying to us even if he did hire us. Up until that moment, we'd nearly forgotten that we were in a strange land where they didn't speak German. The times when Tante Lisa broke into English were merely a joke, and the people at Customs were used to dealing with foreigners who didn't speak English. When I was still in school, I'd started taking some English classes, but I was lazy and couldn't see why I'd ever need them, so I dropped out of them. Ruth was the only one of us who'd learned any English at all, and even she didn't know enough to carry on a basic conversation.

This would have been a good chance for us to become stymied and paralyzed with fear. Thankfully though, Uncle Otto offered to take us around to several places where he knew some people and where they could use people with our skills. The economy was booming too, so there was a good chance that they would hire us.

The first couple places that Uncle Otto took us weren't hiring, but then he took us to an Army / Navy Surplus Warehouse near Albany. Now this was just a few years after World War II, and the military surplus outfits back then were different than they are now. They had a lot of personal gear back then as they do today, but they also had stacks of huge folded up tents, rows of truck and tank engines, piles of unused building materials, boxes of airplane instrumentation panels, crates of pipe fittings taken from dismantled ships, and mountains of spare parts of every description from a myriad of unused or broken somethings that the military no longer had any use for. The warehouse looked like it was several acres in size, and the stuff inside it was strewn around without any apparent order at all, leaving only narrow paths from one pile of machinery to the next.

The owner of this collection had a second warehouse in Troy, just a few miles away, and he wanted to move all this stuff over there and organize it into useful, neat, categorized piles so that it could be put on display for people to sort through and buy. He was also Jewish and spoke Yiddish, which is close to German, so we were able to understand each other. Uncle Otto and he were friends too, so he hired Karl and me to take on the task of cleaning, moving, and organizing his treasures.

Because the owner's intent was to organize all this stuff at the same time as we moved it to the warehouse in Troy, we couldn't just start at one end of the warehouse and load everything in sight onto his flatbed truck until it was full up to the top of its wood slat sides. Instead, he wanted us to collect and move categories of stuff in each truck load, so we had to go rummaging around through the whole place, searching for all of whatever was in each category and load it on the truck like that. This way we could put everything in the one category in one place when we got to Troy.

That meant we had to do a lot of running back and forth to the truck with armloads of stuff from all over the warehouse. He had a couple hand trucks and carts for the bigger stuff, and we even used a fork lift for things like engines and crates of heavy metal parts. This was a very long and labor intensive project, and it took weeks for us to go through it all. We had worked as farm hands and blacksmiths in Germany, so we knew what hard work was all about, but we had never worked on a single large project like this before. It was sort of exciting for us that way, both because of the work and also because this was our first job in America.

We started out making seventy-five cents an hour, so at the end of our first week, the owner paid us $30 each. This was the first American money we'd ever had, and it seemed like a lot to us. Having it filled our hearts with excited dreams of what life in America was going to be like, and we redoubled our efforts the next week. We knew that if we worked hard and acted wisely, anything was possible in this land of opportunity. Of course, we gave all $60 to Papa for him to use towards building the house, and we didn't mind doing that at all. This was the first step towards accomplishing our dream, and it was our part, our contribution, so we were happy to be able to do it.

We also wanted to do a good job to please the owner, and we wanted to show him that we could understand what he was telling us. In many ways, we were proving to ourselves and to America at large that we could do it too, that we could carry our own weight, and that we were worthy of being called Americans. As a result, whenever the owner asked us to do something, which usually involved his discovering some other piece of whichever category of stuff we were loading into the truck right then, we would jump up and run over from where we were to answer his call as quickly as possible.

At first, he was very business-like while doing this. We would be collecting transmission gears from Army deuce and a half trucks, for instance, and he would find another box full of them. So he would politely call us over by name, often from the far side of the warehouse, and after he told us what he wanted us to do, we'd carry the box or whatever over to the truck and load it up. Then we'd go back to looking for more of them. He noticed how energetic we were and how quickly we ran to answer him, and he appreciated that. After two or three weeks went by though, and our enthusiasm remained high, despite our growing familiarity with him, he began to take us for granted somewhat. His calls shortened to just "Hey!" and a beckoning wave of his arm. Then, we started noticing that he was smirking or chuckling as he watched us bounding over the piles of rebar or zig zagging around stacks of landing strip mesh or dodging boxes of M-1 clips. After another couple weeks went by, he shortened his calls further still and started just whistling for us, as if we were his loyal Golden Retrievers. Sometimes he would do this just for the fun of it too, which we could tell because he didn't really have anything for us to carry once we got there. One time, after we had just gotten done answering him the time before, he watched us walking back to the far side of the warehouse, and as soon as we got there, he whistled for us again. When we arrived back where he was, all out of breath from running, he only had a few rags for us to carry, which he could've done himself, and that was the tipping point for me.

We had been becoming progressively more irritated with him over his treatment of us. We didn't mind hard work or even being told what to do. That was how manual labor was. But we did mind being toyed with, as if we were mere ignorant animals. We knew we were ignorant of the American culture and language, and we knew that this made us vulnerable to practical jokes from people who didn't understand. Yet this joke had gone on for way too long, and now I was livid.

I walked up to the owner of the warehouse, who was nearly beside himself snickering at us, and in my very best English, with my face just inches from his, I defiantly told him, "I NO DOG!" Then I turned around and led Karl back to the other side of the warehouse, without even touching the owner's pile of rags.

The owner of the warehouse must not have been all that bad though, because this was the last time he did that sort of thing. The job was nearly done by this time, but we still had several days of work left. He didn't call for us as much after that, and when he did, he was much more respectful and always had serious work for us to do. Nonetheless, our experience with him was quite an eye-opener, and we began to realize that Americans weren't all as magnanimous as Uncle Otto and Aunt Lisa were.

After Karl and I finished cleaning up the warehouse, the owner let us go, so we started looking for work again, with Uncle Otto's help as before. He would take one or the other or both of us to a place and ask to speak with the owner or hiring manager, who he usually knew. Then he would introduce us and explain how we'd come there, what we could do, and what we were looking for by way of work. The owner would inevitably want to ask us questions, so Uncle Otto would interpret for us. Most of the time though, the owner would also want to hear us talk in English, and since we hardly knew any at all, that would be the end of the interview. We'd been in the US for a couple months by this time, so we were starting to pick up some English. We watched TV, listened to the radio, and read the newspaper diligently, every day, trying to learn as quickly as possible. It didn't seem to work for us this time, and several weeks went by without us finding any work.

One such typical interview was at a place called Cronan Brothers Truck Body Shop, in Nassau, where they built custom truck bodies. Harold Cronan was the office manager, while his brother George was the shop manager. This interview ended just like all the others, with one exception. Harold told Uncle Otto, "When the young boy knows more English, he can come back, but he has to know more English." That was somewhat encouraging, but six weeks went by before I was able to revisit that offer.

Harold Cronan, you see, was also a widower of several years, and as God would have it, he became interested in Uncle Otto's daughter, Hilde, who was in her late twenties at the time and still living with Uncle Otto and the rest of us. One day in late winter, Harold asked her out on a dinner date, and she accepted. When he arrived at Uncle Otto's house to pick her up though, she wasn't ready yet, so Harold sat down in the living room to wait.

I'd been using all my spare time to study English, and I'd learned quite a bit, so I saw this as my golden opportunity. I came out of the kitchen and introduced myself. Harold looked vaguely bored or uncomfortable, and he probably didn't really want to talk to me. But I knew that he didn't have much of a choice, so I forged ahead and proceeded to rattle off every single English phrase that I'd learned so far. Then, just as I was exhausting my supply of English words, Hilde came out of her bedroom.

Suddenly Harold found himself in a very awkward situation. He was anxious to leave with Hilde, but he also wanted to impress her. At the same time, everyone in the family knew that I was talking to him because I wanted him to hire me, and he knew it too. I had just finished demonstrating my newfound command of the English language, and now I was waiting for an answer. So he said, "Do you have a job yet?" I said "No," and he replied, "Okay, come to the shop on Monday."

Just like that, I had the job. I'm not sure whether I'd actually impressed him with how much English I knew, or whether he was more concerned about impressing Hilde. He hired me though, and that's all I cared about.

When Monday came, Harold introduced me to his brother George. George showed me all around the shop and told me what all the English words were for every piece of equipment and item of supply that they had. He also explained what I was supposed to do on the job, building the tailgates for his truck bodies. When he went away for a while, I built the entire tailgate assembly, including the hinges, and attached it to the truck. George was impressed later, when he returned and saw that I'd already finished the first one and was working on a second. That set the pattern for the entire week. Every time George told me to do something, I finished it without further instruction and considerably before he was ready for me to finish it. By the time he came by to pay me on Friday night, he asked me if my brother Karl was working yet, and when I said "No," George hired him too.

Meanwhile, Papa got a job at a factory where they made crates for artillery shells. He worked with a saw machine that automatically cut the boards to the right lengths. Unfortunately, that job didn't last very long before they closed the plant down. Things were going very well for us at Cronan Bros. though, so I asked George and Harold if Papa could come and work for them. They agreed, so the three of us got to work together.

Not long after that though, Harold hired a younger fellow to be the shop foreman. This guy was in his early thirties, and although he probably knew a lot about building trucks, he acted like he knew a lot more. Harold and George called everyone together for a meeting to introduce him, and the guy very blatantly announced how highly he thought of himself by saying, "Well, I was made foreman because I know more about building truck bodies than anybody in this place." Everyone just smiled and snorted, but as the days went by, he grew into a source of genuine irritation.

Anyone who has worked with a younger boss who may or may not know a lot more about your job than you do, but who thinks he certainly does, and yet doesn't know his own limitations, knows that this is a recipe for problems on the job. But add to that the problem of not knowing the language or the customs of the land you live in, because you're a new immigrant, and you have the ingredients of an explosion. That's the situation that my Papa found himself in one day with this new foreman.

I was welding the insides of a truck door together that day, when Papa ran up to me with a worried, confused look on his face. He said in German that the new foreman was trying to tell him to do something, but he wouldn't speak slowly enough for Papa to understand him, so Papa asked me if I could interpret for him. Before I could say anything though, the foreman ran up behind Papa and started screaming at him.

He said, "Hey you, didn't you hear what I said? You get the (blankcty blank) back there and put those pieces together like I told you to, or I'm gonna (blanking) fire you!" Then he noticed that Papa was talking to me and ignoring him, so he turned his ire towards me too. "If he doesn't do what I tell him, he will get fired! I'm going to (blanking) fire him! I'm going to give him a (blankety blank) Pink Slip!"

The man's face was red with rage, and his nostrils were flaring. He had no idea what was really going on there, yet he was incensed that Papa wasn't doing what he was telling him to do.

Papa on the other hand, had never had a problem like this on a job in his life. Papa was quite willing to do the work, even the way that the foreman was telling him to. He just couldn't understand what the man was saying. It was strange. In that moment, I saw my Papa, and all the strength and dignity he had as a soldier, blacksmith, Civil Defense Coordinator, Fire Chief, lay preacher, and ex-prisoner of war were gone. Instead, he was confused and frightened, and all because this man with a very small mind did not have the sense to speak slowly in the presence of a foreigner nor the understanding to realize that shouting at someone who doesn't speak English will not make your words any more clear to them.

So in the next moment, I lost it too. Perhaps I was merely defending my Papa, or perhaps I was reacting to months of frustration with a people who, despite their unprecedented level of freedom and their own multicultural roots, had forgotten what it was like to be strangers in a strange land. I held up my hand and said, "Wait a minute." Then in my broken English, I told him, growing angrier with every syllable, "You better not treat my Papa that way. He wants to do the work, and you're raving like that. Come on out. If you want to be a big shot, let's come on out!" By the end of my speech, I was shaking my fist in his face. I turned and marched out to the parking lot, fully expecting him to follow me and give me the opportunity to pound his face in, which I so longed for right then.

When I got out there though, I found that I was alone. He never did follow me. I waited for several minutes, until my own temper had cooled down, and then I went back in and looked around.

Papa was back at his station, with George by his side, patiently showing him what to do. The foreman wasn't anywhere on the shop floor at all, but one of the other workers cast a sidelong glance at the office door in response to my questioning look. I never heard any more about that incident, so I don't know what happened with the foreman, but Papa, Karl, and I kept on working there for months afterwards.

While all of this was going on at work, we were also slowly making progress building our new house. Karl and I both added our salaries to Papa's, and every week we used practically the whole amount to buy more building materials or to pay a contractor to do something. As soon as we'd come home from work at the warehouse or the shop, we'd eat supper and then start working on the house right away. We worked on it all day Saturday too, so the only time off we ever got was on Sunday.

During the winter and again in the summer, we would go into the woods after work and cut down trees. Then we'd use Uncle Otto's tractor to pull the trees out to the road, where we'd load them up on his truck and take them to the local saw mill. We'd trade our freshly cut trees for cured lumber at $19.50 per thousand board feet, which was a pretty good deal even back then. We stored them up over the winter, so that we'd have plenty of lumber to start building with once we got the basement done.

Uncle Otto's son, Herman, knew someone who had a bulldozer, and we contracted with him to dig out the foundation for us. It was still winter then; however, so the ground was hard, and the dozer kept on throwing its tracks. By early spring, we were ready to start laying the foundation, so we rented a small mixer and bought a bunch of bags of cement mix. We made our own forms from plywood and purchased the cement as we went along, doing about one section per week, adding as many rocks as we could find to the mix to cut down on the amount of cement we had to buy.

By summer time, we were putting up the frame and the roof and forming the inside walls on the first floor. The house was a Cape Cod style, with a small covered front porch leading to a hallway inside. We built two bedrooms, a kitchen, living room, and bathroom on that floor, and we managed to get all that part finished by mid-September.

We also had a full basement, which was exposed on the south corner, so we could have a door leading into it, while the other three corners were underground. The house faced northeast, away from the road, and the ground was level with the main floor on that side but sloped steeply down until it was level with the basement floor on the south corner. The road curved around three sides of the house, and on the west end of that curve, it went through something of a saddle between a small hill on its south side and the large hill that our house faced to the north. We started the driveway on that saddle and brought it uphill until it was around in front of the house. Towards the east end of the curve and level with the basement door, was an old abandoned well, made of stone, which I spent one hot summer's day cleaning out and extending to about twenty-five feet deep. That was a lot of hard work, but down in the bottom of the shaft it was much cooler, so I think I had it easier than Karl did, who was helping me by carrying the mud and dirt away as I dug it up.

That fall we roughed out the frames for two large upstairs bedrooms and a big closet, but we didn't get them finished by the time we moved in that December, just two weeks before Christmas, 1952. We also installed a pot-bellied wood stove in the basement with a fourteen-foot horizontal flue to the chimney. Such a long flue extension wasn't really necessary, but Papa wanted it so we could get as much heat as possible from the stove, which was our only source of warmth. We kept the basement door open and the upstairs door closed, and all ten of us slept on the main floor throughout that winter, crowded as it was.

Moving in was the easiest part of the whole building process, because even after thirteen months of living in the US, we still didn't have any furniture and hardly anything else either, except our clothes and personal items. But the Saturday after we moved in, we got an incredible early Christmas present.

We were attending East Nassau Community Church back then, which was a small, closely knit family church, and unbeknownst to us, one of the deacons called Uncle Otto that Saturday to see if we were going to be home. A couple hours later, while we were working upstairs on the unfinished bedrooms, Papa spied a parade of cars and pickup trucks coming up the hill and going into our driveway.

We rushed downstairs to meet our visitors, only to discover practically the entire church at our doorstep, laden with gifts of every description. The women and children had boxes of plates, cookware, kitchen utensils, towels, sheets, blankets, toys, and so on, plus a few pies, a cake, a small Christmas tree, and a bouquet of poinsettias. The men and boys, meanwhile, came up behind them carrying furniture. They had a couple beds with mattresses, a couch, table, several chairs, a couple lamps, and several other things. Papa was totally caught off guard and kept on saying, "What's going on? What's going on?" We had never heard of an American housewarming party, so we were completely floored by it. All our work came to a halt that afternoon, and Mom literally broke down in tears at how compassionate these people were. We laughed and talked with everyone for hours before they started leaving, and then we spent the rest of the afternoon and evening unpacking and arranging all their gifts. Never in all our days had we seen such generosity, and we saw it as a testament to the heart of the American people and as a confirmation of our decision to make our home in America.

Only a few months later, in April, 1953, in time for my twentieth birthday, I received another surprise gift of sorts, from the American people. It came just a week after I nearly severed the middle finger of my left hand with a circular saw while helping finish an addition on our church. It was an invitation to come before the Draft Board in Albany.

Coming into New York Harbor, everyone on the General Taylor was so happy & excited to see the Statue of Liberty

We didn't actually go through Ellis Island, but they recognized us anyway

The Immigration Inprocessing Center on our debarkation pier in New York City

My Parent's Application for U.S. Citizenship

America!

Dad & I on our way to work at Cronin Brothers' Truck & Body Shop

Uncle Otto & Tante Lisa's house, where we lived while we were building our house

Our family around our first car

Mom & Dad in front of our house

Our house in East Nassau, NY, near Albany

Our family, just before I was drafted into the U.S. Army

*Jay Wessel, Myself, &
1Lt. Vertise, while we
were stationed in
Kaiserslautern, Germany,
& ministering in Youth
For Christ*

*The convalescent home
in Engkenbach,
Germany, where the old
man's arm was healed
when we prayed for him*

*Me and two buddies
going on maneuvers
from Kaiserslautern*

*Karl Schafer
advertising an
evangelistic service
that was used to
help start a church
in Heidelberg*

*Me, posing with Uncle
Hans, in Alten Essen,
Germany*

*My
Naturalization
Certificate*

19

Full Circle

The purpose of the Draft Board was to determine if you were eligible for military service. If you were, you got drafted, and if you weren't, you'd be sent home. Because of that, one of the main features of the board was a complete physical, where we had to strip and parade around from one station to another on the cold floor of the Albany High School gymnasium. One of the doctors there noticed my bandaged finger and pulled me out of line to look at it near the end of the process. He took the bandage off and looked it over very carefully, while I stood there shivering. Finally he announced, "Well, you're gonna make a good soldier anyhow." Everyone else got a kick out of that, and muffled laughter broke out here and there. I didn't bother telling them that my wound was genuine.

I passed the Draft Board, and then they bussed me down to Camp Devons, CT, for entrance processing and testing. I wasn't sure how well I'd do on the ASVAB (Armed Services Vocational Aptitude Battery test), since

I'd only been learning English for the last eighteen months, but I scored in the top one-third of the class and nearly made it to Officer Candidate School.

We spent about three days at Camp Devons, and then they put us on another bus and sent us off. This time they didn't even tell us where we were going.

We ended up at Ft. Dix, NJ, where I joined B Company, of the 47th Basic Infantry Training Regiment. I spent the next sixteen weeks there going through the One Station Unit Training (OSUT) Infantry School as an 11B.

Everyone who's ever been in the military has their favorite Basic Training story to tell, and mine has me nearly getting my head blown off during a night attack exercise. We were practicing nighttime fire and maneuver in battle buddy teams, and we were using blanks for ammunition. It was my turn to stop and provide covering fire, while my buddy was supposed to run past me to his next firing position. Somehow he forgot what he was supposed to do or became disoriented or got too excited or tripped or couldn't tell where he was or wasn't quite all there or something, because next thing I knew, he came up behind me and fired his rifle within inches of my head. The blast was so powerful it knocked my helmet off and left me covering my ears with my hands, in pain, trying to get the ringing to stop. I started screaming for the cadre and told them that I wasn't going any further until this guy was taken out of the exercise. They obliged when they heard what he did, and they took him to the hospital for observation.

He got me back though. Later on, when he came back from the hospital, we were cleaning our rifles, and I'd already finished with plenty of time to spare; whereas, he'd barely even started and looked hopelessly lost amidst a jumble of parts and springs. He was my battle buddy though, and the Drill Sergeants said that I was supposed to help him. So I picked up his stock and cleaning kit and said, "Now lets clean your weapon. I'll show you exactly how to strip it and how to clean it, and I'll even clean it for you. I will show you exactly what to do, and then you do the exact same thing, and I will watch and make sure you do it right." I sat down with him and cleaned his rifle until it was spotless, showing it to him and explaining what I was doing the whole time. When I was done, I said, "Now you do it, and I will make sure you do it the right way." But he turned it around on me and said, "Why should I clean it? You just cleaned it." Oh, well.

When I got done with Basic, they sent me home for two weeks of leave. This was a surprise to my family, as they didn't know where I'd gone to begin with, and the Army didn't let me tell them when I was coming home either. When I got there, my brother and sisters wanted to take me around to several church youth groups in the area to show me off in my uniform. Then I spent the rest of my time at home helping Papa and Karl install a new oil-fired furnace in our basement.

After I returned to Ft. Dix at the end of my leave, I had a two-week layover, and then I received orders, along with the rest of my OSUT unit, to go to Zweibrüken, Germany. When my Mom heard about it, she broke into tears and wept long and bitterly, since her brother had been killed near there during World War I.

With that on my mind, I boarded yet another bus and headed for Camp Kilmer, NJ, near the Military Shipping Terminal on the Hudson River, just south of Hoboken. At Camp Kilmer, they put me on another Liberty ship, the USS Randolph, which looked exactly like the General Taylor, and which was bound for Bremerhaven. The irony of it was captivating, since that was the very port that we'd left to come to New York from, in the same type of vessel, exactly two years and seven days earlier. The oddest thing about it was that as a German, I was now returning to Germany as a member of the very forces that were occupying my country, the American Army.

I wasn't bothered by that fact, but it was striking. And it was advantageous too, or at least the other guys on the ship thought so. They were actually envious of me. They would say things like, "You're gonna have a great time. You are gonna go out every night with a different girl, and oh, what a time you are gonna have!" They thought of my knowledge of the land and the language as an advantage when it came to finding girls, and they were eager to enlist my help in their own quests of that nature. That thought scared me, on the other hand, because I was a Christian, and because I wanted to live a clean life, one that was pleasing to God. Yet I knew that my abilities with the locals could also be turned to God's glory, and I was looking forward to that part.

The trip over was mostly uneventful, to me anyway. It was my third ocean voyage, so I was used to it by this time. It wasn't quite as peaceful to most of the other guys though. As we were sitting down to our very first meal at sea, one of them asked me, "I understand you came from Germany on a ship?" I said, "Yes, I did." His face was pale though, and he looked very uncomfortable as he responded, "How was it? Is it gonna get worse than this?"

"Any worse that This," I thought? The sea and the wind were calm, and the day was downright balmy. The ship was gently rocking on some fair weather waves, and there was the rhythmic throbbing of the engines, but other than that, you could hardly tell that we were moving at all. So I said, "Aah, this is nothing.

We're hardly even moving." Obviously comforted by
what I had said, the guy added an extra shade of green
to his face, took his tray over to the tray return, and
then went out and barfed his dinner over the side of the
ship. Inspired by his leadership, a couple other guys
joined him there a minute later.

After that, I spent most of my time on board
helping my fellow soldiers, who seemed to be
continually sea sick. Sometimes I had to roust them
out of bed and get them outside to get some fresh air
and to look at the horizon, which would help their
equilibrium. Other times, I made sure they were eating
properly, since I'd found that a full stomach helps
prevent sea sickness too. Several of them thanked me
afterwards, but I was still amused by how weak and
helpless these otherwise rough and boisterous soldiers
were on that trip.

Once we landed in Bremerhaven, we went by
train to the Army Replacement Center, or "Repo Depot,"
in Zweibrüken, just south of Saarbrüken on the French
border. On our way there, we were served a meal, and
while we were eating, I noticed this German conductor
who looked familiar as he walked by. Later on, I
stopped him and struck up a conversation with him in
German. It turned out he had worked for the dealer
who sold horses to the Swiss Army general when I was
Pieter Mahnke's apprentice in Hedendorf, and he'd
helped me shoe the horses that the general was buying.
This was only a couple hours after landing in Germany,
so I started getting excited. I figured if it only took me
two hours inside Germany to meet someone that I knew
from before, then anything was possible.

We stayed in Zweibrüken for two days to get
briefed on local conditions and policies and to be issued
special gear that USAREUR wanted everyone there to
have. While I was there, I also received a rather

unwelcome surprise when they told me that my readiness status was being downgraded from 1A to 1B. They never told me why, but that meant that I could no longer be an Infantryman, 11B. I was going to have to reclassify to something else, and they gave me the choices of either being an Artilleryman or a Blacksmith Engineer.

If you've read this far, you know that wasn't a hard choice. As a Journeyman blacksmith anyway, I was already qualified for the job, which meant I wouldn't need any additional training. I could keep on doing what I loved to do and get paid for it, even in the Army. In practical terms, it meant that I would be assigned to the 186th Engineering Service Company in Kaiserslautern, only about thirty miles northeast of Zweibrüken.

Kaiserslautern, or K-Town as the Americans called it, was a huge US Army town, with several large logistics bases in the area. It was originally a large rail hub, which was what attracted the Americans to it. They also built a major hospital nearby in Landstuhl, and the Air Force put a fighter base in the area too, at Sembach. Later on, the French built a large air base there too, called Ramstein, which the US Air Force took over as an airlift base.

The 186th was based at the Daenner Kaserne (Barracks), on the east end of the city, just beyond the main city cemetery. We were part of the US Army Headquarters in Europe. Consequently, our mission was to provide support, tents, and electricity for the Army's general staff while they were out in the field with the line units. The generals hardly ever went out in the field, so it was an easy job, mostly just equipment maintenance and guard duty.

When I arrived, our commander was glad to see me, because I was a blacksmith, but my first job a few days later had nothing to do with smithing. He called me into the orderly room and asked if I could read and write German. I said I could, and he said, "I've got a big favor to ask of you;" whereupon, he produced two large shoeboxes full of purchase receipts. These were for things that he'd bought on the local economy with unit funds. Now he had to turn them in to Finance to account for his purchases, but the receipts were all in German, so he needed someone to translate them before he could turn them in. Thus, I spent the next three weeks translating his receipts with the help of his secretary to type them up. This was a good thing though, because it indebted him to me, which came in very handy not long afterward.

I was a PV2 at the time, but the commander rewarded me for translating his receipts by promoting me to PFC before I had finished my required time-in-grade and also before I'd completed the unit's Initial Entry Program (IEP). Newly arrived soldiers were put on IEP status to acclimate them to the area, their job, and base rules. It was a multi-phase program where you were restricted to base for the first phase, and then you were restricted to going within thirty miles of the base for the second phase. Normally you wouldn't get any off-base weekend passes at all during this time, but since I was promoted just before Christmas, I got a four-day pass for New Years weekend, with the stipulation that I stay within that thirty-mile radius of the base.

For most American soldiers this would not have been a problem. Kaiserslautern was a city of about twenty thousand people, not including Americans, so there were plenty of things for soldiers to do right in town. But I was German. I spoke German, I knew how to get around in Germany, and I knew people in Germany. One of those people was a certain pretty young lady named Ilse Corleis, who was the pianist at the church we attended when we lived in Jork. I had a crush on her while we were still in Jork, and after I was drafted and found out that I was returning to Germany with the US Army, I wrote her to suggest that we get together. She wrote back and said she'd like that.

Ilse lived in Hamburg, which was about four hundred miles north of Kaiserslautern. That presented a problem, because my IEP status required me to check in with the Charge of Quarters (CQ) in our orderly room at midnight on Friday night and at 0100 on Saturday night. For some reason though, that didn't bother me, and as soon as I got off base, I caught a bus to the train station and bought a ticket to Hamburg.

On the way there, we stopped in Hanover to change trains. There was an hour's layover, so I went to a café and got a bite to eat. While I was eating, the door opened, and an American MP came in. Now I knew that I was in the wrong, disobeying my pass restriction like that, and my guilty conscience knew that the MPs patrolled train stations, etc, looking for pass violators and AWOL soldiers. So when this MP got his meal and sat down at my table to eat it, my heart was pounding. We talked about this and that, and I tried not to look nervous. Thankfully, he never asked to see my travel papers.

In Hamburg, I stayed with Ilse's family for a couple days, and the two of us went bicycling and got to know each other. I thought I was in love with her, so I asked if I could kiss her. She told me No, and I left it at that. When it was time for me to return to K-Town, I left without making a fuss, though I was rather disappointed.

Once I arrived back at our orderly room though, the knot of guilt returned to my stomach, and a horrible sense of sinking doom filled my being as I approached the log book that I had to sign in with. My name had to

appear among the pass holders signing in on Friday
night and again on Saturday night, and I knew it
wouldn't, because I wasn't there to sign it. The
commander would check the book on Monday morning,
and when my name didn't show up, I would get in
trouble. Something made me flip back through the
pages to see who else was signed in or not on those
days, and when I did, to my amazement, my name was
there, just as if I'd signed in myself. Monday morning
came, and nothing happened out of the ordinary. The
only thing I could figure was that the commander had
come each of those nights to check who had signed in or
not, and he must have filled my name in himself. I was
very grateful for God's allowing for my stupidity, and I
resolved not to tempt His mercy any more.

That weekend brought me back to reality, so I
made every effort to stay clean, obey the rules, and not
provoke either God or the commander. The nature of
our mission at the 186th was very laid back though,
and we hardly had any work to do at all, except when
the generals went out to the field, which wasn't that
often. What little I did do was either equipment
maintenance or pulling guard duty. As a result, I
continued to get weekend passes, and I probably ended
up with more of them than anyone else in the unit.

Since I was now being allowed off base more, and
since I was trying to behave myself and obey God more,
I soon started seeking Christian fellowship in the area.
The first place I looked, of course, was the Base Chapel,
which was right on the outskirts of the base, on
Mannheimer Strasse. The Chaplain there had to
perform three different services every week, one for the
Protestants, one for the Catholics, and another for the
Jews, and none of those services were particularly
exciting to the participants because of that. There was
a soldier helping the Chaplain in the Protestant service

though, and he seemed to hold out the promise of real fellowship. His name was Jay Wessel, and he was one of the leaders of a monthly Saturday Youth for Christ meeting.

The first month after I got off IEP, I attended his YFC meeting, and I was excited by what I found. They had someone playing the guitar and someone else leading praise songs, and then there were worship songs and strong prayer after that. The preaching was relaxed and realistic, and the whole atmosphere was more like the Pentecostal or Baptist services that I was used to. When the service was over, I introduced myself to Jay, and he introduced me to the rest of his YFC group. The other main leader was a Lt. Verthrees, whose wife played the accordion and guitar. He was the main YFC leader, so he spoke at most of the meetings. There was also a Pentecostal sergeant from Texas who played the guitar, though I don't remember his name. Jay and the Verthreeses were Nazarenes, and there was a Baptist in the core group too, but I don't remember his name either. All of us were born-again Christians though, so we didn't care what our other labels might be.

Before I left that meeting, Jay and the Lt (pronounced El-Tee) invited me to come with them to a convalescent home meeting they had on Sunday afternoons. They actually had one on Saturday and another on Sunday, and they visited an orphanage on Saturdays too. I was excited about this, because it would give me something constructive to do on weekends, and it would give me lots of Christian fellowship too.

The convalescent home that they went to on Sunday afternoons was in the small town of Enkenbach, just north of Kaiserslautern, and it was run by some Mennonites. We bought some coffee and cake on our

way there, and after the service was over, we would pass
that out to the hundred or so people in the auditorium.
The Lt's wife played her accordion, while the Texan
Pentecostal played his guitar, and we all sang English
praise songs. Jay did the speaking, but he persuaded
me to translate for him, which is something that I
started doing on a regular basis, regardless of who was
speaking.

That night, I was so on fire for the Lord that I
promised Him that if He gave me the opportunity to
minister on my own, no matter what it was, I would do
it. I prayed long and hard that night, for our YFC
group, for the Germans at the convalescent home, for
my family, for the guys in my unit, and for several other
people; and then I read the Word and then prayed some
more. I hadn't been this enthusiastic for the Lord since
we lived in Jork, and it felt great.

The next week, I went with the YFC group to the
orphanage. We stopped at the Commissary on the way
out and bought three gallons of ice cream, plus some
plastic bowels and spoons. When we got there, the
praise team played for a while again, and then the Lt's
wife got out a flannelgraph and told Bible stories to the
kids. I was ecstatic at being able to interpret for her,
and I began to see that this could be a real calling from
the Lord upon my life. The kids loved listening to us
and they joined right in for the songs and the stories
too. When all that was done, we got out the ice cream
and gave as much to each of the several dozen kids as
they wanted, until it all ran out. After that, we took the
kids out in groups for rides in the Texan Pentecostal's
big Buick. We had so much fun, and it was so exciting
to see the kids be blessed by something so simple.

Once we finished up at the orphanage, we went
on to the other convalescent home that afternoon. This
one was actually a rescue mission for alcoholic men,

operated by the Lutherans. There weren't as many at those meetings, maybe a dozen on a good day, but we gave our testimonies and sang and did some low-key preaching for them, and I interpreted as I had at the other places.

There were also Wednesday night and Sunday night services at the Chapel, and frequently, Jay or the Lt got to speak at those too. I didn't get to attend all of them, because of my guard duty schedule, but I went to all I could. Soon I had become part of the core YFC group, which we called the GI Gospel Team. It was a lot of fun, and it was so exciting, because we could see the impact our simple message was having on people, young and old. Hardly a week went by without someone receiving Jesus into their lives as their Savior, and we could see miracles happening in people's lives. Some of the old men at the rescue mission and some soldiers at the YFC meetings were delivered from alcohol. Families were restored, and hurting children were comforted and encouraged. It seemed as though God was doing something new at practically every meeting, and a sense of expectancy and anticipation pervaded our group, as we wanted to see what God would do next.

After I'd been part of this YFC group for a couple months, I got a first hand opportunity to see what God would do when given the chance. At the end of the YFC meetings, Jay, the Lt, his wife, the Texan Pentecostal guy, and I got together to decide who was going to speak at the next meeting. We did this for the other meetings too, and I'd already given my testimony at the convalescent homes and the orphanage, and I'd interpreted for them as well, but I was shocked when Jay and the Lt invited me to speak at the next YFC meeting. The YFC meetings were larger, with well over a hundred people, and they were more formal too, since they were held in the Chapel and were for American soldiers, rather than for German civilians. I had never given an actual sermon before, and I certainly didn't feel prepared to give a sermon in English to Americans. I might've tried preaching in German, but I was still very halting in my English, so the thought of preaching to Americans scared me.

On the other hand, I remembered my commitment to the Lord after that first convalescent home meeting, where I told Him that I would do anything for Him if He provided the opportunity. I hadn't said anything to Jay or the Lt about this, but God knew my heart. This was obviously God's idea of taking me up on my offer, so there was no way I could turn them down. Now I just had to figure out what to do.

When I got back to my barracks that evening, I started praying feverishly. I needed God to intervene miraculously I thought, so I prayed that He would somehow improve my English skills about a hundred-fold so that I wouldn't be embarrassed when it came time to speak. Hmm. So that I wouldn't be embarrassed. Well, that's what I was praying anyway, but I was also praying for the Lord to be glorified through me, for the Lord to speak through me even in my weakness, and for His Word to go forth from me and have its intended affect on the people in the congregation.

I prayed all that continually for a couple days, but honestly, I was still scared. I knew that I simply didn't have the words in English to say what I wanted to say, and I feared that I would lock up and make a fool out of myself.

Along about Tuesday though, while I was on guard duty, I was praying and crying out to the Lord for help, "Lord You know I don't speak English, and Lord You know my English is so bad. Lord what have I done?

Help me, help me, help me. Lord what have I done?" I prayed like that for a long time. I knew that He could speak through me and that this was all in His plan, so I believed that He would provide the ability when the time came. But that belief was only in my head, not in my heart. In my heart, I was still afraid.

As I was praying at my guard post though, I suddenly and distinctly heard the word, "Fast." I'd had teaching on fasting, but I'd never actually done it, so I was a little hesitant at first. I kept on hearing that in my spirit though, so I determined that I wouldn't eat anything for the rest of the week, until the time of the meeting.

The knowledge that I was obeying God by fasting gave me confidence that He would work it all out, so the nature of my praying changed. Now I was praying for God to show me what I should say and how I should say it. I had been reading the Word regularly in my devotions, but now I delved deeper into it and consumed it during all my spare time. I took notes and started writing down ideas that the Lord put in my spirit as I was reading His Word. By the time Saturday afternoon arrived, I was ready and eager to see what God would do through me as I preached.

During my sermon, I didn't speak any better English than I ever had. I was stiff, halting, and often had to search for words. I preached for half an hour like that, and I finished off with a simple, "Thank you for your attention." But then an Air Force sergeant got up and said, "After what you heard it's not right just to close the service. Let's have an altar call. Who wants to give their life to Jesus?" At first no one moved, but then to my amazement, an Army sergeant came down from the back, knelt at the altar, and accepted Jesus as his Savior. He was the only one that night, but I knew that the angels were rejoicing over that one. I knew that God had used me to bring a man to salvation. That was a very humbling, beautiful experience for me, because to God, there is nothing greater for us to do than to bring someone new into the Kingdom.

The Lord continued to do things like that, and frequently it was at the rescue mission where the most exciting things happened. One time there were eight men there for our service, and when I gave the altar call, seven of them gave their hearts to Christ. That meeting was strange though, because at the end of it, the Lutheran pastor in charge of the place took us aside and said, "I know you boys were well-intentioned, but I really think you went a bit too far there.You shouldn't ask somebody to commit their lives to the Lord in public like that. That is a very private matter." We were polite, but we had to disagree with him. The Scripture is clear about that. You have to make a decision for Christ, and it needs to be in public. So despite what that pastor said, I was glad that I'd given a public altar call. After all, accepting Jesus into your life is so simple, if more people asked people to do that, perhaps more people would receive Him into their hearts.

A few weeks later at the convalescent home, something else exciting happened. Many times after our meetings were over, we would give people the opportunity to come up and ask us questions. No one ever took us up on that, except this one time when the Lt was preaching, with me interpreting, on how God is able to handle any problem you have, whether it's physical, mental, financial, or whatever. He preached, "Whatever problems you have, He has the answers, whether, if it is physically, spiritually, mentally, financially. No matter what it is, God can heal it. If you need healing, He can heal you. If you need finances, He can provide them. If you need mental uplifting or anything, He can do it."

At the end of that sermon, after the altar call, we asked if anyone had any questions, and this one elderly man started speaking to me in German so fast that I couldn't understand him. He also seemed to have a problem pronouncing things. But upon seeing him doing this, the sister that was running the home that day came over to him and said, "Now calm down and speak slowly, so we will understand you."

Then he composed himself and said in his rasping voice, "I was a soldier in Belgium, and there was an explosion next to me, and since then my right arm has been paralyzed, and my speech has not been correct. I want you to pray for me, so God will heal me."

I turned to Lt. Verthrees and said, "He wants us to pray for him for healing, that God will heal his hand."

The Lt's face went pale, and he said, "What are we going to do now?" Several other members of our group let their mouths drop open, as we all became petrified of this man's request. We knew in theory that God could heal people, you see, but we'd never actually seen Him do it, and none of us had even so much as prayed for someone to be healed, at least not directly. Yet we also felt that we couldn't back down from what we'd just preached. Did we really believe what we said, or didn't we? We all believed that, but now we found ourselves backed into a corner which only God could get us out of, and then only by a literal miracle.

The man was waiting for an answer, so I told him, "All we can do is pray for you. God will have to do the actual healing." The Lt, meanwhile, turned around and started leaving, saying, "I am going to pray for awhile." Now only I was there with this old man, and I had to explain why the Lt had just walked off into another room and taken the rest of our group with him.

I was scared stiff. I wouldn't have minded if the ground had opened up and swallowed me whole. I wanted to apologize and explain our way out of it. I was hoping that the man would change his mind and say he didn't want us to pray after all. But instead, I just stood there and smiled at him and everyone else, and we waited for our group to finish praying and come out of the other room.

Finally, the Lt and the others came out of the room and back towards where the rest of us were. Lt Verthrees took his Bible and placed it on the corner of a table near us. Then he reached out and picked up the man's limp hand and placed it on the Bible and put his own hand on top of it. The Lt next said, "Jay Wessel and Herb Flemming," nodding towards the Bible, so we put our hands over the top of theirs too.

Then the Lt prayed, "Lord, You say in Your Word that You answer our prayers, so heal his paralyzed arm." That was about it. Jay and I each added a sentence or so too, and then we all ended with "Amen," but that was all. We didn't scream or holler or jump up and down or get emotional. In fact, we didn't even know about any of that. We prayed very simply, short and to the point, and that was all.

When we were done praying though, while everyone else was wondering what to do next, I surprised us all (myself included) by saying to the man, "Now, let's see what the Lord has done. Lift your hand."

Without thinking, he moved to comply with my request, and under his own power, he raised his arm up to about shoulder height. Then he realized what he'd done, and his eyes became wide as headlights. He hesitated at that point, so I grabbed his arm and raised it the rest of the way. Then I let it go and told him, "Now move it to the right. Now move it to the left. Now put it behind you. Ok, now put it in front of you." Each time, he did exactly as I said, and each time, his mouth dropped a little further towards the floor. The rest of us had already lost our jawbones on the floor tile and were seriously trying to suck up all the air in the entire room, but I wasn't paying them any attention. The Holy Spirit was moving on me and causing me to focus on what He was doing, instead of on what was going on around me.

We didn't know if the man's speech was healed yet, so next I had the three of us put our hands on his head and pray quickly for God to heal his speech too. Then I told him, "Now repeat after me, 'Jesus rettet, Jesus heilt, Preis der Herr.'" (Jesus saves, Jesus heals, Praise the Lord.) And he did exactly that. He spoke those words as plain as day, without any problem at all. After that, we talked some more, and he thanked us for praying for him. Then he walked out of the room and used his healed hand to open the door and to shut it behind him.

On the way back to base in the Lt's car, we couldn't contain ourselves any longer. We were shouting and whooping it up, praising the Lord, and slapping each other on the backs. Right in front of our eyes, God had done a real live miracle. He'd used us too. Us. And we weren't professionals or anything either. We were just soldiers. But God came through and demonstrated His mighty power for us, to bring glory to His Name and to show Himself real. Nothing. Absolutely nothing, could ever convince us that God wasn't Who He said He was from then on. How powerful, mighty, and compassionate He is towards us when we humble ourselves and simply obey Him.

The next time we went to the convalescent home, the old soldier met us outside the door. He was waiting for us. As he saw us drive up, he waved to us with his right hand, the one that was healed. He had a grin on his face that shone like the sun. What an awesome

thing it is to see the Lord answer prayer like that.
Praise the Lord!

God continued to do things like that in our YFC
group while we were in Kaiserslautern, but He was
working through me in other ways too. I became good
friends with Paul Carten, one of the sergeants in our
platoon, for instance. We hung out together nearly all
the time that I wasn't with the YFC group, and we often
stayed up talking about the Lord until late at night. He
frequently came with me to Chapel services, and one
time he even came with me to a Billy Graham meeting in
Mannheim. The next day, we had an especially long
talk about God, and shortly after that, he told me he
gave his life to the Lord. We were walking together, and
he said, "I am so happy, Herb." I said, "Why what
happened? Did your girlfriend write to you?" He
replied, "No it's something more, and a lot better. I am
born again now. You know, after we talked that night, I
went and bought the book, by Billy Graham, 'Peace with
God.' I read it, and I committed my life to the Lord."

Later on, in May of '54, Paul went with me on a
trip to Landau, Germany's "Rose City," to see a friend of
mine from my days in Jork, Aribert Krause. Aribert was
a boy in high school when I met him on a street corner
in Jork. Our church was getting ready to hold some
evangelistic services, and I was helping pass out their
advertising flyers for the meetings. I was walking
around Jork, looking for people to give the flyers to
when I spotted several boys from my high school
standing on this street corner. I was rather intimidated
by them at first, thinking that they would laugh at me,
but I mustered up the courage to go over and give them
each a flyer. There was a boy with them who I didn't
know, but I gave him a flyer too. This turned out to be
Aribert, and he was the only one of them who said he'd
come to the meetings.

Aribert and I arranged to meet at that street corner the next Monday afternoon, which was the first meeting night. Usually I stayed with Mr. Mahnke in Hedendorf during the week, but that week I committed to ride my bike home every night, to be with Aribert at the meetings. Aribert got saved during one of those meetings, and I was able to befriend him and help him start his Christian walk.

When Paul and I went to visit him in Landau, Aribert was working for a horticulturist, preparing roses for sale to tourists. We spent the weekend together and had devotions and that sort of thing. While we were reading the Bible, Aribert said, "You know, when you left for America that time, there were only a few pages opened up in this book, and now all have been opened up." He had read through the entire Bible in the time that I'd been gone. Years later, I met him again in Hanover, and he'd become a pastor. Hundreds of people had received salvation through his ministry. As we talked, it dawned on us what a thin thread there was in people's lives. If I had not had the courage to risk embarrassment for Jesus in front of those boys from my school, hundreds of people may never have received Jesus as their Savior.

Paul didn't come with me on my next trip. I'd saved up some leave, and I decided to use it on a month-long trip around Germany to visit all my relatives. I left on Saturday, May 29, taking the train up to Frankfurt and then over to Heidelburg. From Heidelburg, I went up to Hamburg and spent three days each with Tante Martha, Tante Elfriede, and their families. I brought gifts of nylon stockings from my base PX for all the women, as these were still in short supply back in those days. Then I went to Bremen and then to Delmenhorst, where I had other relatives, spending two to three days at each place, depending on the train schedules. Next I went to Norden and caught a bus to Ostermarsch on the North Sea, where my Tante Bertha and Uncle Frantz lived. I'd pre-arranged which dates I was to be at each of my relatives' houses, and everything was going according to plan, until I arrived at their doorstep.

When I knocked on their door on that 10th of June, 1954, a beautiful young lady whom I'd never seen before opened it. I knew their children were all much older, so I was shocked by her presence, momentarily wondering if I was at the right house. It took me a few seconds to regain my composure and say who I was. She giggled and let me in, calling out to Uncle Frantz that his nephew had arrived.

Uncle Frantz, Tante Bertha, and I went through the usual relative reunion pleasantries, hugging each other and talking about how we were doing and so on. I couldn't concentrate on them though, because I was so distracted by the presence of this beautiful girl in their house. Uncle Frantz introduced her to me as their live-in housekeeper, Frieda Gatzke, after which she smiled and went into their kitchen to continue washing their dishes. Meanwhile, the rest of us sat down in their living room to talk and catch up on family events.

They had me sit on their couch, which I soon discovered had a clear view through the door into their kitchen, where I could plainly see Frieda working on the dishes. Furthermore, the couch and the sink were both backed up against the same wall, so if I turned my head that way, I could see her from her side, probably only twelve or fifteen feet away. I was supposed to be talking with Uncle Frantz and Tante Bertha, but I couldn't resist stealing sidelong glances at Frieda every now and then. I also noticed out of the corner of my eye, that Frieda was sneaking an occasional peek at me too. After a while, Uncle Frantz noticed me looking at Frieda and figured out what was going on, so when Frieda was finished with the dishes, he suggested that we take their bicycles out for a ride and go visit the dike on the North Sea.

Ecstatic, but a little embarrassed, Frieda got her bike, and I got Frantz's bike out of their hallway, and we rode them to the North Sea. Frieda led the way, because she knew her way around. The dike was at the end of a field where local farmers let their cows graze. There was a walkway along the top of the berm, with a pipe rail fence embedded in it and wooden pylons rammed into the ground out beyond it to collect sand and debris from the waves and to provide a buffer against the sea. We walked along and talked, awkwardly at first, but we became more relaxed as we got to know each other. I took a few pictures of her standing against the railing with my garrison cap on, which I had with me because I was still required by Army policy to have my uniform on whenever I was out in public. Just as we were really beginning to feel comfortable with each other though, Uncle Frantz showed up on Bertha's bike and said it was time for us to come home for dinner. He took a few more pictures of Frieda and I together before he left, and then we followed on our bikes.

That night, I lay awake in Uncle Frantz's guest bedroom, thinking about Frieda Gatzke. I'd been praying to God just a few days before leaving on this trip, asking Him for a wife. Back in the early spring, I'd met this other young lady, Helga Hammerschmidt, on the train to Hamburg to visit Tante Elfriede. We liked each other, and she was very interested in me, but she was also Catholic. I had nothing against Catholics per se, but I did know that they didn't believe quite the same about salvation and Jesus Christ as my family did. I knew this would become a problem if we ever got married, because she would want to go to the Catholic church, and I would want to go to a Protestant church, and we'd probably end up arguing over which church our children would attend. We'd been corresponding with each other since we met, but at one point I told her this and suggested that we break off our relationship because of it. She didn't want to hear that though, so she continued to pursue me even as I was becoming excited about getting to know Frieda. Frieda was a Christian. I'd found that out while we were walking at the North Sea. That meant that I could marry her. More than that though, she seemed to be the kind of person I'd want to marry. This put me in a quandary though, because of Helga. Nonetheless, I resolved to get to know Frieda better and to actively pursue an answer as to whether I should marry her.

Although Frieda was Uncle Frantz and Tante Bertha's housemaid, she was also living with them, and they treated her like their own daughter. She was always around, so we got to know each other pretty well, and we spent quite a lot of time together during those two more days that I stayed with them. Unfortunately, I'd made a hard bargain with the German Transportation Authority, and I had a bus and a train to catch. When the time finally came for me to leave, Tante Bertha came with me on the bus to Norden so that she could go shopping. I took that opportunity to ask her several questions about Frieda, such as what kind of girl she was, what her personality was, and so on. Tante Bertha said, "She is a very nice girl, but she's stubborn." I didn't mind about stubbornness though, as I had quite a bit of that myself.

From Norden, I took another train to Essen, where I had more relatives. I spent several days with them, and then I went to several other places until I had visited all of my relatives and went back to Kaiserslautern.

The first thing I did once I got back on base was to take my roll of film down to the PX and submit it for developing. It wouldn't come back for a week, so while I was waiting, I wrote Frieda a letter. I told her that I enjoyed meeting her and having that time with her at the dike and how it was fun the way we'd taken those pictures. When the pictures came back from the developers, I enclosed two of them in the envelope. Then I teasingly added a note at the end of the letter saying that I had about ten pictures of us, but if she wanted to see the rest of them, she'd have to write me back. You see, I didn't have any guarantee that Frieda would really be interested in me at all. Two weeks had already passed by the time I got back off leave, and another week passed while my film was developing, and there weren't any letters from Frieda waiting for me in the mail. So I was trying to provide her with some motivation to write to me. In fact, I had a whole long series of letters all planned out, with gradually increasing levels of interest phasing in and everything. I thought myself quite sneaky for coming up with the idea, though ultimately I don't think it fooled her at all.

Another problem that loomed on the horizon for our ability to have a relationship was that my unit, the 186th Engineering Service Co, was being decommissioned in July. In it's place an Engineering Platoon would be added to HHC (Headquarters, Headquarters Co.), USAREUR, which was located in Heidelburg. Two-thirds of our company were being transferred to other units all over the world or even let go from the Army, and only one-third of us were being moved over to the new platoon in Heidelburg. Thankfully, I was among those being moved to Heidelburg (and so was Paul Carten), but even so, my address was being changed at a critical stage in our relationship.

Somehow the Army Post Office managed to keep track of everyone in our unit, so when Frieda wrote me back, her letter found its way to my new address only a few days later than it should've arrived if I'd stayed in K-Town. The tone of her letter was polite and not overly interested in me, but she did ask me to send the rest of the pictures, and that was enough for right then. When I wrote the next letter, I only enclosed two more of the pictures though, again saying that the rest of them would follow in succeeding letters, as long as she continued to write to me.

She did continue writing me, so that we were writing a letter to each other once or twice a month. At first, I signed all of them, "Your brother in Christ, Herb Flemming." But after I'd sent her all the pictures, and she was still writing me, I started signing them, "Your steadily-thinking-of-you Brother in Christ, Herb Flemming." She didn't seem to mind that when she wrote back, so the next time I wrote, I became a little more bold in the content of my letter, asking her about more details of her life and telling her quite a few of my own too. She responded well to that, so after a couple more letters, I started signing them, "With Love in Christ, Herb;" and after several more letters, this became, "With Love, Herb," and then, "With all my Love, Herb." She kept on writing and answering everything that I asked her, and she didn't seem to mind my more intimate closings, so I became bolder still.

Finally, in mid-November, I asked her what she would think of being called "Mrs. Flemming." In her letter answering that one, she didn't really address that question though. It was as if I'd never asked it. Much later, she told me that she'd shared every one of my letters with a girlfriend of hers, and they'd laughed and had great fun together, reading and making jokes about my letters. This one in particular had them rolling on the floor. Yet she continued to write, and even my oblique suggestion that we get married didn't put her off.

So I next announced that I had enough leave stored up that I could take a couple weeks off over Christmas and come visit her. She thought this would be a splendid idea as December opened, but then things started to go wrong.

In the Army, when you want to take leave, you have to fill out a form to apply for it, and then you hope and pray that the Commander grants you what you asked for. For holidays like Christmas though, everyone was applying for the same days, so we knew that only about half of us would get what we wanted. Sure enough, my squad leader approached me and informed me that I couldn't have both Christmas and New Years off. I'd have to choose between them and then fill out the form again. Oh, yes, and we were going on field maneuvers the week before Christmas too.

Without waiting for Frieda to send me her next letter, I shot off a quick note to her explaining my situation and warning her that I might not be able to take leave as we'd planned. I decided that New Years would be the better one to take off, since I'd get more leave days because of how the days fell. So I filled out and submitted the leave form again. Then I started praying.

Actually, I'd been praying all along, asking God whether she was the right person for me to marry. But now I really got earnest with Him. I needed an answer to that question by the time I went to see her, because otherwise I didn't want to take the risk of asking her. And I was also pleading with Him to work things out with my leave arrangements. I even went so far as to present the leave situation to Him as a fleece, as a litmus test of whether I should ask Frieda to marry me

or not, much like Gideon put out a fleece before the
Lord when the Midianites were oppressing Israel.

All during our time in the field, I prayed and
prayed, asking God if Frieda was the one or not, and
fighting the butterflies in my stomach. Then shortly
before we were to go back to base, merely a few days
before Christmas, my squad leader came to me again
and announced that my leave paperwork had been lost.
I'd have to resubmit the form, again.

Arghh! Now I was desperate. I might not even
have time to mail Frieda another letter, telling her when
I was coming. Or I might not be able to visit her at all.

When our exercises were finally over, and we
returned to base, there was a letter from Frieda waiting
for me. She tried to comfort me and encourage me. She
said everything would be all right, and I'd get my leave
as I asked for it. She also told me that her employer
was giving her New Years weekend and the following
week off as vacation (She was now working as a
housemaid for an architect in Norden.). That meant we
could go somewhere and spend the entire week together.

Alarm bells went off in my head at that. Yes, I
wanted to marry her, but No, I didn't want to sleep with
her before we got married. Practically all of the other
guys in the unit, married or not, had some girl or girls
off base that they'd go and shack up with when they
had some spare time. I was determined before God that
I would not do that with Frieda. Nonetheless, two days
later, when my squad leader told me that my leave had
been approved, and I saw that it was for exactly the
same days that Frieda said she was getting off, I could
barely contain myself. This was the answer from God
that I'd been waiting for! I think I floated all the way to
the train station to buy my tickets.

On the other hand, as I realized on my way back
from buying the tickets, since God gave me an

affirmative answer to my fleece, I was now going to have to ask Frieda to marry me. I'd prayed myself into a corner, God had given His approval, and now I had to come through. I felt my arms and face suddenly drench in sweat, and my stomach wrenched up into a knot. How could I ever do that? What would I say? What if she said No?

Those questions pursued me all the way to the train station in Norden on the Wednesday after Christmas, where Frieda met me as we'd agreed upon. I figured that I had to get it over with quickly, to keep me from chickening out, so as soon as we had a free moment after we arrived at the architect's house where she lived, I pulled her aside and said that I had to ask her a question.

She said, "What, Herbie? What's wrong?"

I looked her in the eyes, swallowed my fear, and asked, "Will you marry me?"

Her face went pale; her eyes got big; and her mouth dropped open. Then she swallowed hard and tried to compose herself. A huge grin flashed momentarily across her face and almost turned into a giggle before she answered, "Um, well, that sounds like a good idea, Herbie, but let me talk to my mother about it first."

Crestfallen, but undeterred, I asked, "Okay, when can we go visit her?"

We talked about it for a while longer, and then she called her mother in Oerel, northeast of Bremen, and arranged for us to take the train there the next day.

My next thought was how to kiss her. We'd not so much as held hands up to this point, and the total amount of time that we'd actually spent together was less than three days. But the last time I'd asked someone to kiss me, which was Ilse Corleis, I'd been turned down. I'd just asked Frieda to marry me, and

she hadn't said No, so I wasn't about to let her turn me
down for a kiss.

I waited until we were alone in the kitchen, and
then I ambushed her as she was turning around,
kissing her lightly on the lips. Frieda's eyes got really
big this time. She sputtered and turned red, looking
around as if her parents were there watching her. Then
she hurried off into the living room for a couple
minutes, where I guess she caught her breath and
collected her thoughts. I didn't follow her, because I
wanted to see what she would do. Soon she returned,
with a smile on her face, and then it was her turn to
join me in a kiss. This time, it was longer though, and
we did some necking too.

The next morning, we caught the train to Oerel,
and once we were at her mother's house, Frieda
introduced me to her mother and her brother. We
talked for quite a while, but after the introductory
pleasantries were over with, she asked to be alone with
her mother, so I went off somewhere with her brother.

Half an hour later, they came looking for us, and
Frieda said, "Mom said it was okay for me to marry you,
so your answer is Yes." I was ecstatic, and relieved. We
spent the rest of the day talking and planning, while
Frieda's mother and brother asked me question after
question about my family, my background, what I
wanted to do with myself, what my beliefs were about
God, and so on. By the end of the day, they were happy
to have me in the family, and I was about as excited as a
young man could get.

On New Years Eve, which was the next day, we
went into town and bought a couple of gold bands for
engagement rings. We had the date inscribed on the
insides of the rings, and we agreed to wear them on our
left hands until we got married, when we would switch
them to our right hands to make room for our wedding

bands.

Admittedly, that wasn't the most romantic way to get engaged, but for a soldier who was struggling to keep his way pure before the Lord, it was enough. We didn't know how to go about making wedding plans either, and neither of us had the money for a big wedding, but we tentatively decided to get married in April of 1955, just before I was scheduled to leave Germany and go back to the US. That was the extent of our planning right then.

Once I was back in Heidelburg, and the impact of what we'd just done began to sink in, I started to do the real planning. First, I wrote a letter to Mom and Papa, announcing our engagement to them. Then told all my friends on base, and finally, I mentioned it to my squad leader. I only told him because I thought that I'd need to take leave again before I was shipped back to the US for my End of Term Separation (ETS). I had no idea what would really be needed.

The next day though, I found out. My squad leader told my commander, and my commander called me into his office.

Since the US Army was still technically an army of occupation in a "hostile" country, and also because of the Soviet threat, I would need to fill out a formal application to be married to a foreigner. Whether the commander approved that or not would depend on whether this girl I was wanting to marry was deemed to be a threat to US National Security and our ability to perform military operations. She would need to provide her birth certificate or an affidavit proving her name and country of origin, and she would have to prove that she was neither a Nazi nor a Communist. I would need to sign a Statement of Financial Accountability, acknowledging that I was aware of the responsibility I was taking on and demonstrating that I had the ability to provide for her, including in case of war and extended deployments.

I thought, "Huh? This is just Frieda. She's not a threat to anything. She's a housemaid. What's the deal?" But I couldn't do anything about that, so I set about trying to comply with my commander's requirements.

As it turned out, Frieda didn't have any documentation at all. It was a good thing she was never arrested. Her family had been living in Poland during the war, and as the Russians approached, they'd fled in a horse-drawn wagon, along with thousands of others. A Russian fighter plane strafed the column of refugees she was in, killing one horse and wounding the other. Her family escaped death only by jumping into the snow by the side of the road, thus getting out of the path of the bullets. Hundreds of refugees were killed or wounded, and panic ensued. Russian soldiers quickly caught up with them after that and killed many more. Their identification papers were lost in the snow when the Russians ransacked their wagon, looking for valuables, and later, a Russian tank ran over the wagon, crushing anything that was left. They were just glad to be alive, and somehow they managed to escape into West Germany, though that is a different story.

Frieda's mother also wasn't her real mother. She'd started adopting Frieda towards the end of the war, but the rapid advance of the Russians prevented them from finalizing it. This meant that she had to fill out an affidavit establishing Frieda's legal identity. Figuring out exactly what had to be on this form and mailing it back and forth took months, and when it was all done, it still had to be translated into English to be acceptable to the Army.

Long before that was finished, we saw that April was out of the question as a marriage date, so we put off planning for our wedding indefinitely. April came, and I had to volunteer to extend my enlistment and my tour of duty by a year so that I could stay in Germany long enough for us to get married.

We finally got the paperwork done in early August, and Frieda came down for a week to visit me and to help me sign and submit all the papers. She stayed with some friends of mine from church, a mechanic from Heidelburg Press, and we got to spend a lot of time together, for the first time since New Years.

By now, even though Frieda and I still hadn't had much time together physically, we had started thinking of ourselves as a couple. Her staying in Heidelburg presented us with a new challenge in our relationship, because this time, no one around us had any real interest in what we did together. The other times that we'd been together, just the fact that we were living with my uncle and aunt or her mother and brother kept us apart sexually. Now, although my friends certainly hoped we wouldn't do anything sexually, they had no responsibility for either of us, so they pretty much left us alone. And the Army didn't even care what we did.

All those long months of writing to each other and laboring through the process of her legalization and our application for marriage now caught up with us. We spent every available minute together, and we quickly grew very physically affectionate with each other. About halfway through that week, I realized that if I wanted to, I could have sex with her. We were right on the brink of doing that anyway, though she was stronger resisting than I was, but instead, we talked about it and decided to back off physically and keep ourselves pure before the Lord. In retrospect, I now believe this was one of the best decisions that I've ever made, and I see that our lives and our marriage have been so much happier because of that.

Towards the end of Frieda's stay in Heidelburg, we decided that the time had come for us to tie the knot and get married. Neither of us had much money, and neither of our families did either, so the wedding couldn't be very big. As it was, I arranged to take another week of leave in early September, and I went up to Oerel again, where we were married on September 10th, 1955, in the small church that her mother and brother attended. We spent a couple more days with them while Frieda got her affairs together, and then we moved what little she owned back down to Heidelburg.

At first, we rented a small apartment in town, but the landlady liked to meddle, and she tried to boss Frieda around. Since Frieda was stubborn herself, that situation was destined to be very short, so after only three weeks, we rented a room from another couple from church, Oma and Opa Schaeffer. We were able to stay with them for the ten months or so until it was time for me to pack my bags and get shipped home to New York, in the United States.

Yes, home was now in the United States. I'd grown up in Germany, and I'd gotten married in Germany, but home was in the United States. When the US Army had first brought me back to Germany, in 1953, I had thought it ironic how as a German, I was now a member of the very forces that were occupying my country. I wondered then if my life had come full circle. But after living there for three years and after marrying there too, I realized that I was desperate to return to the USA. It wasn't just because my immediate family was there either, since I'd learned to live without them, and since I still had lots of relatives living in Germany too. No, the United States had become my home because that's where the freedom was. That's where the freedom to live as myself was, where the freedom to worship God without being interfered with was, and where the freedom to succeed or fail economically, based solely upon my own initiative was. My Papa, Otto Flemming, had raised me to be free, and I had to go where that freedom was.

So in June, 1956, the Army put me on yet another Liberty ship, the USS General Stewart, along with Frieda and everything that we owned, and they sent us home. I was outprocessed from the Army right there at Camp Kilmer, NJ, the same base where I'd embarked on this my German adventure. Frieda and I spent several days in New York City, and then we took a train up to Albany, where my whole family showed up to meet us at the station. We really were home now, and I had finally come full circle.

20

Epilogue

In the years since then, the Lord has blessed us tremendously. We now have four children and seven grandchildren. Our first son, Ronnie, was born in Albany, at the Catholic maternity hospital. Our daughter Nancy was born in New York City, in the Bronx, where we moved after living with my parents for several months. Our third and fourth children, Robert and Sharon, were born after we moved to Succaunna, New Jersey, where I working with M&M Candies in Hacketstown as a mechanic. I am now retired and living in the Shenandoah Valley, where I serve as an usher in an Assemblies of God church. The Lord has given me many opportunities to minister to people, including speaking at various Full Gospel Business Men's and other meetings to give my testimony, and now finally, this book. I pray that this book has been a blessing to you, that you have come to know my Savior, Jesus Christ, in a more personal and powerful way because of reading it, and I pray that it will so bless and inspire everyone who reads it.

As for the rest of my family, Hildegaard, my oldest sister, moved to Laudensville, NY, near Albany where she married a policeman who later became the Director of Communications for the New York State Thruway. Karl first moved nearer to Albany, and later, he moved down near us in Dover, NJ, where he became the Maintenance Supervisor for Sandoes Pharmaceutical. Ruth married a draftsman for General Electric, in Burlington, VT, and after raising a family of her own, she became a nurse at age fifty. Mariann became a school teacher in Queens, NY, where she married the pastor of a German Pentecostal church, though she's now widowed. Waltraut married the pastor of a large Assemblies of God church in New Jersey and has recently become an ordained minister herself. Ursula became a teacher too, in Long Valley, NJ, though she lived in Hacketstown, and she married a computer programmer. She's had to struggle with cancer for several years, but the Lord healed her of it once, and I know He can do it again. And Gerhardt worked for IBM as an engineer in Kingston, NY, among other places, for twenty-seven years, before he retired. All of us are still living in 2004, and thank God, all of us are still mostly in good health.

Mom and Papa lived happily together in the house we'd built in East Nassau, NY, across from Tante Lisa and Uncle Otto, until December 21, 1959, when she went to be with the Lord. We buried her on Christmas Eve, exactly ten years to the day after Papa was reunited with her in Jork, just as he'd asked God for while he was still in the Russian prison. I really appreciate my mother and the role she played in our lives. She was a Godly woman who provided a steadfast foundation for our family during our most desperate days.

Papa remarried about a year later, to a German friend of ours named Bertha. Papa sold the house after marrying Bertha and moved in with her on the outskirts of Nassau. They lived together for another eight years, until she too died. Three years after that, Papa came to live with us in New Jersey. Then, in late May, 1977, he married another woman, named Jan, and they took their honeymoon in Jamaica. He sent us a letter while they were there, telling us how beautiful it was and how much fun they were having, but only a couple days after we'd received it, on June 12, he had a massive heart attack and died instantly, at the age of seventy-three. I am eternally grateful for having been the son of Otto Flemming. He was an honorable, Godly man, and he taught me how to live right, how to pray, and how to serve the Lord. The world would be a much better place if more Papas were like him.

We visited Rothenen on July Fourth, 1999. Some old towns, after a war or some other event carries most of their people away, become ghost towns, with gaunt, hollow structures staring mournfully at their streets. After the Russians annexed East Prussia though, Rothenen simply ceased to exist. The Russians carried everything of value away, and they bombed, burned, or bulldozed the rest. We found a narrow track consisting of two raised parallel cement strips, just wide enough for a car or truck to get by on, running past where the town used to be, but there was nothing else. We could see where our old road used to be because the row of elm trees was still there, now grown huge, but the Russians had even taken the cobblestones. We'd heard that there might've been a single house left standing, but when we arrived, there was nothing. We found where our house had been, but it, the blacksmith shop, our shed, and all the other structures in town had vanished. It was all overgrown with trees and bushes and tall grass, and only an occasional foundation stone remained to hint that there had ever been a town there at all. Yet despite the war and all the horror and suffering that men have caused since then, my God remains real and true. He has proven Himself to me time and time again, bringing us through so many narrow scrapes with death and then healing a man before my very eyes. He has shown Himself loving and trustworthy, a true Papa to all who need one. I owe my life to Him, and this book is my tribute to His power and love at work in my life. He is a God Who answers prayer, and I pray that you will allow Him to show His love to you as well. Amen.

Herb Flemming 2009

Town of Rothenen

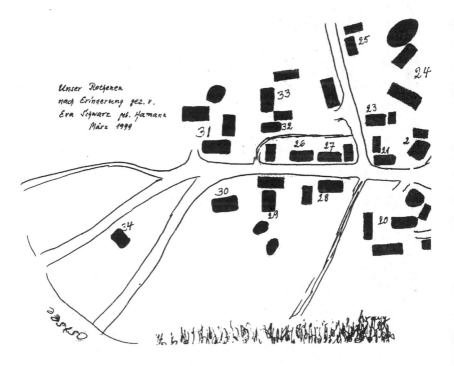

Unser Rothenen
nach Erinnerung gez. v.
Eva Schwarz geb. Hamann
März 1999

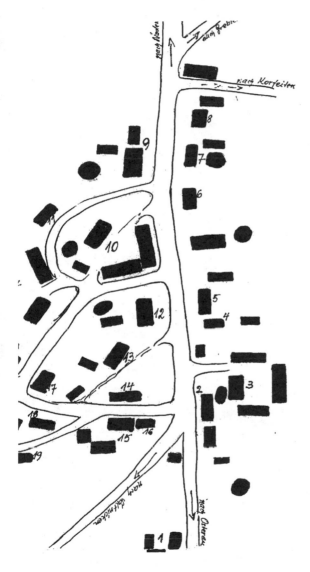

1. „Alt-Audehm
2. Schule
3. Hof Niemann
4.) Insthäuser zum
5.) Hof Niemann
6. „Blaue Villa" zu Hof Dagott
7. Insthaus zu Dagott
8. Schmiede Flomming
9. Gastwirtschaft m. Saal u. Kaufladen Daniel
10. Hof Witthau
11. Pantel
12. Romey (Schuhmacher)
13. Bäckerei Hübner
14. Hinz
15.) Eggert (Stellmachere,
16.) u. Bürgermeister
17. Grohe Gastwirtschaft u. Kaufladen
18. Strauß (Bernstein-Ab
mestelle)
19. Kriegsgefangene
20. Hof Audehm
21. Baumeister Heidt- Rähse
22. Schaack (Rudolf)
23. Baumeister (Max)
24. Hof Dagott
25. Mojelolär
26. Hübner u. Baumei
27. Heysa
28. Insthaus zu Witth.
29. Schaack (Tauster)
30. Hübner (Fritz)
31. Hof Schaack (Karl)
32. Gedenk u. Schpock
33. Hof Rähse (Otto)
34. Heyse, Otti